BRIAN CONROY

HMS Hermes
1923 & 1959

Neil McCart

FOREWORD BY
REAR-ADMIRAL K. A. SNOW CB

HMS Hermes
1923 & 1959

Neil McCart

A magnificent colour photograph of HMS *Hermes* at sea during her second commission between 1962 and 1964. She has Sea Vixens and Scimitars on deck.

(Lt-Cdr Larcombe)

To All Those Who Have Served In HMS *Hermes*
Between 1923 & 1986, And In INS *Viraat*

Front Cover: A magnificent painting of HMS *Hermes* 1959-1986 by artist Brian Conroy, Farnborough, Hampshire.

Cover Design by Louise McCart
© Neil McCart/FAN PUBLICATIONS 2001
ISBN: 1 901225 05 4

Typesetting By: Highlight Type Bureau Ltd,
Clifton House, 2 Clifton Villas, Bradford,
West Yorkshire BD8 7BY, England.

Printing By: The Amadeus Press Ltd,
Ezra House, West 26 Business Park,
Cleckheaton, West Yorkshire BD19 4TQ,
England.

Published By FAN PUBLICATIONS
17 Wymans Lane, Cheltenham, GL51 9QA, England. Fax & Tel: 01242 580290

Contents

Foreword
By Rear-Admiral K. A. Snow CB

As the last Royal Naval Captain of HMS *Hermes* it gives me great pleasure to contribute the foreword to this thought-provoking and historical book on the two aircraft carriers of that name. Having once served for a short time as the RN Liaison Officer on board the aircraft carrier INS *Vikrant,* I am delighted also that the author has been able to find a space to record the time after *Hermes* was bought by the Indian Navy and saw service as the INS *Viraat.* I trust that they found her as sound and effective as I had even after so many years' service.

While reading the book a number of matters seemed to me to stand out. The first is the hesitance with which both ships were built. The lack of faith in the role in which they were to be used, their value as operational units and the inevitable desire by successive governments to reduce expenditure on defence during the period between the wars all contributed to these delays. Yet both were unique in their own way, providing a service when it was most needed, which would have been sorely missed had they not been available. Both also contributed markedly to the better understanding, knowledge and use of naval air warfare. It is sad that the lack of foresight between the wars, and the inter-service rivalry, should have left the Fleet Air Arm so woefully short of modern aircraft in the early years of the Second World War. What became rapidly obvious was that they were no match for the Japanese in either equipment or tactical thinking as regards naval air warfare, and it was these factors that led to the sinking of HMS *Hermes* in 1942.

Of all the events in her successor's long history it is the Falklands War that stands out as the most remarkable. *Hermes'* involvement was critical to the success of the campaign, and without the presence of the Harriers and helicopters embarked in her and *Invincible* it is questionable whether the operation could have been conducted at all. But I would argue that *Hermes'* real legacy is not the question of establishing sovereignty over the Falklands: it is her contribution to the whole future of the Royal Naval fixed-wing operations.

It is worth recalling that in 1981 the knives were being sharpened for RN fixed-wing aviation. John Nott was in the process of conducting a defence review which promised the deletion of the entire capability. Although *Invincible* had just entered service she had already been offered to Australia as a possible replacement for HMAS *Melbourne,* and even on the eve of the Falklands the Australians had every intention of taking her. The future of the remainder of the Invincible class, and of the Harriers, was very much in doubt.

The battle for the Falklands managed to turn the entire argument around in the space of a few short months. Not only did the war throw into stark relief the critical importance of carrier-borne air power as a battle winning capability, but it also vividly demonstrated the versatility it offers. The embarked aircraft not only protected the fleet and provided combat air patrols with notable success, but they also provided an offensive strike capability over the land theatre that could have been achieved by no other means at such a distance from any national airfields which might have agreed to accept our military aircraft. It is this latter theme that has continued to be exploited to such good effect within the context of the present government's strategic review, and on which the future carrier procurement depends. In the current context of expeditionary warfare and the Joint Rapid Reaction Force the carrier plays a pivotal role in shaping the battle space. An exciting maritime fixed-wing future beckons.

Hermes represented one of the last of the 'old style' carriers, providing a transition to the VSTOL world, and has been the springboard to the new era. Aspirations for two 50,000-ton aircraft carriers and the integration of the Fleet Air Arm and RAF crews under the banner of Joint Force Harrier have their genesis in *Hermes* and her contribution during those few short months in 1982 that underlined the versatility and power of naval air warfare. Truly this is a legacy of which to be proud.

Finally, but most importantly, may I pay tribute to all those who served in these '**Happy *Hermes*'** as they were so rightly called. It is, as always, the People who make the ship.

Kenneth Snow

Part One

HMS *Hermes*
1923-1942

Chapter One

A Royal Review And The Mediterranean Fleet
July 1917 - June 1925

On 5 July 1917, the same day that German aircraft carried out an air raid on the East End of London, an order under the Emergency War Programme was placed with the Tyneside naval shipyard of Sir W. G. Armstrong Whitworth & Co for the world's first purpose-designed 'airplane carrier'. It was six months later, however, on Tuesday 15 January 1918, just ten months before the end of the Great War, that the first keel plates for the vessel were laid. With strict news censorship in force the event received no publicity, and even if it had it is doubtful whether the British public would have shown much interest for at that time they were preoccupied with the horrific daily casualty lists from the war, which were showing no signs of letting up, and the introduction of limited food rationing.

In early 1918 aviation in the Royal Navy was not a new idea, indeed, the first seaplane carrier, the modified cruiser HMS *Hermes*, had actually entered service in the summer of 1913, a year before the outbreak of war. However, she carried only three seaplanes and after undergoing seven months of trials which confirmed the viability of aircraft operations at sea, she was paid off. She was followed by more seaplane carriers, all of which were converted merchantmen, the largest being HMS *Campania*, formerly a Cunard transatlantic liner. HMS *Furious*, the fleet carrier which served the Royal Navy for 27 years, was originally designed as a light cruiser. HMS *Argus*, another long-serving aircraft carrier, was intended to be an Italian passenger liner, and HMS *Eagle* was laid down as the Chilean battleship *Almirante Cochrane*.

During the 20 months between the laying of the keel and the launch of the carrier the builders completed the construction of the vessel up to her 'flying deck', as the flight deck was then known, but in the Admiralty it was far from clear exactly what the final design of the new ship would be, and when the Great War ended in November 1918 there was no longer any urgency to complete the carrier. There was even a suggestion that she need not be completed at all, but fortunately this was not taken seriously. Ultimately the main problem for the planners was to decide whether the vessel would have a flush 'flying deck', or whether she would have an island superstructure and, if so, whether the island would be on the port side or the starboard side of the ship. In the autumn of 1919 this question still had not been fully resolved.

Meanwhile, as the debate about the new carrier's design

The hull of *Hermes* in 1920, following her tow from the River Tyne to Plymouth. Her flight deck is incomplete, there is no island superstructure and large sections of her hull plating have yet to be riveted into place. In this photograph she is moored in the Hamoaze awaiting the decision for building work to be resumed. *(Maritime Photo Library)*

dragged on, back on the River Tyne the builders were under pressure to clear the slipways for merchant ship construction which had assumed the utmost importance at the end of the war when the shipping companies needed to replace lost tonnage and at the same time modernize their fleets. During this building boom one lucrative contract won by Armstrong Whitworth's was for a 14,000-ton passenger liner for Cunard's transatlantic service between Liverpool and Canada, although the liner would eventually serve under the White Ensign as the heavy repair ship, HMS *Ausonia*. Under pressure from the builders the Admiralty agreed to launch the aircraft carrier and the date for the ceremony was set for Thursday 11 September 1919. The ship's sponsor was Mrs A. Cooper, the daughter of Mr Walter Long who was the First Lord of the Admiralty in Lloyd George's Coalition Government. An article in *The Times* newspaper described the event thus: 'The airplane-carrier *Hermes* will be launched today from the shipyard of Messrs Armstrong on the Tyne. ...The *Hermes* belongs, among the many miscellaneous types of vessels called for by the Navy during the war, to that special class which became necessary owing to the demands of the Air Service. Most of the vessels in this class, provided for the purpose of carrying planes over the sea, were converted or adapted for that work, but the *Hermes* was laid down as a swift airplane-carrier in January 1918.' The article also gives an indication of the design which the Admiralty had in mind for the carrier: 'As in the case of the *Argus*, the whole length of the flying deck of the *Hermes* will be available for starting and landing the planes, and, by special arrangements for the emission of hot gases and smoke, there will be no funnels or other obstructions. Under the flying deck are the hangars for the planes, as well as the workshops for their repair. Two electrically-controlled lifts are fitted, the one forward and the other aft, for hoisting the planes to the flying deck.' Any thoughts that *Hermes* would be completed in 1920 were soon dispelled when, in his speech at the luncheon which followed the launch, the chairman of Armstrong Whitworth's, Sir Philip Watts, remarked, 'The *Hermes* is one of the last warships which we had in hand before the Armistice, and though launched, she will not be proceeded with at present.'

Having taken to the waters of the River Tyne *Hermes* was laid up at Elswick where she remained for four months, then with the yard due to close she was towed in January 1920 to Devonport and secured to a buoy in the Hamoaze until a decision was made as to her future. By March 1920 the basic design for *Hermes* had been agreed and the Admiralty drawings show a large single island superstructure on her starboard side, which appears to have stemmed from the maritime 'rule of the road', that a ship keeps clear of vessels on her starboard side. At this stage, however, her flight deck was shown as being cut off short of, rather than being faired into, the bow, and her

armament was shown as a mix of 6-inch and 4-inch anti-aircraft guns. The island superstructure, which was kept as narrow as possible, was to house the navigating bridge and charthouse, and the anti-aircraft batteries. The drawings also show a large tripod mast topped by a massive control tower which would not have looked out of place on a battlecruiser of the period. This clumsy looking protuberance was to house an upper navigating position and gunnery control positions, and it was also thought, mistakenly, that it would help to carry the funnel exhaust gases away from the flight deck.

Hermes was, even by the standards of the day, a small aircraft carrier and she was smaller than today's Invincible class of light fleet carriers. She had a displacement of 13,700 tons, a length of 600 feet overall and a beam of 90 feet. She was a twin-screw vessel powered by two sets of Parsons geared steam turbines, which provided 40,000 SHP and gave her a speed of 25 knots. Her six Yarrow water tube, cylindrical return tube boilers were oil-fired and produced steam at a pressure of 235 psi, and she had an endurance of almost 3,000 nautical miles at a speed of 18 knots. She carried a total complement of 700, and many of her pilots, aircrew and squadron personnel were from the Royal Air Force for, in 1918 when the RAF was formed, the Royal Naval Air Service was transferred to that service. This decision ensured the neglect of air power at sea in the Royal Navy until the spring of 1939 when the Navy took control of its own Air Arm once again. Unfortunately, by then another war was only four months away.

The hangar deck in *Hermes* was 400 feet long, 50 feet wide, with a height of 16 feet and she was fitted with two, cruciform-shaped, aircraft lifts. The after lift opened out both to the hangar forward and aft onto the open-sided quarterdeck which was accessible by way of a steel shuttered door and was intended for use as a seaplane operating area. The flight deck was 570 feet long and the round-down aft was exaggerated by a 'hump' which was intended as a rear anchor for the longitudinal arrester wires which were fitted. As to her defensive armament *Hermes* was fitted with six single 5.5-inch guns, three single 4-inch high-angle guns and two quadruple sets of 0.5-inch anti-aircraft guns. In 1924 she could carry 15 aircraft which were made up of Fairey IIID reconnaissance seaplanes and Fairey Flycatcher biplane fighters. The former could operate on wheels or floats, and they were fitted with a Lion IIB, 450hp radial engine which gave the aircraft a speed of 80 knots and a range of 184 nautical miles. The IIID could carry two 230lb bombs and it was also fitted with one .303-inch machine-gun. The Fairey Flycatcher was fitted with a Jaguar 341hp radial engine which gave it a speed of 113 knots and a range of 230 miles. It was fitted with two .303-inch machine-guns and could carry four 20lb bombs.

It was in 1920 that construction work on *Hermes* was resumed at Devonport Dockyard and in February 1923 her

Hermes undergoes her trials in 1923.   *(Author's collection)*

Hermes leaving harbour in 1924, shortly after commissioning for the first time.   *(Maritime Photo Library)*

first commanding officer, Captain The Honourable Arthur Stopford CMG RN, was appointed to the ship. Captain Stopford was an experienced naval aviator who had entered the Royal Navy as a cadet in 1895, long before powered flight had become a reality. In 1917, after service with the Grand Fleet, he was appointed to the Royal Naval Air Service as a pilot and in 1918, as a newly promoted Captain, he transferred to the recently formed Royal Air Force. However, in the following year he returned to the Royal Navy. Six months after his appointment to *Hermes*, at 9am on Monday 6 August 1923, the ship was ready to undergo her initial trials and Captain Stopford commissioned her with a temporary ship's company who had been drafted from HMS *Vivid.* * Two days later the aircraft carrier was towed from No 8 dry dock to No 8 buoy in the Hamoaze and next day she moved further out of the harbour to a buoy in Plymouth Sound. It was at 8.43am on Friday 10 August that *Hermes* slipped her moorings and steamed into the Channel where, for seven hours, she carried out full-power trials before anchoring again in the Sound. After spending the weekend at anchor the trials were due to continue on Tuesday 14 August, but thick fog delayed their resumption until the following day and they then continued without interruption until Monday 20 August with the ship anchoring each evening in Plymouth Sound. On Tuesday 21 August there was a treat for the Portsmouth members of the ship's company when *Hermes* anchored at Spithead for just over 36 hours and leave was granted to those with homes in the city. However, at 7.35am on Thursday 23 August it was back to work when a Fairey IIID seaplane landed in the Solent and taxied alongside *Hermes* for 'hoisting in and out trials'. At just before 11am that day the carrier weighed anchor to carry out her first deck landing trials whilst under way. The aircraft selected to carry out the trials was a Parnall Panther, a rotary-engined, two-seater biplane, which had entered service in 1919 and was, by 1923, virtually obsolete. For almost three hours, whilst *Hermes* steamed into the wind off the south coast of the Isle of Wight, the Panther landed and took off from the 'flying deck' and that afternoon its place was taken by a Nieuport Nightjar, a small biplane fighter which had entered service in 1920 and which would be replaced by the Fairey Flycatcher in 1924. By 4.30pm that day, with the first flying trials having been completed, *Hermes* anchored once again at Spithead for 24 hours, which was good news for the Portsmouth men for they were able to go ashore for the second time. Next day, at 6.25pm on Friday 24 August, *Hermes* weighed anchor and set course for Devonport where, at just after midday on Saturday 25 August, she secured to No 8 buoy in the Hamoaze, close to the battleship *Resolution*.

After a weekend at the buoy, at 5.40am on Monday 27 August 1923, with her initial trials having been successfully

completed, *Hermes* was manoeuvred back into Devonport Dockyard's No 8 dry dock for completion of her fitting out. Three hours later her temporary ship's company were busy packing their kit bags and hammocks, and stowing them on wooden handcarts on the jetty as *Hermes* prepared to pay off. At 10.30am they all mustered at Divisions and marched off to the Royal Naval Barracks, while the White Ensign was lowered as the new 'airplane carrier' was returned to dockyard control.

It was February 1924 before *Hermes* was ready for service and early on the morning of Tuesday 19 February her new ship's company marched down from the Royal Naval Barracks to No 4 basin in the dockyard where they joined the ship. They were closely followed by their kit bags and hammocks which were transported on wooden handcarts, and at 9am that morning Captain Stopford commissioned the ship and the White Ensign was hoisted. That afternoon, as the ship's company were busy stowing their kit and hammocks, *Hermes* was manoeuvred out of the basin and towed alongside the sea wall at No 5 wharf. Six days later, on Monday 25 February, she steamed under her own power out to Plymouth Sound where she put to sea for the first day of her sea trials. On Sunday 2 March, with the carrier firmly anchored in Plymouth Sound, the ship was inspected by the C-in-C Plymouth, Vice-Admiral Sir R. Phillimore. Next morning the C-in-C inspected the ship's company at Divisions in the hangar, and that evening *Hermes* left Plymouth bound for Portsmouth for a four-day visit before going on to Rosyth where she arrived during the early evening of Sunday 9 March. *Hermes* had joined the Atlantic Fleet.

During the eight days spent at anchor in the Firth of Forth *Hermes* was the centre of attention and she received a visit from the C-in-C East Scotland, Rear-Admiral Sir Reginald Tyrwhitt, but on Monday 17 March it was time to get down to serious work and at 9am that morning she put to sea. Two hours later the ship went to Flying Stations and two Fairey IIID aircraft, which had just entered service, landed on safely. For the next 18 days *Hermes* sailed daily from Rosyth to carry out flying trials with the same aircraft, which were, in effect, on trial too. The routine was broken on 7 April when *Hermes* secured to a buoy in Portsmouth Harbour for just over four weeks to carry out maintenance and for seasonal leave to be taken. However, by mid-May she was back at sea off Scotland's east coast and was once again carrying out flying trials with the two IIID aircraft. On the last day of May she embarked a large number of junior officers from units of the Atlantic Fleet and put to sea from the anchorage of the Dornoch Firth to give them a 12-hour flying display, before anchoring at Invergordon for a weekend break. For the officers of the fleet such a flying display would have been a new and unusual experience and it was designed to show them exactly what air power at sea was capable of.

* HMS *Vivid*, the ex-monitor *Marshal Ney*, was the base depot ship.

In early June *Hermes*, together with the battleship *Queen Elizabeth* and a destroyer screen, steamed north to Scapa Flow and down Scotland's west coast where the carrier paid a three-day visit to Oban. From there she steamed down to the Firth of Clyde to carry out further flying exercises, and to enjoy a fleet sailing regatta at Lamlash, before she steamed south once again, this time to Devonport where she arrived during the afternoon of Wednesday 25 June. This was only a five-day break however, and on the last day of June *Hermes* put to sea again, this time bound for Portland. For the next four days, from her anchorage in Weymouth Bay, the carrier sailed daily for flying trials with the IIID aircraft, and they even included a dummy bombing attack on *Hermes* herself. The exercises ended during the afternoon of Friday 11 July, when *Hermes* joined other units of the Atlantic Fleet at anchor in Torbay for a 12-day period of relaxation, with liberty boats providing a shuttle service to Torquay. The final duty for *Hermes*, which would conclude the first half of the commission, was a ceremonial one and when she left Torquay at 5am on the morning of Wednesday 23 July she joined other units of the 1st Battle Squadron to set course for Spithead, where she anchored at 4pm the same afternoon to begin preparations for the Royal Fleet Review by His Majesty King George V.

The Review was held to coincide with the British Empire Exhibition at Wembley, and it also marked the 10th anniversary of that fateful summer when, in response to the European Crisis, over 600 warships of the Grand Fleet were drawn up at Spithead to 'test the efficiency' of the mobilization system for the fleet, in anticipation of war with Germany which was in fact only 19 days away. Paradoxically, only a few weeks earlier, the Royal Navy's 2nd Battle Squadron of the Grand Fleet, including the battleships *King George V*, *Ajax*, *Centurion* and *Audacious*, had paid a successful goodwill visit to Kiel, which was only marred by the assassination of Archduke Franz Ferdinand of Austria-Hungary by a Bosnian Serb, Gavrilo Princip, in the far away Balkan city of Sarajevo, which was then part of the Austro-Hungarian Empire. When the Royal Navy's warships left Kiel on 30 June the Flag Officer in Command, Vice-Admiral Sir George Warrender, had signalled to his German counterpart, 'Friends in past and friends forever'. Sadly it was not to be and the four years of Europe's most destructive war which followed changed the continent's political and financial balances of power forever. In Britain the financial restraints caused by the war had hit the Royal Navy hard and by 1924 the fleet was much smaller than it had been ten years before. In 1914 there had been 54 battleships present, but in 1924 there were

Moored in Grand Harbour with sun awnings rigged.   *(Michael Cassar)*

just ten, *Queen Elizabeth*, (flag of the C-in-C Atlantic Fleet, Admiral Sir John de Robeck), *Barham, Warspite, Valiant, Malaya, Resolution, Revenge, Royal Oak, Royal Sovereign* and *Centurion*. Of the ten only *Centurion* had been included in the visit to Kiel and the Royal Review of 1914, and the newest battleship present was *Royal Sovereign* which had commissioned in 1916. Another indication of the post-war reduction in the Navy's fighting strength was the number of Flag Officers in Command. In 1914 there had been 25 Flag Officers present, but by 1924 this number had been reduced to just eight. However, as in 1914, the fleet was dominated by the battleships and *Hermes*, together with *Argus*, which was the other conventional aircraft carrier present, were included in the official guide under the auxiliary vessels, being listed below the submarine tenders, HMS *Adamant* and HMS *Lucia*.* Of the two aircraft carriers the guide had this to say: 'Of the interesting vessels in the above list, the two aircraft carriers ought to prove the chief source of attraction. The *Argus* has been in service since 1918, but the *Hermes*, the first aircraft carrier to be specially designed and built for the duty, only joined the fleet this year.'

On Friday 25 July 1924, the King travelled by train from London to Portsmouth where he embarked in the royal yacht *Victoria & Albert* that same evening. After dark, and despite the falling rain, all the Review Fleet was illuminated and there was a searchlight display for the holiday crowds who had gathered on the shores of the Isle of Wight and the seafront at Southsea. As it had poured with rain all day it was thought that the proceedings on the following day would be marred by the inclement weather, but Saturday 26 July dawned with warm summer sunshine and blue skies, and for the thousands of people who had packed onto special trains from London and from other south coast towns there was the promise of a lovely day ahead. By mid-morning all the sightseeing boats from Southsea and the Isle of Wight were full and huge crowds had gathered at all the mainland and Isle of Wight vantage points to watch the spectacle. *Hermes* and *Argus* formed part of Line F, headed by the battleships *Barham, Valiant, Warspite* and *Malaya*, between Ryde and Cowes off the Island's north coast, and they were virtually hidden from the sightseers who were watching from the mainland. For the King the morning started with a visit to HMS *Victory*, which was high and dry in Portsmouth Dockyard's No 2 dry dock undergoing essential repairs, and after this he re-embarked in the royal yacht to start the Review.

It was at just after 2pm when the royal procession set out from South Railway Jetty, with the Trinity House yacht *Patricia* leading *Victoria & Albert* out of Portsmouth Harbour, followed by the Admiralty yacht *Enchantress* carrying government ministers, including the Prime

Minister, Ramsay MacDonald, who had become the United Kingdom's first Labour Prime Minister just six months earlier. As the royal yacht turned down the grey steel-walled lines of warships, which were dressed overall, their guns thundered in a royal salute and a haze of blue smoke drifted out over the waters of Spithead. The Royal Marine Bands on board the battleships echoed the royal salutes with the strains of the national anthem while the sailors themselves leapt to attention as *Victoria & Albert* drew alongside their ships. As the royal yacht moved down the lines the rigid formality of the salute was exchanged for terrific bursts of cheering as each ship's company raised their caps and cheered ship. Meanwhile, overhead, flying from RAF Gosport, aircraft from *Hermes* and *Argus* put on an aerobatics display. It was 3.30pm before the royal yacht passed *Hermes*, and the ship's company who were manning the flight deck had been drenched by a sudden downpour of rain, but it did not dampen the enthusiasm of the cheers as the King took the salute from *Victoria & Albert*. With the two aircraft carriers at the end of Line F, as soon as the royal yacht had passed through the line the Review was over and *Victoria & Albert* returned to South Railway Jetty where the King signalled the following message to Admiral Sir John de Robeck: 'It is with much pleasure that I have inspected the fleet under your command, and I am especially glad to have had the opportunity of doing so before you hauled down your flag at the end of your long and distinguished career afloat.* I am proud of the splendid appearance of the ships and their crews, and I know that the conditions of efficiency can only be maintained by that discipline and devotion to duty which animates all ranks and ratings of the Service. Please express to the flag officers, captains, officers and men my appreciation of all I have seen today.'

Following the Review both *Hermes* and *Argus* remained at anchor until 7am on Monday 28 July, when they both put to sea for just over four hours in order to re-embark their aircraft, before returning to anchor once again. Next day they made another early start to rendezvous in the Channel where they exercised together for just over three hours, and aircraft from *Argus* landed on board *Hermes*. However, by 10.30am *Argus* had anchored at Spithead while *Hermes* steamed up harbour to secure in C Lock where she was to undergo her first long refit which would last for over three months.

It was on Monday 10 November 1924 that *Hermes* left the dry dock to secure to a buoy in Portsmouth Harbour, and three days later she put to sea to carry out post-refit trials. For two days she undertook flying exercises with IIID seaplanes, none of which landed on the flight deck, but were hoisted on board by crane after landing alongside the ship. Then at 9am on the morning of Saturday 15 November she weighed anchor and left Spithead to set

* HMS *Lucia* was the ex-German ship SS *Spreewald* which had been captured in September 1914.

* Admiral de Robeck had entered the Navy as a cadet in 1875.

course for Gibraltar and the Mediterranean. After a seven-hour stopover in Gibraltar Bay on Tuesday 18 November for refuelling the carrier resumed her voyage to Malta, but less than 24 hours after leaving Gibraltar she ran into a severe storm with wind speeds of 55 knots and mountainous seas which actually broke the glass in the navigation bridge windscreens and made life uncomfortable for the watchkeepers there. At just before 10am on Saturday 22 November, seven days after leaving Spithead, she secured alongside the Boiler Wharf in Malta's Grand Harbour. After 12 days of maintenance and, for the ship's company some very good runs ashore in Valletta, *Hermes* left Grand Harbour at 8.30am on Thursday 4 December to carry out nine days of flying exercises, anchoring each evening in Marsa Scirocco Bay.* During the exercises the destroyer *Winchelsea* acted as planeguard while IIIDs and Flycatchers of the RAF's 440, 442 and 403 Flights practised deck landings and take-offs. On several days flying was disrupted by heavy rain and thunderstorms, but on the morning of Saturday 13 December, having flown the aircraft ashore, *Hermes* and *Winchelsea* were able to enter Grand Harbour for the Christmas and New Year festivities. During the three-week break leave was granted each day, including Christmas Day, from 1.30pm to 7am

the following morning and even on Christmas Day 'Call the Hands' was at 6am. The bars on Strait Street did a roaring trade, but the hangovers were soon blown away on the morning of Monday 5 January 1925 when, in company with the destroyer *Voyager*, she left Grand Harbour to carry out flying exercises off Malta's south coast. Next day, after leaving her Marsa Scirocco anchorage at 8.30am, she embarked the Rear-Admiral (D) Mediterranean Fleet, Rear-Admiral A. A. P. Addison CB CMG. She then carried out four hours of flying with three Flycatchers and two IIIDs for the benefit of her visitors. That afternoon, after disembarking the VIPs, *Hermes* anchored in Marsa Scirocco Bay again and over the next three days she made daily forays to sea in order to carry out flying operations, but by Saturday 10 January she had returned to Grand Harbour where she secured to buoys in Bighi Bay.

It was Tuesday 24 February when *Hermes* put to sea again, and within an hour of leaving Grand Harbour her Flycatchers had landed on board and were being armed for training exercises which consisted of bombing and shooting up defended bridges ashore. Next day, after leaving Marsa Scirocco at 9am, she landed on four Flycatchers and three IIIDs, one of which crashed on deck when its undercarriage collapsed on landing, but fortunately

*Now known as Marsaxlokk Bay.

Leaving Grand Harbour, Malta, early in her career.

(Michael Cassar)

without any injuries or serious damage. On Friday 27 February she rendezvoused with, and for a short time exercised with, the US Navy's heavy cruiser USS *Pittsburgh*, before returning to Grand Harbour the following day. After a short break in Malta, at 7am on Tuesday 10 March, *Hermes* left to rendezvous with HMS *Eagle* to carry out joint flying exercises. Next day the two carriers joined other units of the Mediterranean Fleet, including the battleships *Barham, Benbow* and *Iron Duke*, the cruiser *Delhi*, the sloop *Snapdragon* and even the minelayer *Princess Margaret,* for exercises which took them as far west as Majorca. On Saturday 14 March *Hermes* anchored for three days in Palma Bay where restricted leave was granted, but by 23 March she and *Eagle* were back in the waters off Malta. After four more days of exercises off Marsa Scirocco, on Friday 27 March *Hermes* berthed alongside Malta Dockyard's Boiler Wharf to undergo a seven-week refit.

The end of the refit also saw the end of the carrier's first stint in the Mediterranean and on the morning of Sunday 17 May 1925 the C-in-C Mediterranean Fleet, Admiral Sir Osmond De Beavoir Brock, visited the ship to inspect Divisions on the flight deck and to say goodbye to the aircraft carrier. Next morning 51 soldiers of the Lancashire Regiment joined the ship for the passage to Plymouth, and at 2pm *Hermes* steamed out of Grand Harbour to land on her Flycatchers and to anchor in Marsa Scirocco Bay for

the seven IIIDs to be hoisted aboard. At 5.40pm, with the operation completed, *Hermes* weighed anchor and set course for Gibraltar where she made a short stop for fuel before anchoring in Plymouth Sound on the morning of Tuesday 26 May when her passengers were disembarked. Later that day she left Plymouth Sound and the following morning she anchored at Spithead where she remained for the day and overnight. At 6.30am on Thursday 28 May *Hermes* put to sea briefly in order to fly off the Flycatchers and IIIDs to RAF Gosport, before anchoring at Spithead for a further 33 hours, which must have been very frustrating for the ship's company who were all eager to get ashore and to their homes. However, finally, at 5pm on Friday 29 May *Hermes* weighed anchor and just over half an hour later she was firmly secured to No 7 buoy in Portsmouth Harbour, but still nobody was allowed to venture ashore. As it was the end of the commission and the carrier had served on a foreign station, at 11am on Monday 1 June, the ship's company mustered in the hangar for a medical examination by the ship's Medical Officer, and next morning the carrier was manoeuvred through C Lock into No 3 Basin where she was taken over by the Dockyard. Finally, at 10.30am on Wednesday 3 June 1925, *Hermes* was paid off and the ship's company marched from the dockyard to the Royal Naval Barracks for leave and to await new drafts.

Chapter Two

The China Station
June 1925 - October 1930

J ust five hours after *Hermes* paid off at Portsmouth a new ship's company joined from the naval barracks at Chatham and at 3pm on Wednesday 3 June 1925 the aircraft carrier was recommissioned. Two weeks later, on 17 June, *Hermes* left Portsmouth and after landing on her aircraft off Spithead she set course for the Mediterranean. During the first few weeks of the commission flying practice was carried out off Malta with her Fairey Flycatchers and FIIIDs. It was during these exercises, on the afternoon of 30 June, that one of the IIID seaplanes was lost when it crashed into the sea and sank, but fortunately the crew were rescued safely. At 9am on Wednesday 15 July, when *Hermes* was moored in Grand Harbour, Captain C. P. Talbot DSO RN joined the ship and took over command from Captain Stopford. Later that afternoon *Hermes* left Malta and set course for Alexandria and Port Said. During the evening of 18 July she started her southbound transit of the Suez Canal, and by the next forenoon she was steaming south through the Red Sea on her way to Aden. After brief stops at Trincomalee and Singapore she arrived in Hong Kong Harbour where, on the morning of Monday 10 August, she secured to a buoy off Kowloon. It was the start of a long period which the carrier would spend away from home, on both the China and Mediterranean Stations.

During the remainder of August and throughout September *Hermes* remained at Hong Kong, with only brief forays to sea for flying exercises. However, although the carrier was moored to No 1 buoy for long periods of time, her aircraft were hoisted out into the harbour for flying exercises on most days and her ship's company were far from idle. On the last day of October three of her IIIDs were hoisted out and flown off to escort the P&O liner, SS *Khiva*, which was leaving harbour with the outgoing Governor of Hong Kong, Sir Reginald Stubbs, embarked. Next day, however, one of the seaplanes was lost when it crashed into the sea off Lantau Island. On 10 November 1925 *Hermes* made her first 'foreign' visit of the commission when she steamed north to the treaty port of Amoy (Xiamen), for six days, but on her departure she returned to Hong Kong to spend three days in the Taikoo Dockyard Company's commercial graving dock at Kowloon.

The last weeks of 1925 and the start of 1926 were spent in and around Hong Kong, but on Monday 1 February 1926 *Hermes* sailed from her base and set course west. Four

days later she called at Jesselton (Kota Kinabalu), and then the small town of Victoria on Labuan Island, where she carried out flying practice before setting course for Singapore. In those days, before the completion of the naval base on the island's north coast, the warships had their own anchorage off the city of Singapore, and after eight days at the port she left for Colombo where she arrived on 20 February. Three days later she set course for Aden and on 9 March she steamed north through the Suez Canal, bound for Malta, and arrived in Grand Harbour on Monday 15 March. During the next few weeks the *Hermes* carried out flying practice off the coast of Malta, and one pilot remembers his first deck landing on Monday 29 March. The *Hermes* had left her Marsa Scirocca Bay anchorage at 8.30am that morning and soon afterwards the first Flycatcher left Hal Far airfield bound for the carrier's flight deck. The pilot takes up the story: 'My number was wirelessed out to the *Hermes* as having started from the aerodrome, and ten minutes' flying south-east of the island brought me within easy visual distance of the ship. I did the customary left-hand circuits round her, waiting for my pennant to go out, and after a few minutes I saw a number seven flag appear on the horizontal signal boom, telling me to stand by to land on. I then took up position astern of the ship, about 1,200 feet up, and waited for the affirmative flag to go out signifying that the ship was into wind and everything was ready for my landing. As I got into position the red and white affirmative flag fluttered out, and I throttled back a bit to make my approach. I had not anticipated the speed of the ship steaming into wind would so affect my judgement of approach, and I was obliged to put on the engine quite a lot to make up the gap between myself and the deck. A little closer to the deck in my approach and I was in the bumpy air caused by the hot airflow and smoke from the funnel, which at this stage of the proceedings was a little disturbing. Luck was with me and I managed to get straight about ten feet over the stern of the ship, pull back my throttle, and glide in the remainder. The relative landing speed was actually very low, as with the ship steaming into the wind to give an air speed over the deck of some 28 knots, combined with the very low landing speed of the Flycatcher with its camber-gear wound down, the movement over the deck was extremely slow. My wheels touched down together and remained steady on the deck with the undercarriage hooks firmly held by the

Hermes moored in Hong Kong Harbour in the 1920s.

(Charles Fisher)

longitudinal wires stretched along the deck. My speed was so slow that I only knocked down two hurdles before coming to rest, but long before I had done so I found each wing being firmly held down by some of the deck landing party who crouch along the sides of the deck in wire-net troughs and leap out directly the landing aircraft has made contact with the deck.' This pilot went on to make three successful landings and take-offs, but next day came the carrier's first fatal flying accident.

Hermes left her anchorage at 8.30am on Tuesday 30 March, and just over two and a half hours later, at 11.11am, a Fairey IIID, flown by Lt Thomas L. G. Bryan RM, approached the ship to make its first deck landing. After what appeared to be a perfect approach and landing on the carrier's deck the aircraft started to swing towards the port side. The pilot attempted to correct the swing, but with two wires engaged in his undercarriage hooks the aircraft pitched up on its nose, fell over the side of the ship and crashed into the sea. The destroyer *Venetia*, which was acting as the planeguard escort, immediately closed the stricken aircraft which was floating with just its tail visible. She had launched her seaboat in an effort to rescue the pilot, but within minutes the plane had sunk. *Venetia* and *Winchelsea* made continuous sweeps over the area for more than an hour and boats from *Hermes* assisted with the search, but it was all to no avail as there was no trace of the pilot. At 1.35pm, with her ensign at half-mast, *Hermes* anchored in Marsa Scirocco Bay. Two days later the C-in-C Mediterranean Station, Admiral Sir Roger Keyes, embarked in the carrier which then weighed anchor and steamed to the scene of the accident, where a memorial service was held. Over the following three weeks *Hermes* continued her flying practice off Malta, and on Thursday 22 April there was another fatal accident on the flight deck when one of the RAF personnel, Ldg Airman H. F. Miles, was killed by the revolving propeller blade of a Flycatcher. Later that day *Hermes* secured to buoys in Grand Harbour to begin a refit which would last for the best part of two months, and would see her dry docked during May and early June.

It was on the morning of Thursday 17 June that *Hermes* put to sea again for post-refit machinery trials and exercises with the destroyer *Viceroy*, before returning to Grand Harbour that afternoon. During the last week of June the carrier exercised in the Adriatic with the battleships *Barham, Resolution* and *Warspite*, and she visited the city of Trieste for ten days. On 5 August Admiral Sir Roger Keyes inspected the ship and eight days later, in the early hours of Friday 13 August, Captain R. Elliot CBE RN, who had been appointed to command *Hermes* three weeks earlier, joined the ship. Next morning, at 11am, he took over command from Captain Talbot who left the ship to await a sea passage home. Following the change of command *Hermes* sailed from Malta on 23 August to carry out flying practice in the Ionian Sea, before returning to Grand

Harbour on 11 September to prepare for another deployment east of Suez. During her nine-day stay in Malta stores and ammunition were embarked, after which she set course for Port Said, commencing her transit of the Suez Canal on 23 September. After making a brief call at Aden and stopping for two days in Colombo, during which time the Governor of the colony was taken for a demonstration flight in one of the carrier's seaplanes, *Hermes* called at Singapore for fuel on her voyage east, and she arrived back in Hong Kong on Monday 11 October, after an absence of eight months. There was a break of five days for the ship's company before the carrier sailed out of harbour to carry out daily flying practice in the South China Sea, following which she anchored each evening in Mirs or Bias Bay, close to the colony. Finally, during the morning of 16 December, she steamed into Hong Kong Harbour where she would remain until the first week of February 1927.

During the 1920s and 1930s the Crown Colony of Hong Kong was not the powerhouse of commercial activity which it became in the post-war years, it was a small colonial backwater with most of the British Empire's trade with China going through Shanghai and, to a lesser extent, other Treaty ports on the Chinese mainland. One important duty of the Royal Navy in the inter-war years was to provide guard ships at the international settlements on the Yangtse River (Chang Jiang River), in order to protect the extensive British trading interests in the city. In early 1927 the civil war in China, between Chiang Kai-shek's Nationalist forces, the various private armies of powerful warlords, and the Communists under Mao Tse-tung, had reached Shanghai, and Britain had dispatched an Army division and additional naval units to the port. In March 1927 the Nationalist forces made an attempt to invade the foreign concessions, and although this had been repelled by the British and Allied forces, tension in the city was high as fighting broke out between Nationalists and Communists. During March and for most of April *Hermes* remained in Hong Kong, venturing to sea only once for 24 hours when she remained in local waters. On the morning of 28 April, however, as part of the British military presence in the area the carrier was sent to the port of Woosung (Wusung), near Shanghai. Three days later she anchored off Woosung, but in the event the fighting had stopped before she arrived and so her visit was brief on this occasion and by 5 May she was back in Hong Kong, where she spent three weeks in the Whampoa Dock Company's Kowloon dry dock. By mid-July, however, she was at sea again and carrying out flying practice in local waters. On Wednesday 13 July one of the carrier's seaplanes went missing during a morning flight and after a long and fruitless search the pilot, Flt-Lt L. W. H. Phillips RAF, was posted as missing believed killed.

On Wednesday 27 July, *Hermes* left the heat and

humidity of midsummer Hong Kong and set course north for the leased territory of Wei hai wei, opposite the Korean peninsula, which was treated by British governments as a Crown Colony. The territory had been leased by Britain in 1898 to offset the Russian acquisition of Port Arthur (Lushun), and the lease was contingent on the Russian presence which, after their defeat in the Russo-Japanese War of 1905, was relinquished. However, far from leaving Wei hai wei at this time Britain stayed on, with the territory's main town and port being renamed Port Edward. Wei hai wei's cooler climate and its fine beaches appealed to holidaymakers who wanted to escape from the frenetic city of Shanghai, or the sweltering heat of Hong Kong's summers. The Royal Navy was no different, and in the summer months, long before air-conditioning became a feature of HM Ships, the fleet would usually steam north for the cooler and more bearable weather at Wei hai wei. After a passage of four days *Hermes* anchored off the island of Liukungtao, which housed the naval base and the fleet canteen, and she remained there until mid-August. During this time the ship's company were granted five hours' shore leave between 4.30pm and 9.30pm each weekday which was not too popular after the fleshpots of Hong Kong, since the only real attraction for liberty men was the ornamental stone fleet canteen on Liukungtao Island. Operationally, in the sheltered waters of Wei hai wei, the carrier's seaplanes were able to continue their daily training flights, so each morning they would be hoisted out into the harbour from where they would take off, and in the late afternoon they would be hoisted back on board to be prepared for the next day's flying. Compared to the hectic routine aboard the post-war carriers of the jet age, life in the pre-war Fleet Air Arm was relatively relaxed.

After leaving Wei hai wei on Monday 22 August *Hermes* steamed south and spent two days anchored off Woosung, before returning to Hong Kong on 30 August. At 4.15am on Thursday 1 September *Hermes* made an early sailing from Hong Kong to rendezvous with HMS *Argus*, which had arrived on station to relieve her, and the two carriers steamed to nearby Bias Bay (which was actually in Chinese territory), to attack pirate junks which were causing a problem for coastal shipping around Hong Kong and Macau. As well as attacking the junks a landing party from *Hermes* went ashore to destroy sampans and houses which were known to belong to the pirates. That evening, with the operation completed, *Hermes* anchored for the night and next morning, with her stint on the China Station drawing to a close, she returned to Hong Kong Harbour.

On the China Station in 1927.

(Fleet Air Arm Museum)

Hermes at Wei hai wei in 1928. As a run ashore it had little to offer but a few beaches and a fleet canteen at Liukungtao Island.

(Fleet Air Arm Museum)

On Wednesday 7 September she left Hong Kong bound for Singapore and her voyage home, and after two days in the man o' war anchorage in Singapore Roads she sailed north to Penang, then on to Colombo and Aden. To everyone's relief she spent just ten hours refuelling at the latter port and on Monday 10 October she made her northbound passage of the Suez Canal. Finally, at just after midnight on Wednesday 26 October, she anchored off the Isle of Wight. Later that day her Fairey Flycatchers were flown off to RAF Gosport, and the following day the Fairey IIIDs departed, with the officers and ratings of 403 and 440 Flights being disembarked soon afterwards. On Saturday 29 October *Hermes* steamed into Portsmouth Harbour where she secured to a buoy, and for the first time in over two years her ship's company were able to go ashore on home soil. It was not, however, the end of the commission and on the last day of October *Hermes* left Portsmouth to set course for Chatham, where after spending the night at anchor off The Nore light vessel, she secured alongside the South Wall of Chatham Dockyard's No 1 basin to start a three-month refit. On Friday 2 December 1927 there was a change of command when Captain G. Hopwood CBE RN relieved Captain Elliot and 12 days later, at 9.30am on Wednesday 14 December, the ship's company were paid off and discharged to the naval barracks, from where they would take their well-earned foreign service leave.

In those days, with a full complement of men being held permanently in reserve in each of the three naval barracks at Portsmouth, Devonport and Chatham, it was quite normal to recommission a ship within hours of paying off and on this occasion *Hermes* was recommissioned with a full complement at 9.30am on Thursday 15 December. It was in the New Year that she was ready for sea once again, and on Wednesday 11 January 1928 the ship's company paraded in the hangar where they were inspected by the C-in-C Chatham. Next day the carrier left Chatham Dockyard and moored at a buoy off Sheerness where, for three days, she took on ammunition from lighters before sailing to Portsmouth to embark stores and the personnel of 440, 442 and 403 Flights. She left Portsmouth during the forenoon of Saturday 21 January, and after landing on the Flycatchers of 403 Flight and the Fairey IIIFs (which had replaced the IIIDs) of 440 and 442 Flights, she set sail.

During her passage east *Hermes* called briefly at Gibraltar and Malta, and on Sunday 5 February, after a day moored in Port Said Harbour, she steamed south through the Suez Canal. After leaving Port Suez early on Monday 6 February she set course for Aden where there was a brief refuelling stop, before she steamed south-east across the Arabian Sea to Colombo and then on to Penang. Early March saw *Hermes* anchored off Singapore City for four days before she steamed north into the Gulf of Siam (Gulf of Thailand), to anchor off Bangkok Bar on the morning of 9 March for a four-day official visit. Because the aircraft carrier was anchored so far from Bangkok the Siamese Navy arranged for their sloop *Chow Phraya** to provide a ferry service into the city. On Monday 12 March, Captain Hopwood and his officers hosted an official lunch on board the carrier which was attended by members of the Siamese Royal Family and British residents of the city. Next day the King of Siam visited the *Hermes* for two hours, during which the seaplanes staged a flying display, after which, at 3pm, the carrier weighed anchor and set course for Hong Kong where she arrived five days later. Her arrival on the China Station meant that *Argus* could leave for home, which she did on Tuesday 20 March, while *Hermes* settled down to life in the exotic east.

Although *Hermes* remained in harbour for four weeks, flying operations were carried out daily and at 11.15am on Tuesday 3 April came the first flying accident of the commission when a Fairey IIIF was lost overboard as it attempted to land on the flight deck. The body of the pilot, Flying Officer Hale RAF, was brought in by the seaboat, but the other two crew members, Lt Graham RN and Telegraphist Jackson, were recovered by the ship's divers that afternoon. Next day the funeral service for the three men took place ashore, and the divers recovered the wreck of the seaplane. After eight days in dry dock at Kowloon *Hermes* sailed from Hong Kong on 18 April to undergo eight days of flying practice in and around Mirs Bay, and on 3 May she sailed from the colony bound for the Treaty Port of Chefoo (Yantai), then Wei hai wei. The visit to the former lasted until 5 June, during which time, with a curfew ashore, leave was terminated at 7.30pm. With such restrictions on the movement of liberty men most members of the ship's company were relieved when, at 11.50am on 5 June, *Hermes* left harbour to make the short four-hour passage east along the coast to Wei hai wei, where she remained for 19 days. During this period flying took place on most days and on Wednesday 20 June there was a fatal accident when Flycatcher 9661, flown by Lt R. A. Aldridge RN, crashed into the sea when attempting to land and sank immediately. The ship's divers and salvage parties were quickly dispatched to the scene, but they were unable to locate the wreckage until the following day when both the body of the pilot and the aircraft were recovered. The funeral for Lt Aldridge took place at Wei hai wei during the afternoon of 22 June, and two days later *Hermes* left harbour bound for the port of Chingwangtao in the Gulf of Pohai. At the port, as well as the cruiser HMS *Berwick* and the destroyer HMS *Somme*, there was an array of international warships, including the US Navy's cruiser *Trenton*, the Italian Navy's cruiser *Libia***, and the French sloop *Regulas*.

During her three weeks at Chingwangtao *Hermes* put to sea regularly to carry out flying practice, and on 9 July one of her Fairey IIIF seaplanes made a forced landing in the sea approximately nine miles east of the ship. Fortunately relations between the Royal and Italian Navies were still good and the Italian destroyer *Muggia* was able to rescue the pilot and tow the aircraft back to *Hermes*. After returning to Wei hai wei the carrier remained at anchor there until the end of July when she steamed south to Shanghai where she was able to secure alongside one of the commercial wharves, close to the US gunboat, *Panay*. It was 12 September before *Hermes* left Shanghai to return to Wei hai wei where the C-in-C China Station carried out his harbour and sea inspections, and it was late October before the carrier returned to Hong Kong where she remained until the end of November with only two days at sea for flying practice. Before Christmas, however, *Hermes* left Hong Kong on a short cruise to Jesselton, where members of the ship's company were given guided tours of a rubber plantation. She also visited Kudat on the northern tip of North Borneo (Sabah), and Manila, where she spent seven days and received a visit from the US Navy's Asiatic Fleet. By Wednesday 19 December 1928 *Hermes* was back in Hong Kong, and during the evening of Christmas Day a fancy dress party was held in the forward hangar.

On Tuesday 1 January 1929 *Hermes* shifted from No 1 buoy in the harbour to the naval dockyard's North Arm to begin a three-month refit, and at 11am on Saturday 16 March Captain Hopwood left the carrier to return to the UK. During his absence the ship's Executive Officer, Cdr R. Ramsbottom RN, assumed temporary command until, on Thursday 28 March the new commanding officer, Captain J. D. Campbell MVO CBE RN, arrived in the colony and took command. It was on Monday 1 April that *Hermes* put to sea again to undergo machinery trials and to embark her seaplanes, and following this she remained in and around Hong Kong carrying out exercises and manoeuvres with the cruiser *Suffolk* and the destroyers *Somme* and *Thracian*. On the morning of Tuesday 8 April, the destroyers of the China Station, which included HMS *Sepoy*, were exercising in local waters when a depth charge which was being prepared on board *Sepoy* exploded and killed an officer and three men outright, and injured three others. The destroyer returned immediately to harbour and next day the funerals, with full military honours, were held for the victims. *Hermes* provided the band along with a full guard of honour and the procession was led by the C-in-C China Station, Admiral Hill, who was followed by men from all the military units in Hong Kong, including contingents from US, French, Italian and Portuguese warships as well as many civilians. In late April aircraft from *Hermes* escorted *Suffolk* with the Duke of Gloucester on board as the cruiser left for a visit to Japan, and in mid-

*The *Chow Phraya* was the ex-Royal Navy sloop HMS *Havant*.
**The ex-Turkish cruiser *Drama*.

23

Another view of *Hermes* at Wei hai wei.

(*Fleet Air Arm Museum*)

May there came another fatal accident. It was on 13 May, whilst *Hermes* was operating her aircraft off Hong Kong, that a Fairey IIIF crashed into the sea after landing on the flight deck. The pilot and a passenger were rescued alive by *Thracian* but, despite a long search by *Hermes* and the destroyers *Sepoy*, which was back at sea after the explosion on board, and *Thracian*, there was no sign of the third occupant, AC (1) J. A. C. Willis of the RAF. Three days later a memorial service was held over the spot, before *Hermes* set course for the city of Nanking (Nanjing) on the Yangtse River. The passage up the river took 24 hours, during which she anchored overnight before resuming her progress and arriving off Nanking at 10.20am on 21 May. During the nine-day visit *Hermes* undertook the duties of guardship, but with shore leave restricted to just a few organized trips to the tomb of Sun Yat Sen, everyone on board was relieved when the carrier steamed back down the Yangtse, a passage which again took the best part of 24 hours. Once clear of the river, *Hermes* set course for Wei hai wei, where she remained for four months, putting to sea on occasions to carry out flying exercises and manoeuvres with other units.

The carrier's summer visit to Wei hai wei came to an end on Monday 23 September when she sailed for the Treaty Port of Tsingtau, where she stayed for five days. The port had formerly been administered by Germany, and although it had been taken by the Japanese during the Great War, the foreign presence was still dominated by Germany. When she left the port, with the cruiser HMS *Kent*, she was bound for Japan, a cruise which proved very popular with the ship's company. After eight days in Yokohama she left Tokyo Bay and steamed down the coast to Suruga Bay for a seven-day visit to the small town of Shimizu, and from there she sailed into the Inland Sea for six days at Kobe, where she was able to secure alongside the harbour breakwater. After leaving Kobe *Hermes* made a five-day passage back to Hong Kong, where she moored in the harbour at 11am on Tuesday 29 October. No sooner had she secured to her buoy, however, than one of her Flycatcher aircraft was involved in a fatal accident when it crashed into the harbour close to the carrier whilst landing. Unfortunately, despite the prompt dispatch of the crash boat the pilot, Flying Officer A. R. Ward RAF, lost his life and later that afternoon the ship's divers recovered his body and the wrecked aircraft.

The remainder of 1929 and most of January 1930 were spent in and around Hong Kong, but on 28 January *Hermes* embarked the British Minister to China, Sir Miles Lampson, and sailed for Nanking where he was disembarked five days later, for talks with Chinese Government representatives about the Japanese invasion of Manchuria which had started in November 1929. *Hermes* herself spent the rest of February as the guardship at Nanking before, on 2 March, she steamed down the

Yangtse River to Shanghai where she joined the cruiser *Cornwall*, the destroyers *Somme* and *Stirling* and the river gunboats, *Aphis, Ladybird, Peterel* and *Tern*. In addition to the Royal Navy's presence in the city, there were also three US warships, two Italian, one French and one Japanese (the cruiser *Hirado*) moored offshore. To the delight of the ship's company the stay in Shanghai lasted for three weeks, but by the end of March the carrier was back in Hong Kong, in whose vicinity she would remain until mid-June. During this period the carrier underwent a four-week refit, but on 10 June she left for the cooler climes of Wei hai wei, from where she operated until late July when she set course for Hong Kong once again. This time, however, she was homeward bound at the end of another commission on the China Station.

Hermes left Hong Kong on Thursday 7 August to steam home by way of Singapore, Colombo and Aden. She made her northbound transit of the Suez Canal on 7 September, and after two nights in Port Said, with shore leave granted until midnight, she left Egypt on 9 September bound for Malta and Gibraltar. At 8.10am on Tuesday 23 September, those on watch on *Hermes*' bridge sighted St Catherine's Light on the Isle of Wight, and later that morning all the aircraft were flown to RAF Gosport. During the afternoon she steamed up harbour to secure alongside Portsmouth's Pitch House Jetty, and once again she was home.

After six days in Portsmouth *Hermes* left at 9.30am on Monday 29 September for Chatham and that same evening she secured to a buoy off Sheerness. Three days later, at 10.20am on Thursday 2 October, the carrier's new commanding officer, Captain E. J. G. Mackinnon RN*, joined the ship to take over from Captain Campbell and three hours later the ship's company were paid off.

* Rear-Admiral Mackinnon lost his life on 17 September 1940 when, having been recalled to the Royal Navy from the Retired List, he was Commodore of Convoy OB 213 in the Ellerman City liner, *City of Benares*, which was torpedoed and sunk in the Atlantic with heavy loss of life, including 77 children.

Hoisting a Fairey Flycatcher onto the flight deck.

(Fleet Air Arm Museum)

Chapter Three

Return To China And A Royal Review
October 1930 - June 1937

At 10.30am on 3 October 1930, just 24 hours after her change of command, the RFA *Nimble* secured alongside *Hermes* at Sheerness with a new ship's company for the carrier, and one hour later, at 11.30am, the ship was recommissioned for further service east of Suez. Before leaving, however, she was taken into Chatham Dockyard for a short refit and it was Monday 3 November before she left to carry out two days of trials before setting course for Spithead and Portsmouth Dockyard. At Pitch House Jetty *Hermes* embarked the Fairey Flycatchers of 403 Flight and the Fairey IIIFs of 440 Flight, all of which were brought alongside by lighter and hoisted on board. In addition she also embarked six Blackburn Ripon torpedo-bombers to deliver to HMS *Eagle* which was with the Mediterranean Fleet and operating from Malta.

Hermes left Portsmouth on 12 November and eight days later, when she was off Malta, the Ripon bombers were flown off to join *Eagle*. After spending nine days in and around Grand Harbour *Hermes* sailed for Port Said and in the early hours of 1 December she cleared the Suez Canal and set course for Aden. To everyone's relief the stay in Aden lasted less than 24 hours before she set course for Colombo and Singapore, where she was to spend Christmas. After fuelling at Singapore's Keppel Harbour, just west of the city, on the afternoon of Monday 22 December the carrier sailed round to the north-east coast of the island to anchor in the Johore Strait, off the naval dockyard which was under construction. Next day she was manoeuvred into the Admiralty floating dock which, at that time, was the only naval dry docking facility available in Singapore and she remained there for four days. For the ship's company the naval base was not as popular as the man o' war anchorage off Singapore City itself, for it meant a round journey of over 40 miles for liberty men. Apart from the fleet canteen within the naval base, only the villages of Nee Soon and Sembawang were within easy reach of the dockyard. New Year's Eve was spent in the South China Sea, en route to Hong Kong, and it was during the forenoon of Friday 2 January 1931 that the carrier arrived back in Hong Kong Harbour.

During the three months which followed her arrival on the China Station *Hermes* operated out of Hong Kong, and she was inspected by Vice-Admiral Sir W. D. H. Kelly, the C-in-C China Station. In early April she began an eight-week refit in the colony's naval dockyard, which was completed at the end of May when she carried out her post-refit trials. On Friday 5 June, after carrying out several days of deck landing practice, *Hermes* left for the cooler climes of Wei hai wei where she was to spend the summer. Four days later, at 1.35pm on Tuesday 9 June, when *Hermes* was in a position Lat 37° - 28'N/Long 122° - 44'E, she received an urgent signal reporting that the submarine HMS *Poseidon* had sunk outside Wei hai wei. Captain Mackinnon immediately increased speed to 21 knots and just over an hour later the carrier anchored close to the scene of the tragedy. *Poseidon* had left her depot ship, HMS *Medway*, at just before 9am that morning and after carrying out submerged control trials, she surfaced to carry out the firing of a torpedo at the 'target', which was the minesweeper, HMS *Marazion*. However, at 12.12pm the submarine was accidentally rammed by the 1,753-ton merchantman, the coaster SS *Yuta*. The terrific impact punched a 'V' shaped hole about nine feet deep through the submarine's saddle tank and about four feet into the pressure hull. Although five officers and 28 ratings managed to scramble to safety before she sank, 18 ratings were trapped in the compartments abaft the engine room, with six ratings and two Chinese civilians trapped in the forward torpedo compartment.

Fortunately *Marazion* and *Yuta* were able to rescue those who had managed to escape from the stricken submarine, and *Marazion* was able to buoy the position of the wreck so that rescue attempts could begin as soon as possible. *Hermes*, the cruisers *Cumberland* and *Berwick* and the submarines *Osiris* and *Pandora* were all soon at the scene and Captain Mackinnon, as the senior officer present, took charge of the rescue mission. He immediately called for all ships' divers to be mustered and for all the diving gear from ships in harbour to be made available, while at the same time he organized boats from the rescue ships to patrol the area from which bubbles and oil could be seen rising to the surface. It was not long before the first diving boats were over the position, but in the cold and dark forward torpedo compartment the survivors, under the leadership of the submarine's coxswain, Petty Officer Patrick H. Willis, were organizing their own escape. With the aid of the Davis Submarine Escape Apparatus they managed to flood the compartment and force open the forward torpedo hatch. Six of the eight men reached the surface and they were taken to *Hermes'* sickbay, where two subsequently died.

That evening, at 10pm, Lt-Cdr G. A. M. V. Harrison,

A Fairey IIIF takes off from *Hermes'* flight deck.

(Fleet Air Arm Museum)

from *Hermes*, located the wreck of *Poseidon* with a grappling hook and divers were sent down to attach lines to the submarine. Unfortunately, weather conditions were poor and soon they became too severe to allow diving to continue, but next morning hawser wires were attached to the wreck. In the evening the US Navy's specialized submarine salvage vessel, USS *Pigeon*, arrived on the scene to help, and her divers reported that *Poseidon* had sunk some five feet into the mud and so any immediate plans for the salvage of the submarine were abandoned. Although HMS *Medway* took over command of the salvage operations, divers from *Hermes* continued to descend on the wreck in order to assess the damage but, finally, during the afternoon of Saturday 13 June, the carrier weighed anchor and steamed into Wei hai wei harbour, leaving the divers from *Pigeon* and *Medway* to continue working on the wreck of the *Poseidon*.

During the remainder of June and through to the last week of August *Hermes* operated out of Wei hai wei, with only a short visit to Chefoo to break her daily flying routine. With Wei hai wei having been handed back to China on 1 October 1930, the Navy wished to maintain good relations with Commissioner Hsu who, on 4 August, was taken for a flight in one of the carrier's seaplanes, following which he watched a flying display by the Flycatchers and IIIF seaplanes. On Saturday 29 August, the *Hermes* left Wei hai wei and set course for the Treaty Port of Hankow, some 600 miles up the Yangtse River. There can be few people who have not heard of the mighty Yangtse River, but for the sailors on the Royal Navy's China Station of the inter-war years it was very familiar for most ships would, at some time during their tenure, navigate the 600 miles between the sea and the port of Hankow. Even in those days it was estimated that 150 million people lived along its banks, and as the ships steamed slowly up against the fast flowing currents they would pass dozens of large towns and hundreds of villages. At its mouth the river is over 30 miles wide and even at Hankow it is still a mile across. Although Britain had surrendered her leasehold concessions to China in 1927, there were still considerable business interests in the city and a cruiser, together with river gunboats of the China Fleet, were permanently stationed there. The city itself had a two-mile-long Bund which, like that in Shanghai, was adorned with many fine European buildings. The waterfront was always massed with steamers of all sizes and nationalities, and behind this lay a considerable European town with shops, hotels, clubs and even a racecourse. For ships' companies, however, shore leave was usually restricted to daylight hours which was not popular. At 1am on 31 August *Hermes* anchored off Woosung at the mouth of the Yangtse, and later in the morning she weighed anchor to begin her passage. That evening, at just before dark, she anchored for the night and next morning she continued her passage, anchoring off Nanking later in the afternoon. On the evening of 4 September she anchored at Chicken Reach, and next day, at 3pm, she finally reached Hankow after a river passage of over 100 hours.

The carrier was being sent to the port for two reasons, firstly because there had been some unrest and mutinies aboard a number of British-owned merchant vessels, and secondly to assist with flood relief measures. As soon as *Hermes* was safely anchored, armed guards were sent to various merchant ships, including the SS *Siang Wo*, whose local Chinese crew had started the unrest. That year floods along the Yangtse River had been more severe than usual and it was estimated that over a million people had drowned in this natural disaster. One naval officer summed up the scene at Hankow thus: 'It was an extraordinary sight; a sea horizon, although 600 miles inland'. The seaplanes from *Hermes* were to be used to carry out detailed flood surveys for the Chinese Government, and for the operation they had Chinese identification characters painted on their fuselages. Also in Hankow at that time was the celebrated American pilot Colonel Charles Lindbergh with his wife Anne, who was also a very competent aviator. They had arrived in China from Tokyo on a much publicized round-the-world flight in their specially built Lockheed Sirius seaplane. Whilst in China Lindbergh was asked by President Chiang Kai-shek to assist with the aerial survey of the Yangtse River just as aircraft from *Hermes* were doing, as they were the only machines in China with the capability of flying the long hours required; Anne Lindbergh would pilot the aircraft whilst her husband drew the detailed maps of the area. During their stay in Hankow the C-in-C China Station invited the couple to use *Hermes* as their base and they arrived in the river alongside the carrier during the afternoon of 30 September to be hoisted on board. Next morning at 10.30am, the Lockheed Sirius was hoisted out to continue its survey flights, before being brought back on board later that afternoon. On the following day the Lindberghs climbed into their seaplane at 9.45am and whilst being lowered into the river to prepare for take-off, the strong current caught it and flipped the plane onto its back pitching both Lindbergh and his wife into the muddy waters of the Yangtse River. Happily they were both quickly rescued by one of the ship's boats which had been stationed downstream, unfortunately not before they had both swallowed mouthfuls of the murky water, and after they had both taken great pains to avoid drinking

and cleaning their teeth in anything but pure bottled water. In fact the cable holding the plane had been too taut to detach the hoisting hook and as the aircraft touched the water Lindbergh had revved the engine in an attempt to maintain the plane's equilibrium while they tried to release the hook, but as they struggled with the cable one of the plane's wings dipped into the water capsizing the whole machine. As the hook was still attached to the seaplane it was quickly hoisted back onto the carrier's flight deck, but having been damaged it was in need of repairs and Captain Mackinnon offered to take the couple and their seaplane downriver to Shanghai. The Lindberghs accepted his offer and at 3.30pm on Saturday 3 October the *Hermes* weighed anchor to make a four-day passage to Shanghai, where the Lockheed Sirius was disembarked onto a lighter and the Lindberghs left the carrier for a hotel in the city.

After disembarking her guests *Hermes* remained at Shanghai until Monday 2 November, and during the visit there were many social events, with a dance in the hangar for the officers which lasted until the small hours of the morning. Despite the guests having to endure a rather cold journey downriver in a tug, most of 'social Shanghai' attended. There were football and hockey matches against Army and RAF units, and a billiards match was arranged at Shanghai's Union Jack Club between *Hermes* and an Army team. At 8.20pm on 3 November, the day after leaving Shanghai for Hong Kong, she received an SOS message from a Japanese merchant ship, SS *Ryinjin Maru*, which had run aground on the Tan Rocks off the Chinese mainland at the northern end of the Taiwan Strait. The carrier immediately increased speed and on arriving at the scene at 11pm she anchored as close as she could to the stricken vessel. Because of heavy seas, however, she was unable to give any practical assistance that night, but next morning she was able to move closer to the wrecked ship and by 9am a cutter was on its way over to the *Ryinjin Maru*, where it rescued nine crew members. It then set out, under sail, to make a second rescue attempt, but rough seas and high winds forced it to return to the carrier and the efforts were abandoned for the day. Next morning the Japanese destroyer *Nashi* arrived on the scene to take on board the survivors from *Hermes* before assuming the rescue operation. Later that day *Hermes* weighed anchor to set course for Hong Kong once again and at 6.45am on Saturday 7 November the aircraft were flown off to Kai Tak airfield, with the carrier securing to No 1 buoy in the harbour two hours later.

Hermes remained in and around Hong Kong through to late April 1932, with both Christmas and New Year being celebrated in the colony. On Tuesday 29 December 1931 Captain Mackinnon was taken ill and he left the ship for the Royal Naval Hospital ashore, with command temporarily passing to the Executive Officer. On Thursday 25 February 1932, the carrier's new commanding officer,

Colonel Charles Lindbergh's specially built Lockheed Sirius seaplane is hoisted aboard at Hankow. *(Fleet Air Arm Museum)*

Captain W. B. Mackenzie RN, who had been appointed to the ship on 8 January, arrived in Hong Kong by sea to assume command of the ship. In early March the *Hermes* started a six-week refit in the dockyard, including two weeks in dry dock, and it was 23 April before she left harbour to undergo engine trials. In the last week of April she left Hong Kong, in company with the destroyer *Whitehall*, to steam north for a short visit to the Treaty Port of Amoy. After leaving Amoy early on the morning of 29 April the two ships steamed north for Wei hai wei, but they soon ran into thick fog which, on the evening of 1 May, caused them to heave to for over an hour. Next morning, with the fog having cleared somewhat, the carrier received a distress call from the Japanese merchant ship, SS *Kirim Maru*, which was in trouble some 60 miles south-east of Wei hai wei. In the event Captain Mackenzie dispatched the faster *Whitehall* to her assistance, but before she arrived

the request was cancelled and at 7pm that day both units anchored at Wei hai wei.

During her summer at the north Chinese port *Hermes* carried out flying practice and manoeuvres in local waters, often in company with the *Whitehall* or the *Wishart* and at 11.25am on Wednesday 22 June, whilst coming in to land on the flight deck, Fairey IIIF, S1477, crashed over the port side of the flight deck and into the sea. *Hermes* immediately turned to port and stopped her engines, but just as the crash boat was being lowered, the destroyer *Wishart* rescued the pilot, Captain R. Giddy RM, and the observer, Lt-Cdr E. R. Dymott RN. Seven days later a Flycatcher, S1414, crashed into the sea, fortunately not far from the cruiser *Suffolk* and the pilot, Lt Chaseley RN, was rescued safely. As for runs ashore, there was the fleet canteen on Liukungtao Island, and the occasional visit to the Treaty Port of Chefoo, but on 17 September the *Hermes* left Wei

Hermes at sea with Fairey IIIFs on deck.

(*Lt-Cdr Larcombe*)

hai wei for a much anticipated visit to the Japanese port of Nagasaki. From Japan the *Hermes* returned to China and the city of Shanghai, where she remained for four weeks before returning to Hong Kong on 28 October.

Hermes remained in and around the colony for the remainder of the year, and in January 1933, after exercising with the cruiser *Devonshire*, there came a complete change of scenery when the carrier set course for the port of San Fernando in the Philippines, at the north-west of Luzon island. After two days at anchor *Hermes* carried out high-level bombing exercises before mooring in Manila Harbour where she remained for 11 days, and which proved to be a popular run ashore. By mid-February, however, she was back in Hong Kong and in early April she underwent a refit in the naval dockyard. Although she steamed north to visit Tsingtao and operate from Wei hai wei, the carrier's commission on the China Station was drawing to a close and in mid-June she left Hong Kong to begin her voyage home. She steamed west by way of Singapore, Colombo and Aden, and on Sunday 9 July she made her transit of the Suez Canal, arriving in Malta's Grand Harbour four days later. By the afternoon of 15 July, however, she was steaming west once again and at just after midnight on the

morning of Saturday 22 July Alderney Light was sighted. *Hermes* then made a fast passage up the Channel to secure to No 7 buoy at Sheerness that same evening, with leave being piped for the off-duty watch as soon as the mooring ropes were secured. Two days later large groups of Portsmouth and Devonport drafts left the ship and on 25 July the carrier shifted berth to Chatham Dockyard's No 3 basin. Saturday 5 August saw the start of Navy Week, the forerunner of today's Navy Days, and for seven consecutive days *Hermes* was opened to visitors each afternoon, following which the task of destoring ship got under way. During the afternoon of Wednesday 6 September *Hermes* left Chatham and set course for Devonport, arriving at the Cawsand Bay anchorage 24 hours later. After three days in Plymouth Sound the carrier steamed up harbour to secure alongside No 5 wharf of Devonport Dockyard. For 13 days the job of destoring and deammunitioning ship continued, but on the morning of Friday 22 September the remaining officers and men of the ship's company left, and at 9am *Hermes* paid off into dockyard control for a 12-month refit.

Hermes' first major refit was designed to give her at least another eight years of operational life, but given the carrier's small size and the increasing weight of naval

Hermes in her China Fleet livery alongside at Devonport in September 1933.

(*Lt-Cdr Larcombe*)

aircraft as aviation technology developed, there was little that could be done to increase her aircraft capacity. She was, however, fitted with arrester wires, and all her main and auxiliary machinery was thoroughly overhauled.

On Wednesday 15 August 1934, Captain The Hon G. Fraser DSO RN was appointed as the carrier's new commanding officer and a few weeks later, on Tuesday 18 September, the ship was commissioned with a full engine room complement, but with only half her complement of seamen, for engine trials. It was 10.30am on Friday 5 October when *Hermes* left Devonport Dockyard's No 7 wharf and put to sea for her trials, but a boiler defect soon forced her back to Plymouth Sound for repairs to be made. It was not long before she was back at sea again, but further machinery problems caused the trials to be abandoned and she steamed back to the dockyard for full repairs to be carried out. Fortunately the machinery problems were not difficult to rectify and on Thursday 1 November the carrier's full complement of seamen joined the ship. Six days later the C-in-C Plymouth, Admiral Sir E. J. A. Fullerton, carried out his inspection, before *Hermes* steamed east to Portsmouth for trials of the new arrester gear and the arrival of the Hawker Osprey, two-seater spotter/reconnaissance aircraft of 803 Squadron and the Fairey Seals, the three-seat torpedo-bombers of 824 Squadron. The latter aircraft was the successor to the Fairey IIIF and it had originally been designated as the IIIF Mk VI. It was the last of the Fairey III series of seaplanes which had first appeared in 1917, and it would eventually be replaced by the Swordfish. The Osprey was the naval version of the RAF's Hawker Hart bomber with folding wings for shipboard stowage and both it and the Seal were designed to make possible the rapid interchange of wheeled and float landing gear.

After landing on her aircraft *Hermes* returned to Portsmouth for seven days, then on Sunday 18 November she sailed for the Far East. After a brief call at Gibraltar *Hermes* arrived in the area off Malta where she operated her aircraft and spent two days in Grand Harbour. On Tuesday 4 December she made her transit of the Suez Canal, and called at Aden and Colombo before setting course for Singapore. Christmas Day was spent at sea steaming south through the Strait of Malacca and despite the steaming heat and humidity, the cooks in the galley worked hard to produce a magnificent traditional Christmas dinner. With the mess decks all decorated with streamers, they served roast turkey, pork and Christmas pudding, while later in the day, for tea, there was ice cream, Christmas cake, mince pies and fruit and nuts. Early the following morning *Hermes* anchored off Singapore City where leave was piped, and two days later she sailed round to the naval base in the Johore Strait, where *Eagle* was moored with her ship's company who were all eager to head west for the Mediterranean on the first stage of their voyage home. On

New Year's Day 1935 *Hermes* left Singapore bound for Hong Kong, where she arrived, after an absence of some 19 months, five days later.

Since her last deployment on the China Station there had been far-reaching political changes in the Far East, with a powerful and aggressive Japan making her presence felt by having warned the Western powers to keep their 'hands off China'. Following the successful invasion of Manchuria, Japan increasingly considered China to be within her own exclusive sphere of interest and her naval units were very much in evidence all along the coast of China. The first incident in which *Hermes* was involved, however, did not involve Japan but the problem of pirates on the China coast. The saga had started at Shanghai on 29 January when the China Steam Navigation Company's coastal passenger steamer *Tungchow* embarked her passengers, who included 70 British and American children who were returning to their mission school at Chefoo. Although *Tungchow* was registered at Shanghai and most of her crew were Chinese, she was British owned with British officers and White Russian security guards. Among the deck passengers who embarked that day were 12 heavily armed pirates and at 6pm that evening, when *Tungchow* was at sea, they attacked the ship's bridge in their attempt to take over the vessel. A Russian security guard, who put up a brave fight, was shot dead, as was one of the ship's British engineers who went to the guard's assistance. Following this bloody skirmish the pirates quickly took control, seized all arms and turned the ship southwards towards their base at Bias Bay near Hong Kong.

For three days they looted the ship, but they treated the passengers courteously, their only inconvenience was being herded into the ship's saloon. During the time they were in control of the *Tungchow* the pirates repainted the ship's funnel red and white, and they also replaced the name *Tungchow* with the Japanese name *Toa Maru*, a ship which was derelict at Hong Kong. Meanwhile, however, as soon as the *Tungchow* was reported as overdue at Chefoo the Royal Navy dispatched the sloop HMS *Sandwich* from Wei hai wei, and the cruiser HMS *Suffolk*, together with three destroyers, from Hong Kong to search for her. In addition, *Hermes*, which was operating from Hong Kong's Tolo Bay, was ordered to send her aircraft out on reconnaissance missions. At noon on Friday 1 February *Tungchow* arrived off Chilang Point, Bias Bay, where a junk was waiting to convey the looted stores and cargo ashore. Soon after the start of this operation, three Seals took off from *Hermes* at 12.50pm to carry out a search of the area and within minutes they had spotted the suspicious 'Japanese' steamer which was anchored in Bias Bay. As soon as they had flown low overhead and 'buzzed' the ship, the pirates clearly realized that the game was up and they hurriedly made their escape in the junk and one of the ship's boats, taking with them as hostages the steamer's Chief Officer, wireless

Having made a successful landing, a Fairey Seal is taken in hand by the flight deck handlers.   *(Anthony G. Myers)*

A Hawker Osprey is prepared for take-off.   *(Anthony G. Myers)*

Hermes at anchor with awnings spread and Fairey IIIFs on the flight deck.

(*Fleet Air Arm Museum*)

operator and the Chinese passengers. Once ashore they smashed up the boat and left the passengers unharmed, but stranded on the beach. Fortunately they were soon rescued and *Tungchow* herself steamed into Hong Kong Harbour where, it was said, the schoolchildren were delighted with the unplanned extension of their school holiday. This was just one, highly-publicized, example of the continual war which was waged against marauding pirates on the China coast during those inter-war years.

During the following weeks *Hermes* continued to operate out of Hong Kong and in April she underwent a refit which kept her in dry dock until early May, when she returned to No 1 buoy in the harbour. On Monday 6 May she, like all the other warships in the harbour, was dressed overall for King George V's Silver Jubilee celebrations. After ceremonial Divisions a make and mend was granted and the gangway was opened to liberty men at 1pm. That evening *Hermes* was illuminated and she put on impressive searchlight display across the harbour. Eleven days later she left Hong Kong to steam north for her summer base at Wei hai wei, where she operated with the cruisers *Berwick, Capetown* and *Kent* (flag C-in-C China Station), the destroyers *Decoy* and *Duchess* and the sloop *Falmouth*.

In early September 1935, with Italian troops about to invade Abyssinia (Ethiopia), it was decided to station *Hermes* closer to East Africa, where she could be called upon should any British and French intervention in the

crisis be ordered by the League of Nations. It was on Thursday 12 September that she left Wei hai wei in very stormy weather, bound for the naval base at Singapore where she was to spend the rest of the year and the first few weeks of 1936. Just an hour after sailing, at 9.45pm, with severe gales blowing and high tumbling waves, the carrier's commander, who was carrying out his rounds of the weather decks, saw that the heavy rolling had tilted one of the ship's boats and he ordered seven of the duty watch ratings to get into the boat and try to right it. One of those men, 'Jock' Begg, remembers the incident: 'The attempt to right the boat was unsuccessful and he ordered the gripes to be released. Immediately we did this the boat swung outwards and at the same moment a colossal wave lifted the boat, with us in it, above the falls. When we crashed back down again the stern release gear was torn from its sockets, the boat upended and we were all catapulted into the raging sea. As I was on top of one of the waves I remember seeing the lights of the *Hermes* disappearing into the distance, and as I was thrown into the trough I thought my end had come, particularly as I couldn't see any of my mates. I don't know how long we were in the water, but suddenly I smelt oil and at the same time the sea around me was lit up by searchlights from the ship, which had returned. I heard splashes around me and realized I was being thrown heaving lines, and I grabbed hold of one immediately. I then felt myself being pulled towards the

Hermes steams past Drake's Island in October 1934 as she returns to Devonport from sea trials.   *(Maritime Photo Library)*

huge bulk of *Hermes*. I still have vivid memories of seeing the ship's propeller as she was lifted out of the water, but the thought of sharks spurred me on and I was hoisted up on board where many hands grabbed me as I came over the side. We were all taken to the sickbay where we were treated for shock, but the only man injured was Norman Tapscott who suffered two broken ribs.' Fortunately, prompt action and skilful navigation as the carrier executed a circle to port had brought her back to the scene, and prevented the drama from turning into a tragedy on that dark and stormy evening in the Yellow Sea.

After a seven-day passage *Hermes* arrived off Singapore City on 19 September and after flying the aircraft to RAF Seletar she anchored in Singapore Roads which, for liberty men, was handy for the city. On 3 October, however, she steamed up the Johore Strait to spend five days in the floating dock at the naval base, where she also took on a replacement cutter. In the second week of November, whilst at anchor in Singapore Roads, *Hermes* was ordered to stand by to sail should she be required to assist in the search for two missing aviators. On Wednesday 6 November, a distinguished Australian pilot, Air Commodore Sir Charles Kingsford-Smith, and his co-pilot, Tom Pethyridge, had left Lympne aerodrome, Kent, flying their Lockheed Altair monoplane, *Lady Southern Cross*, in an attempt to break the speed record between Britain and Australia. An hour after taking off on their flight to Sydney they were seen flying over Paris, and they made their first refuelling stop at Marseilles. Despite the fact that weather conditions in the Bay of Bengal were described as 'unfavourable', they pressed on, calling at Athens and Baghdad for fuel. They landed at Allahabad in India at

5.25pm on 7 November for further refuelling, then they took off an hour later en route to Singapore where they were due to land at the island's Kallang Airport early the next morning. They were seen over Akyab (Sittwe), on the coast near the India-Burma border, before they headed out into gale force winds over the Bay of Bengal. During the early afternoon of Friday 8 November, when they were several hours overdue at Singapore, the Air Officer Commanding the Royal Air Force in Singapore ordered aircraft from *Hermes* (which were ashore at RAF Seletar) together with RAF flying boats from the base and from Rangoon to search the Bay of Bengal. *Hermes* was also ordered to immediate notice for steam and a Qantas airliner also took part in the search, but after battling with severe storms all the flying boats returned to their bases without having sighted the missing plane. The search continued until 6 December but, with no trace having been found of the missing airmen, it was assumed that they had crashed into the sea and lost their lives.

For the next two months *Hermes* operated out of Singapore and in mid-December she paid a four-day visit to Port Swettenham (Pelabulan Kelang), the port which served the Malayan capital, Kuala Lumpur. Christmas 1935 and the New Year were spent at anchor in Singapore Roads and for the first seven weeks of 1936 *Hermes* operated from Singapore. On Wednesday 15 January, whilst operating off Singapore City, *Hermes* saluted the outgoing C-in-C China Station, Vice-Admiral Sir Frederick Dreyer, who was homeward-bound in the P&O liner, SS *Carthage*, which had left Singapore's Keppel Harbour at 11 am that morning. As she steamed out of Singapore Roads, *Hermes* and the cruiser *Cornwall* kept

High and dry in the floating dry dock in the Johore Strait off Singapore Naval Base during October 1935.

(Fleet Air Arm Museum)

station alongside her and, with the ships' companies manning the decks, salutes were exchanged, with the two squadrons flying over the departing liner in formation. In the first week of March *Hermes* returned to Hong Kong, where she underwent a refit before leaving the colony on 21 April with the destroyers *Delight* and *Duncan*, for a cruise to Japanese ports. The first call was Kobe where she spent two weeks before moving on to Kagoshima for a four-day visit, and finally to Nagasaki where she spent five days. After leaving Japan on 25 May the carrier set course for Wei hai wei, which, after the exotic Japanese ports, seemed rather an anti-climax. During her stay at the northern Chinese base she carried out fleet exercises with other units and her ship's company took part in the annual fleet regatta. At the end of July she visited the Japanese-controlled Treaty Ports of Port Arthur and Tsingtao.

On Monday 7 September 1936 *Hermes* hoisted the flag of the C-in-C China Station and put to sea for a day of flying and gunnery exercises, and later that month he carried out his harbour inspection of the ship. In mid-October the carrier made a nine-day call at Shanghai, where the more relaxed atmosphere of the 1920s and early 1930s had given way to tensions with the Japanese who controlled most of the city, and strict curfews were in force. As she steamed south to Hong Kong there was a brief call at Amoy, but the rest of the year was spent moored to No 2 buoy in Hong Kong Harbour, with only one day at sea to undergo a full-power trial. The New Year of 1937, however, brought a change of scenery for *Hermes* when, on 4 January, in company with the cruiser *Dorsetshire,* and the destroyers *Diana* and *Duncan*, *Hermes* left the China Station for the last time to steam south for a series of visits to ports in what were then the Dutch East Indies, but are now part of Indonesia. On Thursday 14 January, for the first time in her career, *Hermes* crossed the equator and the event was marked with a full ceremony on the flight deck. Next day she anchored at Macassar, Celebes (Ujong Pandang). From there she steamed across the Java Sea to Partai Barat (Denpasar), where Captain Fraser granted make and mends each afternoon of the three-day visit. The final port of call was Sourabaya (Surabaya) on the island of Java, where the carrier was able to secure alongside the harbour wall. During the seven-day visit the ship was opened to visitors each afternoon, and the Dutch Governor of East Java paid an official visit to the ship where he was entertained by Captain Fraser. During the afternoon of Saturday 30 January the carrier left the Dutch East Indies to steam north to the naval base at Singapore.

For *Hermes* the whole of February 1937 was spent operating from the naval base at Singapore and her Seals joined up with the RAF's torpedo-bombers based at Seletar to make very successful mock torpedo attacks on the cruisers *Cumberland* and *Dorsetshire*. Any lessons learned, however, were subsequently lost because four years later, in

waters not far from where the exercises were carried out, the Japanese Navy used similar tactics against the Royal Navy, with devastating results. Later in the month the carrier spent five days in the floating dock at the naval base before, on 17 March, she left Singapore to make a leisurely voyage home. On the following day she anchored off Little Dindings Island, near Lumut on the Malayan mainland, where recreational leave, complete with a 'picnic party' was granted - clearly a forerunner of the popular post-war banyans. She spent six days at Penang, four days at Colombo and, to everyone's relief, less than 24 hours in Aden. On 16 April the carrier passed through the Suez Canal and spent three days in Malta before, on 26 April, putting in to Gibraltar for three days.

At 2.55am on Monday 3 May came the welcome sight of the Eddystone Light and at daybreak all the aircraft were flown off to Roborough Airfield outside Plymouth, before *Hermes* anchored in Plymouth Sound. Two days later she moved up harbour to secure alongside No 5 wharf where destoring and deammunitioning began. Not only was this the end of *Hermes'* fourth commission, but it also appeared to be the end of her operational career, for she was to be reduced to reserve. With the new aircraft carrier *Ark Royal* having been launched just three weeks before, and with the keels of *Illustrious* and *Formidable* having been laid, the aircraft carrier tonnage allowed under the Washington Naval Treaty was urgently required for these modern fleet aircraft carriers for, even by the standards of early 1937, *Hermes* was outdated and obsolete. Before she was laid up, however, she had one more important function to fulfil, the Coronation Fleet Review for King George VI, at Spithead.

The last time *Hermes* had taken part in a Royal Review was in 1924, when she and *Argus* had been lined up with the capital ships, but this time with pride of place going to the fleet carriers *Courageous* and *Glorious*, she was representing the Reserve Fleet, and she was placed among the line of destroyers. She left Devonport on the morning of Tuesday 18 May and that afternoon she entered the waters of Spithead by way of the Needles Channel, to anchor in E-Line, off Browndown Point and next to the destroyer *Kepenfelt*. The Review took place on Friday 21 May and the start of proceedings was signalled at 1.30pm by the firing of a saluting gun on board the battleship *Nelson*. At 3.05pm the royal yacht *Victoria & Albert* slipped from South Railway Jetty, and at the same time the ships of the Review Fleet were manned by their ships' companies. As *Victoria & Albert* passed between Southsea Castle and Spit Fort a 21-gun royal salute was fired simultaneously by all the capital ships as the royal yacht entered the lines of warships at the eastern end of the fleet. It was 3.50pm before the King passed by *Hermes* to the sound of cheers from her ship's company, and by 5pm the Review was over. That evening *Hermes*, like the other ships, was illuminated and she also contributed to the spectacular firework display. Next day, at 5pm, the carrier followed other units of the Reserve Fleet out of the Needles Channel before her main engines were worked up to full power for a fast passage to Devonport, where she anchored in Plymouth Sound at 11.30pm. Next morning she steamed up harbour to secure at No 8 buoy in the Hamoaze and on 24 May, with her boilers and engines shut down, she was towed into No 4 basin and secured alongside the south wall, where destoring and deammunitioning was completed. By 9am on Friday 11 June her ship's company had been discharged and a draft of officers and men of the Reserve Fleet had joined the ship. Half an hour later, at 9.30am, HMS *Hermes* was paid off into the Reserve Fleet, and few observers ever expected to see her as an operational aircraft carrier again.

Following the 1937 Coronation Fleet Review *Hermes* returned to Devonport where she was laid up in the Reserve Fleet.
(Maritime Photo Library)

Chapter Four

Tragedy In The East
June 1938 - April 1942

In 1938, in response to the deepening political crisis in Europe between Germany and Czechoslovakia, Britain's rearmament programme was accelerated, and in the spring of 1938 naval ratings became eligible to qualify as pilots in the Fleet Air Arm. Men from all branches of the service could apply and those who were successful underwent a 14-month course, the last two months of which were spent in a training carrier. In order to provide additional training facilities it was decided that *Hermes* would become a harbour training ship, and at just after midnight on Saturday 16 July 1938 she was transferred from the Reserve Fleet to independent command at Devonport. She was moored at a buoy in the Hamoaze with Commander C. N. Lentaigne RN appointed as her commanding officer. It was not long before the first officers who had been accepted into the Air Branch on short service commissions joined the ship, but *Hermes* remained firmly moored to her buoy. When Stan Curtis joined *Hermes* on 1 January 1939 the carrier was secured to No 3 buoy opposite Devonport Dockyard's South Yard.

Her ship's company consisted of a small care and maintenance complement, and there were classes of Boy Seamen on board who were preparing to pass out as Ordinary Seamen. The Boys' instructor was Leading Seaman 'Yorkie' Garbett, who was a very strict disciplinarian. Stan became the coxswain of the motor cutter, which was the same boat that would be involved in the depth charge attack on the French battleship *Richelieu*. During her two years of inactivity at Devonport the carrier was fully maintained and when, in the summer of 1939, with the clouds of war gathering over Europe, it was decided to recommission her as an operational aircraft carrier, it was a relatively simple task.

In early August 1939, with war just a matter of weeks away, *Hermes* was given a short refit and on 23 August her new commanding officer, Captain F. E. P. Hutton RN, was appointed to the ship from the cruiser *Penelope*. *Hermes* was commissioned the following day and at 2.23pm on Friday 1 September 1939 she left Devonport to fly on the 12 Swordfish aircraft of 814 Squadron, which was to be

Hermes at sea during the Second World War.   *(Lt-Cdr Larcombe)*

her wartime complement of aircraft. At 4pm that afternoon, having safely landed on the squadron, she set course for her war station at Portland which she was ordered to reach before dark, and in the event she anchored in Portland Harbour at just after 8pm that evening, close to the *Courageous*. Two days later, at 11am on Sunday 3 September, when hostilities commenced against Germany, *Hermes* was still at anchor in Portland Harbour and apart from a day at sea when the gunners were given a chance to practise, she remained at Portland until 12 September when she returned to Devonport. It was from this base that *Hermes*, together with the fleet carrier *Courageous*, carried out anti-submarine patrols in the South Western Approaches. The dangers of using aircraft carriers on such patrols in coastal waters was tragically illustrated on 17 September when the *Courageous* was lost, along with 518 officers and men, to a U-boat some 50 miles north-west from where *Hermes* was patrolling. Next day, at 9.15am, *Hermes* reported a submarine contact which her escorts *Imogen* and *Isis* depth charged, but without result. That evening *Hermes* was ordered back to Devonport and on 27 September she entered the floating dry dock for six days for her underwater hull to be scraped and painted and degaussing gear to be fitted.

When *Hermes* left Devonport Dockyard again on Tuesday 3 October it was to carry out her final patrol in the South Western Approaches and later that same day, when she was an hour out of Plymouth Sound, she suffered her first fatal casualty of the war when Air Mechanic H. W. Friday was lost overboard. The escorting destroyers, *Witherington* and *Wolverine*, were dispatched to search for the missing rating, but they could find no trace and he was posted as, 'missing presumed drowned'. On Saturday 7 October *Hermes*, escorted by the destroyers *Keith* and *Vesper*, left Plymouth Sound to rendezvous with the French battleship *Strasbourg* and her escorts off Brest, and together the squadron steamed south to much warmer waters, arriving at the French naval base at Dakar on the morning of 16 October. Ironically, over the next few days the Swordfish of 814 Squadron practised dummy torpedo attacks on the French ships that were in the harbour. Stan Curtis, who was serving in *Hermes* at the time remembers that during their time in Dakar a beer canteen was set up on the jetty, which doubled as the mail office and which became known as 'The Bag of Mails'. It was thought that Captain Hutton preferred his men to use this canteen rather than some of the dubious bars in the town of Dakar. On Monday 23 October, together with *Strasbourg* and other French units and designated as 'Force X', *Hermes* left Dakar to carry out the first of many patrols of the Atlantic Ocean covering the area as far west as Pernambuco and to the south of the island of St Helena, and to act as an escort for some of the many convoys which were passing the coast of West Africa. Each patrol would end at Dakar, where

Hermes was able to secure alongside one of the jetties in the harbour.

On Monday 13 November two Swordfish aircraft were lost within 20 minutes of each other when they crashed into the sea. The first incident took place at 11.28am and the crew were rescued by one of the French escorts. Then, 20 minutes later, an aircraft crashed over the bows on take-off, but once again the French escorts rescued the crew. Later that month the carrier patrolled with the French cruiser *Foch*, and spent two days in the British port of Freetown, which was far less attractive than Dakar. The patrols from West Africa continued into December 1940, but at the end of that month *Hermes* took over the escort of a northbound convoy and maintained it right up to the South Western Approaches, where she handed over to other escorts and set course for Devonport. She secured alongside the dockyard wall at 12.30pm on Tuesday 9 January 1940 for a four and a half-week refit and, for the ship's company, some well-earned leave.

Hermes left Devonport again on Saturday 10 February and once at sea she rendezvoused with the destroyers *Acasta* and *Viscount*, before landing on her aircraft and anchoring in Plymouth Sound for the night. Next day she sailed for Dakar, and as she left Plymouth Sound it was the last time that she and many members of the ship's company would see the shores of home. During the passage the Swordfish practised dive-bombing on towed targets, and she arrived in the French naval base on 19 February. During the three weeks following her arrival *Hermes* spent only two days at sea, but on 9 March, with the French battleship *Provence*, the cruiser *Duquesne*, and the destroyers *Decoy* and *Defender*, she put to sea to search for German commerce raiders and blockade-runners in the Atlantic Ocean. The first patrol took the carrier as far south as the equator and on 14 March the force was ordered to search for two Portuguese merchantmen, *Garda* and *Mauzinho*, which were reported to be carrying German nationals. The first vessel was stopped by HMS *Decoy*, but the latter was not found and next day the force returned to Dakar. The patrols continued until the end of March, and in early April *Hermes* operated out of Dakar on a daily basis, with her aircraft carrying out dive-bombing exercises.

On Wednesday 24 April *Hermes* left Dakar to carry out a patrol off the African port and to search for the SS *Jobshaven*, which was suspected to be an Axis blockade-runner. After having been located by air reconnaissance from the carrier, the vessel was intercepted by the cruiser *Shropshire*, and *Hermes* steamed into Freetown Harbour where she remained until mid-May. On Thursday 16 May *Hermes* embarked the C-in-C South Atlantic and sailed to a position just off the coast of Sierra Leone where her aircraft were launched to make dummy bombing attacks on the Freetown defences. Sadly, however, at 2.30pm that afternoon, one of the planes crashed into the sea with the loss of its three crew members. Despite a search of the area there was no trace of the aircraft or the crew, and at 5pm the carrier returned to Freetown where the C-in-C was disembarked and *Hermes* left for Dakar where she arrived on the morning of Saturday 18 May.

By the time *Hermes* arrived at Dakar the devastating German invasion of France and the Low Countries was making rapid progress through a 50-mile-wide gap in the Allied defences and although there was a great deal of anxiety at the French base, there were no problems with the Anglo-French alliance. On Saturday 25 May there was a change of command on board *Hermes* when, at 9.10am, Captain R. F. J. Onslow DSC MVO RN, who had been appointed 18 days earlier, joined the ship to take over from Captain Hutton, who left at 4pm that day. Captain Onslow had entered the Royal Navy in the years before the Great War, and in August 1914 he was serving as a midshipman in the battleship *Queen Mary*. As a sub lieutenant he served in the destroyer *Zulu*, which was engaged on the Dover Patrol, and HM Ships *Thames* and *Arrogant*, former light cruisers which had been converted to depot ships. In January 1919 he was appointed to the cruiser *Theseus*, and later that year he served with the Caspian Naval Force, followed by a spell with the Naval Mission to Persia (Iran). During the 1930s, having been promoted to Commander, he served in the royal yacht, *Victoria & Albert*, and the cruiser *Coventry*, which is where he was on the outbreak of war in 1939.

Three days after taking command, Captain Onslow took *Hermes* to sea for the first time on a routine patrol to Freetown. By this time, with the Belgian Army having surrendered, the British Expeditionary Force having been evacuated from Dunkirk and the German Army having taken the towns of Ostend, Ypres and Lille, the military situation for the French Army looked bleak, but throughout the following weeks *Hermes*, together with the cruisers *Delhi* and *Shropshire*, continued to operate from Dakar. At 4.10pm on Sunday 23 June, whilst *Hermes* was secured alongside No 51 berth at Dakar, the brand new and powerful battleship *Richelieu*, whose building had not quite been completed, arrived in the port from the French Navy yard at Brest. She had escaped before the port was occupied by German troops, and it was intended that her fitting out should be completed at the West African port. On Wednesday 26 June, *Hermes* left Dakar on patrol and she returned three days later to anchor in the outer harbour. Nine hours later, at 6pm, having received urgent orders from the Admiralty, the carrier weighed anchor and slid quietly out of Dakar Harbour, having been instructed to start a blockade of the French port which, over the past eight months, had provided a friendly and welcoming base for her. Two and a half hours later, having reached international waters, she started her patrol, this time with the objective of stopping any French ships from entering or leaving the port.

With France having formally surrendered to Germany on 21 June, and with the colonial Governor of Senegal having declared the colony's allegiance to the Vichy Government of Marshal Petain, Dakar was now a hostile port. The carrier's new base became Freetown and she put into the harbour to refuel on Tuesday 2 July, sailing again the following night at 11pm to rendezvous with the cruisers *Australia* and *Dorsetshire* and the sloop *Milford*. Captain Onslow, who had been temporarily promoted to Acting Rear-Admiral to command the operation, had been ordered to carry out an aerial torpedo attack on the battleship *Richelieu* and to supplement this it was decided to carry out a night depth charge attack using *Hermes'* crash boat. On 7 July, with the force back in international waters off Dakar, *Hermes* refuelled *Milford*, and that afternoon the crash boat was painted a matt black colour to give it some camouflage protection. The boat was manned by a volunteer crew of ten commanded by Lt-Cdr R. H. Bristowe RN, and it included Commissioned Gunner F. W. Grant as his second in command, two ERAs, a leading telegraphist, a leading seaman, two able seamen and two Royal Marines who would man the Vickers machine-gun which was fixed to the bows of the motor boat.* Their orders were to proceed inshore with *Milford*, to a position within ten minutes of Dakar Harbour when the motor boat, which had been nicknamed 'The *Hermes'* Coffin', would be on her own. They were to get through the port's boom defences and drop four depth charges under *Richelieu's* stern, as close as possible to her 'A' brackets. Having accomplished this the boat was to attempt to return safely to *Milford*.

At 9pm on the evening of 7 July the freshly painted crash boat was manned and 25 minutes later it was on its way to *Milford* to pick up depth charges. Once alongside the sloop, with a considerable swell running and in the dark, the task of embarking the depth charges proved very difficult and one of them fell on Mr Grant's head, almost knocking him unconscious. Despite this, in the words of Lt-Cdr Bristowe, 'he managed to work harder than usual in a semi-unconsious state'. Another depth charge fell on the port engine, cracking the cylinder head but, finally, at 9.45pm, *Milford* got under way with the motor boat following at 12 knots which, with depth charges slung on the side of the motor boat, made it an extremely perilous trip. As the motor boat made its way to the harbour mouth it encountered the cruiser *Australia* which for a few moments in the darkness was almost mistaken for *Richelieu*. It was after midnight on the morning of Monday 8 July that the crash boat took its departure from *Milford* and, after lifting the last depth charge into position, it

* The other crew members were: - Ldg Seaman P. J. Kearns; ERA C. Ford; ERA A. V. Westmore; Ldg Telegraphist R. E. Tuffnell; AB J. Quinn; AB A. Cookson; Marines W. S. Robinson and G. T. Youndle.

Hermes in wartime dazzle-paint camouflage.

made its way inshore. At 12.15am Goree Island loomed into sight and soon afterwards the boat was almost run down by a patrolling French destroyer. Fortunately, although the warship followed the motor boat, it was clear that they had not been seen and at last the outer boom came into sight. As they went over the obstacle the boat's engine was stopped, and as soon as it was restarted the noise appeared to the crew to be deafening, so they tried to muffle the sound by keeping the engine cover on.

As they made their way into the harbour they passed an armed merchant cruiser and they were convinced that the vessel ahead of her was the huge bulk of *Richelieu*. However, as they approached they recognized it as a sloop and they moved slowly away hoping that the noise of their boat would not be heard by the quartermaster whom they could see on deck. After moving round the harbour's inner boom they at last sighted their quarry, but to their dismay there was a merchant ship anchored immediately astern of her, which was going to make their approach and attack even more difficult. Then, as they got closer they sighted a harbour launch which was under way just astern of *Richelieu*, but nevertheless they decided to continue with their operation. As they approached the battleship, however, red and white lights flickered out a challenge and Lt-Cdr Bristowe ordered the attack at full speed. As they sped in towards their target they were challenged six times and, not having answered any of them, they fully expected to be shot at. Once they closed *Richelieu* they spotted a lighter lying aft on the port side and a quarter boom with a boat alongside it, but the coxswain, Ldg Seaman Kearns, skilfully brought them alongside the battleship about 30 yards from its stern. As they dropped the depth charges the French quarterdeck staff were standing looking idly over the guard rails, clearly puzzled as to what was going on, but they did not seem unduly alarmed. Once they realized, however, that the crash boat was dropping depth charges, they hurriedly withdrew, obviously to get help. To the disappointment of the crash boat's crew none of the depth charges exploded, which later was put down to the shallowness of the water.

As the motor boat withdrew from the harbour a challenge came from an armed merchant cruiser, whose crew hailed them and to which Lt-Cdr Bristowe replied, 'passant', which seemed to satisfy those on board. *Richelieu*, however, sent out a general alarm signal which was answered by the ships in the harbour and by the shore batteries, and the crash boat's crew, expecting to be floodlit by searchlights at any second, tried to get under cover of a merchant ship's hull. However, when no searchlights were switched on they decided to get out of the harbour at full speed but, to their dismay, their boat's starboard engine gave up completely. For about 20 minutes they lay drifting while the two ERAs, working feverishly in the pitch dark, got the port engine working and this, when it started, made

a noise which seemed as loud as a thunderclap. As they waited for the engineers to start the engine there was what appeared to be a loud explosion in the harbour, which the crew took to be one of their depth charges exploding. Unfortunately, it was not, but it cheered them all up and soon they were under way again. Before they reached the harbour boom they were chased by an auxiliary launch which, to their delight, got caught up in the boom nets. Just as they thought they had shaken off their pursuer, however, a second launch took up the chase, but this time with some skilful manoeuvring they managed to shake it off, although they were expecting to be fired on at any time.

Much to their surprise the boat's crew found themselves safely out of the harbour, but by this time it was 3am and they realized that they stood little chance of making their rendezvous with *Milford*, so they decided to try to reach the main force of the cruisers and *Hermes*. At 3.55am they made radio contact with the carrier, to report, 'Dropped four depth charges under stern of *Richelieu* at 02.10.' As they made their way north-west they heard more heavy explosions in Dakar Harbour, which they took to be a heavy bombardment, but which was actually an air attack by the Swordfish of 814 Squadron, one of which actually flew over them on its way back to *Hermes*. In fact, at 4.15am that morning six Swordfish aircraft, all armed with torpedoes, took off from *Hermes* to attack *Richelieu*. Despite a heavy anti-aircraft barrage the attack was pressed home successfully, and with damage to one of her propellers the battleship was temporarily disabled. All six aircraft returned safely to *Hermes*, but at 9.28am French planes attacked the force for over 20 minutes, although with *Hermes* and the cruisers putting up a terrific barrage, there were no casualties and no damage was suffered.

Meanwhile, as dawn broke, the motor boat's crew, who had heard the torpedo attack and the subsequent explosions, could see *Richelieu* about two to three miles away shrouded by a pall of yellow smoke. Having altered course to avoid the anti-aircraft barrage put up by their own defences, one of the French aircraft spotted the motor boat and as she made her way back to the safety of *Hermes* several more planes flew overhead, but without taking any offensive action. As they made their way back to the force they had to take avoiding action to keep clear of a French armed merchant cruiser, and at about 5.45am they decided that it would be impossible to reach the carrier so they set course instead for Bathurst, Gambia, which was British territory about 70 miles away. At this point Lt-Cdr Bristowe decided that the crash boat's engines should be overhauled, but whilst they were stopped their only navigation chart was blown overboard and a volunteer was called for to dive in and rescue it. Happily, the chart was rescued and within minutes of the man being hauled back on board a large shark appeared alongside the boat. The adventure was, however, almost at an end, for a signal was received from *Hermes* instructing them to stop engines and wait to be picked up. Finally, at 11.43am, with the cruisers forming a screen round *Hermes*, the carrier stopped to embark the boat and 20 minutes later the gallant crew were safely back on board.

In his report to Rear-Admiral Onslow, Lt-Cdr Bristowe described his crew's conduct thus: 'The behaviour of my crew, throughout a very exciting operation, inspired very largely by Mr Grant's imperturbable cheerfulness, was exemplary. I couldn't have wished for a more cheerful, a more sporting or more loyal company, and any success which we may have achieved is entirely due to their wholehearted co-operation.' In the event Lt-Cdr Bristowe was awarded the DSO, Commissioned Gunner Grant the DSC, ERA Ford and Ldg Seaman Kearns the DSM, and the remainder of the crew were Mentioned in Dispatches. In addition two officers of 814 Squadron were honoured with the DSC and a Mention in Dispatches for their part in the torpedo attack.

Less than an hour after the boat's crew arrived back on board, French bombers made their final attack on the force as it steamed towards Freetown, but once again there were no casualties or damage. Two days later, at 3.06am on Wednesday 10 July 1940, when the force was in a position Lat 09° - 10'N/Long 15° - 48'W, disaster almost struck for *Hermes*. At 8.50am on the previous day, the armed merchant cruiser, HMS *Corfu**, had left Freetown escorting a convoy which was bound for Greenock. In the early hours of 10 July, on an inky-black night and during a heavy rainstorm, *Hermes* and her escorts found themselves in the middle of the convoy. Suddenly, a lookout on *Corfu's* bridge shouted, 'Object bearing ten degrees', and at the same time the officer of the watch in the armed merchant cruiser sighted what looked like phosphorescence in the water about half a cable (100 yards) away. For a split second he took it to be a fish, but almost immediately realized that it was a ship's bow wave and before he could take any action *Hermes* loomed up out of the darkness and mist, crashing into the *Corfu's* starboard bow. The carrier's stem had ripped into the armed merchant cruiser's No 2 hold, which was acting as her forward magazine, and she pounded away on hundreds of 6-inch shells. The impact of the collision punched a huge hole into the AMC's bow, and 30 feet of *Hermes'* bow was crumpled and pushed back. Given the force of the impact it was surprising that only three members of the carrier's ship's company were seriously injured, one of whom, PO Blacksmith Crabb, died later in hospital. On board *Corfu* there were no casualties as all the damage had been caused to cargo holds. As soon as Rear-Admiral Onslow had taken stock of the situation he realized that neither ship was in any immediate danger of sinking, and he ordered most of *Corfu's* crew to

be evacuated on to the carrier's flight deck which, as the two vessels were locked together, meant walking from one ship to the other. Meanwhile, on board the armed merchant cruiser a volunteer detachment of engineers pumped out ballast tanks to lighten the ship forward, and on board *Hermes* the engines were manoeuvred at Full Astern before, with a terrible grinding and screeching of tortured metal, the two ships were pulled clear of each other. *Corfu* was then towed stern first to Freetown, where she arrived three days later. With damage to her stem and bows, mainly above the waterline, *Hermes* made the passage to Freetown at 12 knots with relatively few problems, although at one stage she had to reduce speed when one of her starboard bow plates started dragging in the water and threatened to tear away a large section of the ship's side. Fortunately the offending piece broke off and speed was increased again, with the carrier arriving at Freetown at 6pm that evening. In the event a subsequent Court of Inquiry found that neither ship was to blame for the accident.

With the completion of the operation to immobilize *Richelieu* Rear-Admiral Onslow reverted to his substantive rank of Captain, and on Monday 5 August *Hermes* headed a southbound convoy, arriving in Simonstown Harbour 12 days later where she was dry docked for repairs. It was Saturday 2 November 1940 before *Hermes* was moved out of dry dock with her hull now repaired and five days later she sailed to land on the Swordfish of 814 Squadron. After seven days of trials off Simonstown, where storing and ammunitioning was completed, *Hermes* sailed north once again for Freetown, arriving on the afternoon of Friday 29 November. On Monday 2 December, having been inspected by the C-in-C South Atlantic, *Hermes* put to sea again to join the elderly light cruiser HMS *Dragon*, to carry out search operations for enemy raiders and blockade-runners in the South Atlantic, between Rio de Janeiro and the coast of West Africa. On the morning of Wednesday 4 December air patrols from *Hermes* spotted what was thought to be a blockade-runner, but when *Dragon* investigated the ship it turned out to be the British merchantman *Ocean Emery*. On Tuesday 10 December *Hermes* and *Dragon* anchored off Jamestown, St Helena, where they fuelled before sailing again late that evening. During the remainder of December the two ships operated from St Helena, with only brief periods at anchor for refuelling, and on 20 December they rendezvoused with the armed merchant cruiser, HMS *Pretoria Castle **, to search for the German raider *Admiral Scheer*. On Christmas Day the force was in a position Lat 25° - 04'S/Long 06° - 35'W, with the carrier's aircraft flying reconnaissance patrols from dawn to dusk. On New Year's Eve, with the force having completed refuelling at St Helena, they weighed anchor and set course for Simonstown where, to

*HMS *Corfu* was an ex-P&O passenger liner which was eventually scrapped in 1961.

* HMS *Pretoria Castle* was an ex-Union Castle mail liner.

The damage to *Hermes'* bow following her collision with the armed merchant cruiser *Corfu*.   (*Fleet Air Arm Museum*)

the relief of the ship's company, they arrived on Sunday 5 January 1941.

On Monday 20 January 1941, when *Hermes* left Simonstown again, she steamed north-east into the Indian Ocean to patrol off the South African coast in an effort to locate Vichy blockade-runners from Madagascar. At 1.45pm on 26 January, when the carrier was some 200 miles south of the island, reconnaissance aircraft sighted the Vichy ship, SS *Santry*, and shadowed her for a time before she returned to Madagascar. Two days later the aircraft were flown off to Durban and on the following day, 29 January, *Hermes* secured alongside at Durban Docks, where she remained until 4 February.

On 19 January 1941, British and Indian troops, commanded by Lt General Sir Lewis Heath, had invaded the Italian colonies of Ethiopia, Eritrea and Somaliland from the Sudan before advancing towards the Ethiopian capital of Addis Ababa. Although they moved successfully into the weakly defended colonies, they were sadly lacking in air support, and when *Hermes* sailed from Durban with the cruiser *Shropshire*, it was to head north for Mombasa to

refuel before rendezvousing with another cruiser, HMS *Hawkins*, to mount a blockade of the Somali port of Kismayu (Kismaayo). The port was under siege by South African Army forces which had invaded Somalia from Kenya and the naval force was there to prevent reinforcements getting through. On Wednesday 12 February, reconnaissance aircraft from *Hermes* located a number of enemy merchantmen, including the Italian vessels *Askari* and *Pensilvania*, which they bombed in the approaches to Mogadishu Harbour (Muodisho). Three more enemy vessels were captured by *Hawkins* and at 11.05am *Hermes* sighted the Italian merchant ship, *Leonardo da Vinci*, just east of Kismayu and ordered her to stop. Ten minutes later a boarding party left *Hermes* and by 12.30pm the Italian ship was bound for Mombasa, flying the White Ensign. Four days later Kismayu fell to the South African Army and that same day *Hermes*, *Hawkins* and *Shropshire* set course for Mombasa, where they arrived on 18 February.

Having now joined the East Indies Station, *Hermes* left Kilindini Harbour on 22 February and steamed south-east into the Indian Ocean to patrol the shipping lanes between Mombasa and Ceylon. On Tuesday 4 March 1941, after an absence of four years, *Hermes* moored in Colombo Harbour from where she would operate for most of the month. In April she continued her patrols with calls at the Seychelles, where she refuelled from the RFA tanker *Pearleaf*, but later that month, with British and Indian troops having landed at the port of Basra under the terms of the 1930 Anglo-Iraqi Treaty to overcome a pro-Axis rebellion in Iraq, *Hermes* was ordered to the Persian Gulf. With the land force opposed by an Iraqi Army of 9,000 men *Hermes* was to provide air support for the British Army. The move was complicated by the fact that a large quantity of the carrier's frozen food stores had to be jettisoned owing to a refrigeration failure, but for five days her aircraft carried out daily bombing missions on Iraqi positions. On 21 April the ship's company enjoyed a break when *Hermes* anchored off Bahrain and shore leave was granted, but eight days later she was at sea again and operating with the cruiser *Enterprise* about 70 miles off the coast of Saudi Arabia, just south of the border with Kuwait. In the early hours of Tuesday 6 May, as the aircraft were being prepared for a dawn bombing raid, Sub-Lt Leslie Herbert RNVR was killed instantly when he accidentally walked into a running propeller on one of the planes, and later that day he was buried at sea. That same day there was a minor diplomatic incident when one of the Swordfish pilots flew over neutral Saudi Arabian territory, but for the remainder of the month, in the sweltering heat of the Persian Gulf, raids and reconnaissance missions were flown daily without any incidents. Such was the heat in the Persian Gulf that men on watch in the boiler and engine rooms were fainting from heat exhaustion, and in an attempt to relieve the hardships the normal four-hour watches were cut to two hours. This meant that the additional personnel required to man these vital compartments had to be drawn from other branches.

In mid-June 1941, to everyone's relief, operations in the Persian Gulf came to an end and *Hermes* returned to the fresher and cooler air of the Indian Ocean as she, together with the cruiser *Enterprise*, continued to patrol between Ceylon (Sri Lanka) and the Seychelles. On Saturday 5 July the carrier spent a few hours in Colombo Harbour where the C-in-C East Indies Station, Vice-Admiral Sir Richard Leatham, addressed the ship's company. Throughout the rest of that month and into August the monotonous task of patrolling the sea lanes of the Indian Ocean continued, with regular stops at the Seychelles where *Hermes* would anchor off Port Victoria, the largest town on Mahé Island, to refuel. On Sunday 10 August there was a break in the routine when the carrier put into Mombasa's Kilindini Harbour for three days before returning to the sea lanes of the Indian Ocean. In late August information was received that Vichy French merchant vessels were sailing from

Saigon in French Indo-China (Vietnam), to Madagascar and from there to Dakar, Casablanca and Marseilles. On 7 September a small French convoy left Saigon to cross the Indian Ocean and *Hermes*, together with the cruisers *Enterprise* and *Mauritius*, was deployed on a search for them which was code-named 'Operation Snip'. Despite long periods at sea which took the force as far south as Port Louis on Mauritius Island, the operation was not a success and on Monday 29 September *Hermes* and the three cruisers anchored at Port Louis for five days. On the final day of the visit the colony's Governor, Sir Geoffrey Clifford, was taken to sea to watch ten of the carrier's Swordfish aircraft being put through their paces. After leaving Port Louis during the afternoon of 4 October *Hermes* and *Enterprise* steamed north-west to Mombasa, where they arrived six days later. After flying 814 Squadron off to Port Reitz airfield, just outside Mombasa town, the carrier entered harbour to start a nine-day maintenance period, and the ship's company had a reasonable run ashore to Mombasa, or to the nearby beaches at Nyali and Bamburi.

When *Hermes* left Kilindini Harbour at 9am on Sunday 19 October, she landed on her aircraft and rendezvoused with the ill-fated battlecruiser HMS *Repulse*, and the two vessels remained together until the end of the month, patrolling the shipping lanes of the Indian Ocean between Trincomalee and the Seychelles. During the late afternoon of Thursday 23 October, whilst landing on three aircraft, one of the planes was lost when it veered to port and went over the side. Fortunately, however, the three crew members were rescued by the crash boat. Over the following weeks *Hermes* continued to patrol the shipping lanes of the Indian Ocean, but on Tuesday 18 November she arrived at Simonstown to begin a long-overdue refit.

For *Hermes'* ship's company the weeks spent at the South African naval base were a happy interlude after long periods at sea carrying out trade protection duties and searches for Vichy blockade-runners, tasks for which the small aircraft carrier was ideally suited. However, before the refit was completed the war situation in the Indian Ocean would be completely transformed and *Hermes* would be up against a powerful, aggressive and ruthless Imperial Japanese Navy. This was a formidable task even for one of the new armoured fleet carriers of the Illustrious class, but if the small, outdated and obsolete *Hermes* were to come up against Vice-Admiral Chuichi Nagumo's Air Attack Group of six fast fleet carriers with their complement of over 300 fast and modern Zero fighter bombers, there could only be one outcome. In November 1941, with *Hermes* in Simonstown's main dockyard basin and with plenty of shore leave to nearby Cape Town, the Japanese threat to South-East Asia seemed a long way away and on Saturday 6 December the carrier was moved into the dockyard's dry dock for hull maintenance. Next day Japan entered the war in the Pacific and South-East Asia with a devastating air attack on Pearl Harbor, accompanied by powerful invasions of Thailand, Malaya, Hong Kong and the Philippines, as well as the occupation of the International Settlement at Shanghai. All over South-East Asia the weakness of the Western colonial powers, including Britain, was starkly highlighted as the Japanese Army made rapid advances throughout the region. On Wednesday 10 December came a devastating blow to the Royal Navy, when the battleship *Prince of Wales* and the battlecruiser *Repulse* were sunk by a ruthlessly efficient force of Japanese Navy torpedo-bombers, for the loss of only half a dozen enemy aircraft. On Christmas Day the British garrison at Hong Kong surrendered, and by the end of 1941 the Japanese Army had pushed the British forces in Malaya into a headlong retreat towards the island of Singapore. The capture of Penang Island had closed the Malacca Strait to British and Allied shipping and it would not be long before the eastern side of the Indian Ocean was dominated by Japan.

On 10 January 1942 a single Allied command area was formed under the supreme command of General Archibald Wavell, which was known as the ABDA area (American, British, Dutch and Australian sea, land and air forces), covering all South-East Asia from Formosa in the north to Port Darwin in the south, and from the Caroline Islands in the Pacific to Burma and the Andaman Sea. Unfortunately, with the rapid advance of the Japanese forces, most of this area was soon overrun, with Singapore surrendering on 15 February, and as the Japanese advanced swiftly through Java and Sumatra, on 25 February the ABDA command was dissolved and replaced by the ANZAC Command under Vice-Admiral H. F. Leary USN. The ANZAC naval force would be made up of the remnants of Allied Navies that had survived the Japanese onslaught, and they were to be reinforced by *Hermes*. It was intended that this naval force would cover the eastern and north-eastern approaches to Australia and New Zealand in order to protect coastal shipping in the area, and while working closely with the US Pacific Fleet with its aircraft carriers still intact, would help regain the initiative in the Pacific Ocean. This, then, was the long-term plan for the deployment of *Hermes*.

Meanwhile, as these momentous events were taking place in the Pacific and South-East Asia, *Hermes* was still undergoing her refit in Simonstown and it was not until Saturday 31 January 1942 that she left the dockyard basin to carry out her post-refit trials. Next day, at 1am, *Hermes* left South Africa to rejoin the East Indies Fleet temporarily at Colombo which was being organized as a base for a new Eastern Fleet since Singapore was now untenable as a naval base. After refuelling at Port Louis on 7 February *Hermes* arrived at Colombo a week later, on the day before the garrison at Singapore surrendered, to embark her squadron personnel and stores that had been left behind the previous November. Five days later, on Thursday 19 February, she

put to sea in order to land on the 12 Swordfish aircraft of 814 Squadron and to rendezvous with the Australian destroyer, HMAS *Vampire*, which was one of the few Allied naval units that had been successfully extracted from the debacle in Malaya and Singapore. *Vampire* had been with *Prince of Wales* and *Repulse* when they were sunk off Kuantan, and she had helped to rescue survivors from the waters of the South China Sea. In late January she and HMS *Thanet* had been involved in a spirited action off Malaya's east coast when they had vainly tried to prevent a Japanese landing at Endau. During the action *Thanet* had been sunk, and the *Vampire* had only just managed to escape under cover of a smokescreen. She was then ordered to sail for Colombo, after which her fate would now be linked to that of *Hermes*.

After leaving Colombo *Hermes* and *Vampire* carried out a patrol about 200 miles south of Ceylon, with the Swordfish aircraft carrying out anti-submarine patrols armed with depth charges. During the afternoon of 20 February there was a lucky escape for one aircrew, and for *Hermes* herself, when Swordfish 'G' crashed on landing and ditched over the port side of the carrier. Fortunately the crew were able to get out of the aircraft which sank rapidly and, as it reached a pre-set depth, the depth charge detonated underwater with a massive explosion. The three aircrew members were picked up by *Vampire* and transferred back to *Hermes* that evening. On the morning of Monday 23 February, with the patrol over, *Hermes* and *Vampire* entered Trincomalee Harbour where, two days later, ten of the remaining 11 Swordfish were flown off to the airfield at China Bay, and the squadron personnel were disembarked.

One Boy Seaman who had joined *Hermes* in November 1941 was Peter Babtie who, after completing his training on the Isle of Man, embarked on the troopship *Durban Castle* for the long voyage round the Cape of Good Hope to Bombay (Mumbai). From there he had a three-day train journey to Trincomalee where he joined the Boys' messdeck in *Hermes*, and took up his duties as Captain's Messenger. These duties brought him into contact with various officers and he recalls that during March 1942 one of the pilots of 814 Squadron offered him a flight in a Swordfish. He remembers that his Divisional Officer thought he was mad, but nevertheless he signed the authorization form. Peter remembered that the flight was 'hair-raising', while the landing on *Hermes*' flight deck was 'breathtaking'. Any ideas of an idyllic war in 'spiced tropical waters' were, however, soon dispelled for, with the fall of the Malayan defensive barrier, the whole of the Indian Ocean was vulnerable to Japanese attack. In fact on 9 March 1942, Vice-Admiral Nagumo was ordered to carry out an aggressive raid on Ceylon and any British shipping in the Bay of Bengal in order to sweep the area clear of Royal Navy units, and to prevent any attacks on the Japanese

An aerial view taken by a Japanese pilot of *Hermes* on fire and listing to port shortly before she sank after an onslaught by Japanese Navy bombers. Bomb holes can be seen in the flight deck and the forward lift has been blasted right out of the lift well.

(Lt-Cdr Larcombe)

supply routes. To carry out the raid Admiral Nagumo had at his disposal a force of five fast aircraft carriers with approximately 330 of the latest naval fighter bombers, supported by four fast battleships, two cruisers and eight destroyers, accompanied by six oil tankers. The Japanese force sailed from Staring Bay in the Celebes on 26 March 1942 and steamed into the Indian Ocean towards Ceylon. In mid-march *Hermes* and *Vampire* were ordered to leave Trincomalee and steam for Fremantle where they were to form part of the ANZAC command, but after three days they were recalled back to Trincomalee where the carrier joined the elderly battleships *Ramillies, Resolution, Royal Sovereign* and *Revenge* as part of Force B.

On 28 March, just 48 hours after taking command of the Eastern Fleet, Admiral Sir James Somerville received a report of the Japanese force which, it was thought, was going to attack Ceylon on or around 1 April. In fact, just as he had done at Pearl Harbor, Admiral Nagumo had chosen a Sunday morning - Easter Sunday, 5 April - for his raid. The 70 Zero dive-bombers were opposed by 42 Hurricanes and Fulmars which, despite being outnumbered and

outclassed, shot down 19 Japanese aircraft for the loss of 16 of their own. *Hermes*, as part of 'Force B', was at sea with the rest of the fleet, but she and *Vampire* were sent back to Trincomalee to prepare for 'Operation Ironclad', the occupation of Vichy-occupied Diego Suarez in Madagascar.

Peter Babtie remembers that for him Wednesday 8 April was spent in taking live torpedoes out to buoys in the harbour to which they were secured as an anti-invasion measure. He recalls that at about 8am his boat was hoisted back onto its falls as *Hermes* was made ready for sea. Some men were ashore enjoying beer and a meal at the fleet canteen when the recall sounded and patrols directed everyone back to their ships, but for others who were stuck on board and engaged in cleaning the after boilers, there came the order to, 'close up the water drums and prepare to raise steam'. Another member of the ship's company, Stan Curtis, remembers that 'buzzes (rumours) were flying round the ship like seagulls after scraps', but it was noticeable that most of the other ships had left the harbour. Eventually, however, the ship's company were told that *Hermes* and *Vampire* had orders to clear the harbour and proceed to sea. Stan remembers that Special Sea Dutymen were closed up at about 10.30pm, and shortly afterwards the carrier, accompanied by *Vampire*, sailed from Trincomalee. He recalls the events of that night: 'I don't think anyone turned in that night, we were all keyed up with tension, not knowing what to expect. I had the middle watch at my post as a breach worker on P1 5.5-inch gun, but as we were not at Action Stations, after a turn on the headphones for any orders from gunnery control, we could get our heads down. I don't think anyone slept though, I certainly didn't; I just lay on the deck using a coil of rope for a pillow and gazing at the deckhead. As the middle watch came to an end dawn broke over the Indian Ocean, and one of our "stringbags" took off for an air patrol. After it returned all our aircraft were flown ashore and soon after their departure Action Stations was sounded. We, on P1 gun, were already closed up, so we put on our anti-flash gear and lifebelts, opened up the ready-use ammunition lockers and prepared for action. Then, over the tannoy came the voice of Captain Onslow who read out a signal he had received from the C-in-C to the effect that the Japanese had sighted us and we could expect to be attacked at any time. I can remember he stressed that RAF fighter aircraft were being sent for our protection. He then went on to tell us that the Japanese had carried out a heavy air attack on Trincomalee Harbour and our air base at nearby China Bay and that they had spotted us whilst returning to their carriers.'

On the morning of 9 April, with the sighting report of *Hermes* having been intercepted at Colombo, the carrier was ordered to return to Trincomalee with the 'utmost dispatch', while fighters should have been providing her with air cover. Unfortunately, however, the order did not reach the fighters in time for them to save the carrier from attack. At 10.35am that morning, with *Hermes* in a position Lat 07° - 35'N/Long 82° - 05'E, about 20 miles south-east of Batticaloa, more than 80 Japanese Zero fighter-bombers, each armed with a 250lb bomb, were sighted on the starboard quarter diving out of the sun at about 10,000 feet. *Hermes* opened fire with every gun that would bear as the enemy planes came within range, but it was clear that without fighter support she was virtually helpless against this skilful and determined attack by well-trained, modern dive-bombers. The story is taken up once again by Stan Curtis: 'It was always said that because *Hermes* had spent most of her life in eastern waters the Japanese knew as much about her capabilities as we did and, apart from a few near misses, every bomb was on target. They went through the flight deck as though it were tissue paper, causing appalling destruction below decks, and one of the first bombs hit the forward aircraft lift blowing it into the air to land upside down on the flight deck. All personnel on duty in that part of the hangar were killed instantly. Captain Onslow was doing his best to

dodge the hail of bombs, we were steaming at over 25 knots and the ship was shuddering from stem to stern - from both our speed and from the pounding we were getting from the bombs. All the anti-aircraft guns, mine included, were firing flat out at the never-ending stream of bombers that were hurtling down out of the sky. Suddenly, there was an almighty explosion that seemed to lift the whole ship out of the water, followed by another which came from the island superstructure on the starboard side, and from that moment we had no further communication with the bridge. Only about 15 minutes had passed since the start of the action, but fires were raging in the hangar and the ship was listing badly to port. I heard the whistle of a bomb just aft of our position, and I saw it penetrate the deck just yards from us and explode in the galley. Then there was a near miss right opposite our gun, and what seemed to be a huge tidal wave of water knocked us all clean off our feet. Picking myself up and finding no broken bones I called out to the gun's crew, and I got a reply from each of them. At this stage *Hermes* had a severe list to port and the sea was only a few feet below our gun deck. It was obvious that we were sinking rapidly and I gave the order, "Over the side lads, every man for himself!" I was the last in and I hit the water at 11am, which is the time my non-waterproof watch stopped. In fact the order to abandon ship had been passed round before we went, but events had overtaken the ship before it reached us. Once in the water I swam away from the ship as fast as I could as she still had way on and bombs were still exploding in the water. As I swam away I noticed that the colour of the sea had turned from blue to black, from the fuel oil that was gushing from *Hermes*. It was impossible to escape from it and I was soon covered from head to foot in the foul-smelling oil. Having swum for 200 to 300 yards, with my eyes smarting badly from the oil, I turned over on my back and witnessed the end of *Hermes*. She was listing heavily to port and her forward end was already under water, with her propellers almost vertical in the air. She was on fire from end to end when she just vanished under the waves, leaving a mass of floating wreckage and hundreds of men fighting for survival. Once the bombing stopped there was an uncanny silence and we were able to organize ourselves with a few carley floats that the flight deck party had managed to cut loose, and we set about getting the injured and non-swimmers on to them which was not easy as we were all covered in thick, greasy oil. Some of the very severely wounded were given morphia injections by Lt Smart, who was the only Medical Officer to survive, but for many it was too late. Very soon the carley floats were full and many of us, including myself, just hung on as tightly as we could to the ropes which were on the sides of the rafts. We sang all the usual songs such as "Roll Out the Barrel", and it was after 4pm, when I had been in the sea for five hours, that I was rescued by the hospital ship *Vita*, where I was reunited with my two mates Bill and Dennis.'

Peter Babtie, who was also manning a gun on the port side of the ship, remembered that as the list of *Hermes* increased men were jumping over the side. He also remembered his shipmate Joe O' Neale struggling to escape, having had both legs blown off, and the cries of another friend who was trapped in the ship. He never saw either of them again and, like Stan Curtis, he was rescued by *Vita*. For *Hermes* the end had come quickly, while the damage control party was still hoping to reduce the list, and as she sank beneath the waves one gun was still firing. One survivor, who was on the bridge at the time, remembers that literally moments before the ship sank, Captain Onslow, 'went down the forward ladder, I can only assume to his cabin'. Seconds later the flight deck was awash as the ship listed further to port and she sank beneath the waves. As soon as the carrier had disappeared, the enemy bombers turned their attention to *Vampire* and she too was quickly sunk. From *Hermes* 19 officers, including Captain Onslow, and 288 ratings were lost, in addition to which *Vampire's* commanding officer and seven ratings lost their lives.

As for Admiral Nagumo's force, his aircraft also sank the corvette *Hollyoak*, the RFA *Athelstone* and the merchantman SS *British Sergeant*, before they left the Indian Ocean and returned to Japan where they arrived on 18 April 1942, just in time to hear that 16 US Army B25 bombers, operating from the aircraft carrier USS *Hornet*, had bombed Tokyo.

Part Two

HMS *Hermes* & INS *Viraat*
1959 - 2001

Chapter Five

A Slow And Uncertain Start
July 1943 - November 1959

Even before the ninth *Hermes* was sunk by Japanese bombers in April 1942 it was recognized at the Admiralty that aircraft carriers had succeeded battleships as the fleet's new capital ships, and plans were in hand for new classes of light fleet carriers. In order to ensure that the new aircraft carriers were built quickly and to enable all large British shipbuilders to tender for contracts, the hulls of these new carriers were based on merchant ship designs although, in the event, none of the 18 carriers that were built would take any part in the Second World War. The first eight vessels of the Colossus class were laid down in 1942 and 1943, and they were followed by six ships of the Majestic class, all but one of which were sold to overseas navies and the one which remained at home was never completed. The third class of light fleet carriers was the Centaur class, whose vessels were larger than the Colossus and Majestic classes, with considerably higher speeds and the capacity to operate larger aircraft. Originally it had been intended to build eight ships of the Centaur class which would have been named *Albion, Arrogant, Bulwark, Centaur, Elephant, Hermes, Monmouth* and *Polyphemus*. The first seven vessels were to be built by commercial shipbuilders, with the *Polyphemus* being constructed by Devonport Dockyard which already had the Majestic-class carrier HMS *Terrible* in hand.

On Monday 12 July 1943 the Deputy Director of Naval Contracts wrote to the Chief Executive of the Barrow-in-Furness shipbuilders, Vickers Armstrong Ltd: 'I have to request that you will proceed with the construction and completion in all respects of one in number Light Fleet carrier for His Majesty's Navy.' This, then, was the letter which set in motion the events which, 16 years later, would culminate in the commissioning of HMS *Hermes*, but in 1943 it was proposed to name the Barrow-built aircraft carrier *Elephant*, with *Hermes* being earmarked as the name for a sister ship which would be built in Birkenhead by Cammell Laird & Co. The first of the class to be laid down was *Albion* on 23 March 1944, at Swan Hunter's shipyard on the River Tyne, and she was followed by *Centaur* on 30 May 1944 at Harland & Wolff's Belfast shipyard. The first keel plates for *Elephant*, which at Vickers' yard was known as 'Ship No 928', were laid on 21 June 1944, 15 days after D-Day in Europe and the day after the decisive Battle of the Philippine Sea in the Far East, when the US Navy sank three Japanese aircraft

carriers, *Hiryu, Shokaku* and the brand new *Taiko*. It was an appropriate date, for it was aircraft from the first two of these Japanese aircraft carriers which had been responsible for sinking the ninth *Hermes*.

Between June 1944 and the end of the Second World War on 2 September 1945, the shell of *Elephant* was built up to middle deck level and her main internal bulkheads were completed, but with the war over, the nation's shipbuilding priorities altered and work on the hull was stopped. The only warships which were being completed were those whose construction was well advanced and which had, in most cases, already been launched. However, even some ships which had taken to the water were cancelled or work was halted, one case being the Majestic-class aircraft carrier *Leviathan* which had been launched with great ceremony on 7 June 1945 by the Duchess of Kent. In May 1946 work stopped on both *Leviathan* and *Hercules*, both of which were fitting out on the River Tyne, and although *Hercules* was eventually completed and sold to India, *Leviathan* remained an uncompleted hulk until she was scrapped in 1968. As for the Centaur class, a few weeks after the end of the war, in October 1945, four of the proposed carriers whose keels had never been laid, the *Arrogant, Hermes, Monmouth* and *Polyphemus*, were cancelled. In the following month, with the original *Hermes* having been discontinued, the Admiralty decided to perpetuate a name that had close connections with the birth of the Fleet Air Arm and *Elephant* was renamed *Hermes*. However, although she had been renamed, the future for *Hermes* did not look bright since all construction work on the carrier had been stopped and the hull remained on the slipway, with a small care and maintenance party carrying out essential work such as coating the steelwork of her hull with oil to prevent corrosion. In the drawing office of Vickers Armstrong, however, there was a glimmer of hope for some work did continue as various modernization amendments were made to the original design.

In the late 1940s Vickers Armstrong at Barrow-in-Furness were tendering for some very lucrative contracts for the construction of two large passenger liners for the Orient Line as merchant ship tonnage now had a higher priority than warship building. After a great deal of pressure by Vickers Armstrong, in 1949 the Admiralty agreed that work could be resumed on *Hermes*, in order to complete the ship up to launching stage so that the slipway

The tenth *Hermes* is launched by Mrs Clementine Churchill, the wife of the Prime Minister, at Vickers Armstrong's Barrow-in-Furness shipyard on Monday 16 February 1953. *(Lt-Cdr Larcombe)*

could be cleared. The ceremony took place at midday on Monday 16 February 1953, over eight years after the first keel plates had been laid, and was performed by Mrs Clementine Churchill, the wife of the Prime Minister, Winston Churchill. The event was watched by the hundreds of workmen who had helped to construct her, and with all work temporarily halted, thousands of spectators crowded the shipyards and the hulls of the vessels there. It was a cold, cloudy day at Barrow, with a light wind and a mist and at 12.10pm, after a short religious service, Mrs Churchill released the mechanism which operated four 120-ton triggers. Slowly at first *Hermes* moved down the slipway, but she soon gathered speed as the crowd cheered her and exactly 61 seconds later, the seven massive drag chains weighing 770 tons in all brought her to a stop ready for the eight waiting tugs to take her in tow. As they began to attach the towing lines, VIP guests were entertained to lunch by the shipbuilding company and in a speech to those assembled Mr J. L. P. Thomas, the First Lord of the Admiralty, reported that when completed, *Hermes*, with an angled flight deck, a steam catapult and a side lift, would be the most modern aircraft carrier in the world. He went on to explain how these innovations would remove the usual limitations found in older light fleet carriers and would enable her to operate efficiently the most powerful naval aircraft which were under development. He went on to say: 'Her flight deck is larger than a football field; her distilling plant is sufficient for most small towns; her generators could supply 10,000 homes without fear of power cuts, and two games of badminton could be played on the after lift.' He continued by telling his audience that, unlike the ships' companies of earlier light fleet carriers, the whole of *Hermes'* complement of over 1,000 men would sleep in bunks instead of hammocks and that they would be provided with dining halls instead of having to eat and sleep in the same compartment. At 3pm that afternoon, as the VIP guests left the shipyard, *Hermes* was secured alongside her fitting-out berth in the Buccleuch Dock, but it would be a long time before she was ready for sea.

Despite the First Lord's optimistic speech, however, there were no early plans to complete *Hermes* and, once launched, she was again laid up with a small care and maintenance party responsible for her preservation. It was two and a half years after her launch, in September 1955, that the Admiralty decided that work should be resumed on *Hermes* and that this time she should be completed. First, however, she had to be dry docked so that the underwater hull could be scraped and painted and she was towed to the Gladstone Graving Dock in Liverpool where the work could be carried out and her propellers could be fitted. It was *Hermes'* first foray to the open sea and there was drama on her return passage, however, when as she was being towed down the River Mersey, a sudden gust of wind

caught her and blew her onto a marker buoy. Although five tugs pulled her clear the buoy remained wedged under one of her propeller brackets, but nevertheless she had to continue the voyage. Once into the Irish Sea the weather suddenly deteriorated and the four tugs in whose charge she was had great difficulty controlling her so urgent messages were sent out for assistance. Two powerful 1,200 horsepower vessels were sent out from the Clyde and it was thought that they would be able to get her to more sheltered waters off the Isle of Man to ride out the storm, but in the event they had to tow her to Belfast Lough where she remained until the weather moderated and the six tugs were then able to tow her back to the safety of Vickers' yard at Barrow-in-Furness where, at long last, work got under way to complete her.

When the new Admiralty plans arrived at the shipyard it was clear that this was not just a case of making modifications to the existing design, but of virtually building a new ship within the confines of the original hull. Perhaps the biggest difference was the armament, for with the development of guided missiles the need for a multitude of medium and close-range weapons had gone. The planned 4.5-inch guns, together with all but ten of the 40mm Bofors and 20mm Oerlikans, were removed and all the magazine stowage areas and ammunition supply hoists were modified or taken away altogether. Two steam catapults were built into the forward end of the flight deck and this proved a particular headache for the builders. To allow for the tremendous increase in thrust and the heavier aircraft which would be handled, the ship's structure had to be considerably strengthened. New and heavier longitudinal bulkheads supporting the catapult troughs and machinery were fitted, and additional stiffening was necessary on several of the decks below. The deck edge aircraft lift on the port side posed further problems. This type of lift was common to the US Navy's carriers, but its first application in a British carrier, HMS *Ark Royal*, was not particularly successful because part of the lift encroached on the internal space within the hull. In *Hermes* it was decided that the whole lift would be outboard of the ship's side. This, however, required greater strengthening of the surrounding areas of shell, hangar deck plating and hangar bulkheads in order to support the overhanging load, and consequently it was found necessary to build the lift supports and other adjacent structures of special steel. The island superstructure was completely redesigned and, in place of the proposed foremast, provision was made for a new Type 984 Comprehensive Display System radar antenna, with its huge 'searchlight' scanner which weighed 28 tons. New and heavier aircraft meant strengthening the flight and hangar decks, and increasing the size of the after lift well.

Perhaps one of the biggest changes which had to be allowed for was the increase in complement. As laid down,

Hermes was intended to carry a ship's company of 1,000 officers and men, which included squadron personnel, but with her new design and with her aircraft and electronic equipment there would be an increase of at least 770 on that number. Not only had messing space to be provided, but additional galley, storage and recreational areas were required. Down below in the machinery spaces, to meet the demands of possible nuclear warfare, a remote control system for the engine and boiler rooms was devised so that, if necessary, the ship could continue to steam without a single man in any of the main propulsion machinery compartments. All the pumps and fans had to be capable of remote control from the machinery control room, and in addition a separate system of air supply for the boilers had to be arranged so that air intakes for the boiler furnaces would not contaminate air in the boiler rooms. Finally, prewetting equipment had to be provided on all exposed decks.

As jet aircraft use different fuel from piston-engined machines, two separate fuel systems, Avcat (jets) and Avgas (piston-engined), had to be fitted, as well as an Avlub lubricating oil system, which meant a big increase in fuel stowage space, pumps and fuel lines. One of the most complicated changes which had to be made was the changeover from a DC to AC electricity supply. The original electrical equipment was designed on a ring main system requiring the use of low voltage relay open breakers controlled from one main and four unit switchboard rooms. This comprised a 220 volt DC system of distribution involving the use of turbo and diesel DC

Hermes alongside the fitting-out berth in Buccleuch Dock, Barrow. Her steam catapults are still covered over and scaffolding festoons the mast. In the background is the minesweeper *Laertes* which was awaiting demolition. (*Barrow Museum Service*)

Inclination trials whilst still alongside. The Reserve Fleet minesweeper *Niger* is in the background.

(*Barrow Museum Service*)

Hermes is manoeuvred from the Buccleuch Dock to Ramsden Dock at Barrow. *(Barrow Museum Service)*

generators. All the drawings for the DC system were completed before building work had started on the new design, and the switchboards had been delivered and were nearly ready for installing. Some generators and much wiring had already been fitted aboard when it was decided that the ship should become AC, with a distribution system of 440 volt, 60 cycle, three phase. This meant that all motor auxiliaries would be supplied at this voltage and that lighting would have a supply of 115 volts, transformers being used for this purpose. The changeover from DC to AC in *Hermes* made close collaboration between the Director of Electronic Engineers at the Admiralty and the electrical drawing office at Barrow necessary. Originally, the ship as designed would have been capable of producing 3,200 kW, but after the conversion her output was 5,400 kW, and the cost of the conversion was £1½ million.

Some of the other alterations in the plans which were as a result of the change in design included the fitting of a sponson on the port side for the mirror landing aid; the provision of air-conditioning in offices and living spaces; the fitting of liquid oxygen making equipment; the removal of separate accommodation for warrant officers and a corresponding increase in wardroom accommodation; new all-electric equipment in the galleys, the removal of hammock hooks and the provision of improved laundry and bathroom facilities. The ship's company would find the new mess decks well-lit and cheerful, with comfortable bunks which could be collapsed during the day in order to provide maximum recreational space and no more wooden-topped mess tables. There would be full canteen facilities with food cooked in up-to-date galleys and served in dining halls. In addition plenty of bathrooms and showers were installed, along with a modern laundry, a barber's shop and a well-stocked library.

As completed *Hermes* was a vessel of 27,800 tons with an overall length of 741ft - 6in, a beam of 144ft - 6in, and a draught of 28ft. She was armed with ten 40mm anti-aircraft guns in twin mountings, all of which were radar controlled. She could carry an air group of 20 aircraft and eight helicopters and, with the squadrons embarked, she would have a complement of 2,100 men. Like her half-sisters *Albion, Bulwark* and *Centaur*, the *Hermes* was a twin-screw ship powered by two sets of Parsons geared turbines in two engine rooms, which developed 80,000 SHP and gave her a speed of 28 knots. The steam for the turbines was supplied by four Admiralty three-drum, superheat boilers in two boiler rooms. She was fitted with a $6^{1}/_{2}°$ angled flight deck, and two 151-ft steam catapults.

In spite of the varied and large-scale alterations to the original design, Vickers was able to give the Admiralty a firm delivery date of 31 October 1959, which meant that at times more than 2,000 men were working to complete the ship. The first naval personnel, commanded by Cdr (E) A. H. Carmichael RN, joined the ship in July 1956, and until the accommodation became available they lived and worked in the Algerine-class minesweeper, HMS *Pluto*, which soon became known as 'Heartbreak Hotel'. In May 1959 *Hermes* was ready to undergo her builder's sea trials, but before these could take place she needed to be dry docked for her underwater hull to be scraped and painted, and her underwater fittings inspected. This time it was decided to send her to Southampton, and she left Barrow-in-Furness on the morning of Sunday 24 May to make the passage south under her own steam. It was during this voyage that *Hermes* was again involved in a drama at sea when one of Vickers' workmen, 63-year-old George Bourne, fell down a lift shaft on board and was seriously injured. The carrier was off Land's End at the time, but a rough sea prevented any vessel from making the 20-mile round trip to take off the unfortunate man, so a helicopter was summoned from RAF Chivenor, 90 miles away in North Devon. So it was that the first deck landing on to *Hermes*' flight deck was actually made by the RAF, but the mission was successful and ten minutes after landing the helicopter was airborne once again and flying the injured man to Penzance Hospital. Next morning *Hermes* steamed up Southampton Water and, guided by five tugs, she was berthed in the port's King George V Dry Dock. Once the maintenance work was finished the carrier completed her builder's trials on the return passage to Barrow, and by mid-June she was back alongside the fitting-out berth at Buchleuch Dock, Barrow-in-Furness.

As she leaves Buccleuch Dock *Hermes* has to pass through the Buccleuch bascule railway bridge and this shot shows just how little room there was to spare between the bridge and the overhang on the port side of the flight deck. *(Barrow Museum Service)*

On Monday 19 October 1959, *Hermes'* first commanding officer, Captain David S. Tibbits DSC RN, was appointed to the ship. Captain Tibbits had entered the Navy at the Royal Naval College, Dartmouth, in 1925, and during the Second World War he had helped to set up the Naval Radar Plotting School. He also served as the Navigating Officer of the battleship HMS *Anson*, and he was present for the surrender of the Japanese in Hong Kong. Between 1956 and 1959 he commanded HMS *Manxman* and the shore establishment HMS *Dryad*, which was the Navigation and Direction School. *Hermes* was to be his last command before retirement.

At 8am on Friday 23 October, four days after Captain Tibbits joined the ship and over 15 years after the first keel plates had been laid, *Hermes* was commissioned. The 74 officers and 281 men who had been standing by the ship were finally able to move on board and most of the day was spent transferring heavy baggage from HMS *Pluto*. Later that afternoon a further 236 ratings arrived in Barrow on a special train which had been laid on from London's Euston Station and this brought the carrier's steaming crew up to strength. Next day, as the ship had not been handed over to the Navy, the Red Ensign was hoisted and during the afternoon of 25 October the Admiralty approved a special open day when the builder's workmen and their families were invited on board, with 13,000 people taking advantage of the offer. On Thursday 29 October, Captain Tibbits hosted a luncheon on board for 85 guests, including the Mayor of Barrow-in-Furness and the senior management from the shipyard. That same afternoon, just half an hour after the visitors had left, the fire alarms sounded for the first time, but fire parties quickly extinguished the small fire which had been caused by overheated lagging in the junior rates dining hall. At 1.15pm on Friday 30 October it was time for *Hermes* to leave Buccleuch Dock and prepare for her final departure from Barrow, but it was not going to be an easy task as the overhang of her angled flight deck meant there would be very little room to spare. As steam was raised for the main engines four tugs stood by to assist in easing her through dock bridge lock. Although she passed through the lock without any problems, as she was being turned to berth alongside Quarantine Wharf she grounded off Whelpsford Point, but the tugs quickly pulled her stern to starboard and she was able to secure alongside safely. Later that evening the carrier's Sailing Master, Captain C. H. Campbell DSC RN (Retd), joined the ship and, finally, at 7.27am on Sunday 1 November, the mooring ropes were slipped and *Hermes* left Barrow for good. Three hours later she was out in the Walney Channel, passing Piel Bar Light and heading south into the Irish Sea.

As *Hermes* steamed south boiler trials were carried out, and at 12.30pm on Monday 2 November she passed within nine miles of the Eddystone Light. That afternoon, as she steamed up Channel, aircraft from Culdrose and Yeovilton made dummy attacks on the new carrier, and at 10.20pm, as she was off Start Point, speed was reduced. Next morning, at 8.15am, she stopped off the Nab Tower to embark the pilot and three hours later she was passing the Shaw Savill passenger liner *Southern Cross* as, for the second time that year, the tugs manoeuvred her into Southampton's King George V Dry Dock. The docking period lasted for 15 days, during which time the Controller of the Navy, Admiral Sir Peter Reid, visited the ship for a day. At 10.30am on Tuesday 17 November 1959, under the command of Captain Tibbits, but with Captain Campbell as Sailing Master, *Hermes* was warped out of the dry dock by tugs before setting course down Southampton Water. Although the carrier was manned by naval personnel, all her machinery was operated by employees of Vickers Armstrong and their sub-contractors. Calshot Spit was cleared at noon and the Nab Tower was reached by 1.15pm, where four hours were spent adjusting compasses before the ship sailed up the Solent to anchor at Spithead at 6.52pm. It had been planned that senior executives of Vickers Armstrong and 45 press representatives would embark from the tug *Forceful*, but strong winds and tides gave no lee to the tug and so *Hermes* weighed anchor and steamed slowly through the Solent with *Forceful*, to the discomfort of her passengers, riding alongside. At this stage, with a strong south-easterly wind, and an overhot port engine which could not be put astern, *Hermes* was not handling easily, so it was with some relief when, at 8pm, the carrier was able to stop and all the passengers were embarked. By 8.55pm *Hermes* was under way and proceeding down the Nab Channel and out to the open sea.

While steaming across the Channel in the direction of Le Havre the main machinery control systems received their final adjustments, and at 2am on the morning of Wednesday 18 November the ship was headed up Channel to be off Dieppe by dawn. At 8am *Hermes* was steaming at full power down Channel on her acceptance run, which was successfully completed at 10am, having achieved a speed of 28.7 knots. Being a fine day, and with the ship some 20 miles off the Isle of Wight, the lower deck was cleared onto the flight deck at 10.40am and, with a Royal Marines guard stood to attention directly behind their table, Captain Tibbits accepted *Hermes* into naval service from the General Manager of Vickers Armstrong (Shipbuilders) Ltd, Mr Leonard Redshaw. Having handed over the vessel, Mr Redshaw told those assembled that, having regard to the long periods of enforced idleness, Vickers considered that they had actually built the ship in four years. In all the cost of building *Hermes* was £20 million, which was roughly what it had cost to modernize *Victorious*. Another short ceremony on the flight deck followed at 11am when, after buglers had sounded the General Salute, the Red Ensign was lowered and the White

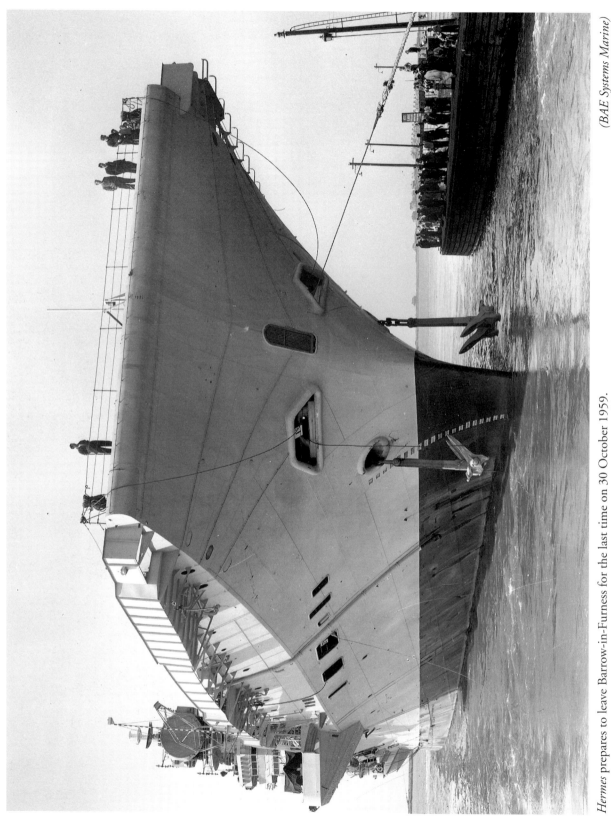

Hermes prepares to leave Barrow-in-Furness for the last time on 30 October 1959.

(BAE Systems Marine)

Ensign was run up. Meanwhile, down below, following the successful completion of the acceptance trials, naval personnel took control of all machinery and the carrier steered what was described by Captain Tibbits as, 'an erratic course back to Portsmouth while members of the press went around the ship in a helicopter for aerial views under way.' At 1.08pm *Hermes* passed Outer Spit Buoy and, after a very smart entry into Portsmouth Harbour, she secured starboard side to, alongside Pitch House Jetty at 1.30pm. Her first arrival at her home port was an auspicious one, for the Sea Lord of the Admiralty and most of the C-in-Cs of the various stations in the Royal Navy happened to be at a meeting on board HMS *Tyne,* and they watched her enter harbour. *Hermes* did not let anyone down and she berthed beautifully, as if she wanted to be there. On the bridge there were sighs of relief and a great satisfaction. As soon as the brow was in place all but ten of the Vickers Armstrong personnel left the ship and she was, at long last, firmly in naval hands.

The carrier is manoeuvred stern first through the final lock.

(BAE Systems Marine)

Chapter Six

The First Commission
November 1959 - September 1961

On Friday 20 November 1959, two days after *Hermes*' arrival in Portsmouth after having been accepted into service, another 200 ratings joined the ship to bring her ship's company up to a full trials complement. Five days later the Commissioning Ceremony was held in the hangar, with the first of 3,000 guests, including relatives and friends of the ship's company, starting to arrive at 10am. The three senior guests of honour were Admiral Sir Manley Power, the C-in-C Portsmouth, Admiral Sir Leonard Durnford-Slater, the C-in-C Nore and His Honour Judge Leslie Block, the latter two being survivors of the ninth *Hermes*; Admiral Durnford-Slater had been her Executive Officer and Judge

Block the Navigating Officer. The only serving member of the ship's company to have been on the previous *Hermes* was Petty Officer Cook J. Nicholas, who was also a survivor of the sinking in April 1942. The ceremony got under way at 11am when Captain Tibbits read the Commissioning Warrant, and it was followed by a religious ceremony which took three-quarters of an hour and then all the guests were treated to a buffet lunch. On the following morning it was down to business for the ship's company when, at 7.45am, *Hermes* slipped her mooring ropes and set course for Gibraltar to carry out initial trials. Captain Tibbits described the passage: 'It was just the sort of day that the Captain of a new ship would wish to have. There was a

Framed by palm trees, *Hermes* lies in the picturesque setting of Malta's Grand Harbour for a ten-day maintenance period.

(Terry McKee)

strong south-westerly wind and quite heavy seas off the Isle of Wight, so everybody had to take considerable pains to look after their part of ship and it was possible to see straightaway what needed securing and what, if any, were the deficiencies. As she proceeded westward down Channel, she very soon steamed clear of the bad weather, so that conditions were pleasant across the Bay of Biscay and down the Spanish and Portuguese coasts. Trials of the stabilizers for the big radar set, and many drills and tests in various departments were carried out and this was all valuable. We entered the Strait of Gibraltar during the night and arrived off the Rock about 9am on 30 November. The ship steamed round close to the Spanish shore and in through the North entrance. This was an anxious moment, for it was not at all well known how the ship would handle and what she would do in a fairly strong wind and a confined space. As at Portsmouth she came into the harbour and went alongside as if she liked doing it, and was berthed without incident on the South Mole. That night Gibraltar experienced one of the worst gales ever recorded there, which was indeed, a "baptism of fire" for a new ship and her company. Happily she rode well at her berth, and tested the strength of the nylon hawsers now supplied to the fleet.'

While the colony was buffeted by severe gales, wind speeds of 90 knots were recorded during the night of 1 December and on board *Hermes* all hawsers were doubled. The ship rode well at her berth, but the 17,000-ton passenger liner *Braemar Castle* was not so fortunate and she ran aground off Capiamento on the Spanish side of Algeciras Bay. Fortunately, she was soon refloated and towed into Gibraltar where she was berthed astern of *Hermes*. Her unscheduled stay alongside meant that 75 of the liner's passengers, along with 400 local schoolchildren, could take the opportunity to visit the Navy's latest aircraft carrier. After four days alongside, at 10am on Friday 4 December, *Hermes* left Gibraltar to return to Portland. For the first part of the passage home the weather was excellent and everything went smoothly, but on passing Cape Finisterre, however, the weather forecast showed a very large and severe depression sweeping across the Atlantic, and this reached Ushant at the same time as the ship. The final 24 hours of the passage were a real test for *Hermes* as the heavy seas washed over her flight deck and rolls of 11 degrees were recorded. When she arrived off Portland on 7 December the weather was too severe to carry out trials and so the carrier remained at sea for the day, before starting the tests on 8 December. Once they had been completed and Customs' clearance had been obtained, *Hermes* returned to Portsmouth and at 10am on Friday 11 December, having spent the night anchored at Spithead, she secured alongside Pitch House Jetty. It was the end of her maiden voyage and *Hermes* would not venture to sea again until the New Year of 1960.

Two days after her arrival in Portsmouth the first

christenings took place on board when the infant sons and daughter of Sub-Lt Johnson and Petty Officers Watson and Parrott were baptized in the ship's chapel. On Tuesday 19 January, with everyone back on board following seasonal leave, *Hermes* left Portsmouth for Portland where she completed her radio and radar trials which had been postponed before Christmas on account of the severe weather. On conclusion of these the carrier secured to C buoy in Plymouth Sound for three rainy days and the West Country men enjoyed a welcome break before, on 25 January, she left and returned to Portsmouth.

It was Tuesday 9 February when *Hermes* sailed again, setting course for Portland and the Lyme Bay area. Next day, at 9am, the first fixed-wing aircraft, two piston-engined Sea Furies from RNAS Yeovilton, landed on board for a brief visit and later that morning they left the ship. The first phase of the carrier's trials and work-up was completed on 18 February when she returned to Portsmouth, but two weeks later she was at sea again to complete her various evolutions in the area between the Isle of Wight and Portland. On Friday 18 March there was a break in the routine when *Hermes* made her first foreign visit, a long weekend in Le Havre. On two afternoons the ship was opened to visitors and more than 8,000 local people took the opportunity to look over *Hermes*. During the visit the Royal Marines Band gave an impressive display when they Beat Retreat in the hangar in front of 300 port officials and their families. A similar display in the town centre, which was advertised in the press as a spectacular 'Beat Retraite' performed by the, 'batalion de fusilier marin', was well attended by a crowd of several thousands, who showed their appreciation by taking the musicians to a nearby restaurant where they were plied with wine. *Hermes* left Le Havre during the afternoon of Tuesday 22 March, and after carrying out gunnery trials she returned to Portsmouth three days later.

Hermes remained alongside Portsmouth's Middle Slip Jetty during the whole of April when the opportunity was taken for the ship's company to take their seasonal leave. On Tuesday 3 May the C-in-C Portsmouth, Admiral Sir Manley Power, inspected the carrier and six days later the trials teams joined the ship. At midday on Tuesday 10 May *Hermes* left Portsmouth to start her initial flying trials and an hour and a half later, with the ship off the Isle of Wight, 'Flying Stations' was piped. At 2.32pm came the first operational deck landing when a Gannet of 849C Flight landed on board. During the following 20 minutes two Gannets made three more deck landings and take-offs before, at 3.30pm, the first jet aircraft, a Sea Hawk, landed on. Two hours later a second Sea Hawk landed safely and next day the two planes performed numerous launches and landings. The flying trials continued for another ten days and on 21 May, after an air direction exercise in conjunction with RNAS Brawdy, *Hermes* anchored off

An extremely smart *Hermes*, with the ship's company manning the flight deck, prepares to enter Algiers Harbour. *(Terry McKee)*

Steaming to her berth alongside the Quai Antiles on the morning of 18 August 1960.

(*Terry McKee*)

Refuelling from RFA *Wave Baron* during 'Exercise Swordthrust' which took her north of the Arctic Circle. The destroyer *Defender* looks on.   *(Terry McKee)*

Milford Haven for the night. The respite was only brief, however, and next day the trials resumed, continuing until 9pm on Monday 23 May when the carrier anchored at Spithead. Next morning a tug from the dockyard drew alongside the carrier and relatives of the ship's company were embarked for the first Families Day. After weighing anchor at 10.30am the carrier steamed out into the Channel, south-west of the Isle of Wight, where the two Sea Hawks put on a flying display before leaving the area, following which *Hermes* steamed up harbour and secured alongside Pitch House Jetty at 1pm.

Four days after her arrival alongside tropical clothing was issued to the ship's company, although there were still five weeks to go before she was due to sail, and while the ship was alongside deadload trials were carried out with two bright-yellow, trolley-like contraptions, named 'Effie' and 'Lucy', which were catapulted over the bows at regular intervals. Also at this time a reunion was held on board for survivors of the ninth *Hermes*, and the first deck landing of the new Westland Wessex helicopter took place. Finally, however, with a full complement of 189 officers and 1,643 ratings, at 9.20am on Tuesday 5 July, *Hermes* left Portsmouth and sailed out to Spithead where she would

anchor for the night. Next day she weighed anchor at 11am and spent the rest of the day, until 7pm, embarking her full air group for the first time. By the end of the day the Scimitars of 804 Squadron had arrived from Lossiemouth, the Sea Vixens of 890 Squadron from Yeovilton, as well as the Gannet AEW3s of 849C Flight and, appropriately, the eight Westland Whirlwind helicopters of 814 Squadron. It was the Swordfish aircraft of this squadron that had served in the previous *Hermes*, from September 1939 until she was sunk in April 1942. From the moment that 'Flying Stations' sounded in the morning until the last recovery that evening, the ship was a wasps' nest of frenzied activity with all efforts focused on the safe recovery of every aircraft. Finally, however, *Hermes* set course for Gibraltar and her first deployment during which she would carry out her operational work-up, which was divided into three phases with visits to Malta, Messina and Algiers.

On Saturday 9 July *Hermes* paused briefly off Gibraltar before setting course for Malta and two days later, under a scorching Mediterranean sun, 'Hands to Bathe' was piped for the first time. Next day, with the ship in the exercise areas off Malta, flying operations started in earnest and continued for seven days, with only a short break on 16

July when *Hermes* anchored in Marsaxlokk Bay. The first phase of the work-up ended on Friday 22 July, when *Hermes* put into Messina for a weekend break, but in the following week flying started again, this time off the coast of Tripoli with the RAF base at El Adem being designated as the diversion runway. On the morning of Saturday 30 July the squadrons were flown off to Hal Far and *Hermes* entered Grand Harbour for the first time to secure at buoys in Bighi Bay where she joined *Ark Royal* which had arrived the day before, and at last the ship's company had a welcome opportunity to escape from the constant uproar of jet engines.

During the ten-day maintenance period in Malta the ship's company were able to enjoy the 'delights' of Strait Street or 'The Gut' as it was better known, which had changed little since the pre-war visits of the ninth *Hermes*. For those who wanted a little more relaxation there were the beaches of St Paul's Bay or a soccer match against *Ark Royal's* team, although the latter beat *Hermes* by seven goals. The visit ended on the morning of Tuesday 9 August when *Hermes* left Grand Harbour with *Ark Royal* to continue her work-up off Malta, and on the following day the Governor of the colony flew out to watch the flying

operations. The two carriers rendezvoused with the cruiser *Tiger* and units of the US Navy's 6th Fleet, including the aircraft carrier USS *Forrestal,* for 'Exercise Royal Flush III', which was primarily an air defence exercise. As such it was an ideal opportunity for *Hermes* to show off her Type 984 CDS radar, while intercepting 'hostile' raiders from *Forrestal* and *Ark Royal.* With the final stages of the exercise having been completed off the Algerian coast *Hermes* was able to enter Algiers Harbour at 8am on the morning of Thursday 18 August, and with the aircraft ranged on deck and the ship's company manning the flight deck she presented a magnificent sight as she secured alongside the Quai Antiles. Despite the unrest against French rule which pervaded Algeria at the time, the French population were very hospitable and the visit was a success.

By this time the Flag Officer Aircraft Carriers, Rear-Admiral Smeeton, had hoisted his flag in *Hermes*, and after the long weekend of relaxation in Algiers it was time to get back down to work as he carried out his Operational Readiness Inspection. *Hermes* then returned to the UK and on 26 August arrived in Falmouth Bay where she paused to fly off 814 Squadron, before setting course for Scotland's east coast. During the passage the Scimitars flew off to

An impressive bow shot of *Hermes* at speed in the Mediterranean. *(Terry McKee)*

Hermes, in the background, exercises with *Victorious* and *Ark Royal* off Malta on 3 December 1960. *(Fleet Air Arm Museum)*

Lossiemouth, and once in the North Sea *Hermes* rendezvoused with *Ark Royal* once again to practise manoeuvres prior to her next major exercise. For two weeks *Hermes* carried out flying operations off Scotland before putting into Rosyth Dockyard on 5 September and securing alongside the South Arm. Ten days later the C-in-C Home Fleet, Vice-Admiral Sir Wilfred Woods, visited the carrier and an hour after his departure *Hermes* slipped her moorings and put to sea to rendezvous with *Ark Royal*, the cruiser *Gambia* and the destroyers *Camperdown, Daring, Defender* and *Saintes*, as well as the RFA *Wave Baron*. The ships were to take part in 'Exercise Swordthrust', which was described as, 'a supreme test for the air defence organization', particularly for the Sea Vixens of 890 Squadron who flew 81 sorties, during which 76 day and 26 night interceptions were successfully carried out in the face of ferocious American opposition. For the ship's company it was a busy, but bleak time, without sight of land and with only brief glimpses of other warships, but having crossed Latitude 66 degrees 32 minutes North they had entered King Neptune's northerly kingdom and so received their 'blue nose' certificates. During the course of the exercise both *Hermes* and *Ark Royal* had their own Russian trawlers shadowing them, only leaving when, on

the morning of Sunday 2 October, the two carriers anchored off Greenock. Unfortunately, the run ashore was disrupted by strong winds and a choppy sea, but the ground parties of 824 (Whirlwind) Squadron were embarked before, on 6 October, *Hermes* left the Clyde to take part in her next exercise, which was code-named 'Rumtub III'. This time it was an anti-submarine exercise in the Western Approaches, and after embarking the Whirlwind helicopters of 824 Squadron *Hermes* rendezvoused with other units taking part, including British submarines and the US Navy's brand new nuclear-powered submarine, USS *Scorpion*,* which proved to be a most worthy adversary for the energetic Whirlwinds. At 8.35am on 7 October, Whirlwind 282 was forced to ditch in the sea, but fortunately the machine was close to the frigate *Blackpool* at the time and the crew were rescued safely. Later that day there was a break in proceedings when *Hermes* anchored in Northern Ireland's Lough Foyle, where she was joined by the Flag Officer Flotillas (Home), Vice-Admiral Sir Charles Madden. Next day the exercise resumed, with *Hermes* operating closely with *Blackpool* and

*Tragically, USS *Scorpion* was lost with all hands in May 1968, south-west of the Azores.

the cruiser *Gambia*. Finally, after six days of exercises, *Hermes* returned briefly to Lough Foyle where Admiral Madden was disembarked and the carrier then set course for Plymouth, where she arrived on the following day to disembark the helicopters and ground staff of 824 Squadron. The carrier did not linger in Plymouth Sound for long, however, and early on 16 October she anchored at Spithead, moving up harbour the following day to berth alongside Middle Slip Jetty. During the period between 5 July and her return to Portsmouth the *Hermes* had spent 78 days at sea, and during that time she had steamed some 22,514 miles.

Hermes remained alongside at Portsmouth for three weeks before sailing again at 2pm on Monday 7 November, this time bound for the Far East Station. Before leaving home waters, however, she operated in the North Western Approaches and the Irish Sea for a few days, and the Vixens spent some time firing Firestreak missiles at a target from RAE Aberporth in Cardigan Bay. During the passage south to Gibraltar the carrier encountered severe gales which caused damage to the starboard forward catwalk, but by 11 November she was off Gibraltar and carrying out flying operations. Four days later, after flying the Vixens off to RAF North Front (the Scimitars of 804 Squadron flew from the UK direct to Gibraltar), *Hermes* was safely berthed in Gibraltar's No 1 dry dock where, over the next 13 days, the underwater hull was scraped and painted.

It was on Tuesday 29 November that *Hermes* left Gibraltar and steamed east to Malta where, four days later, she rendezvoused with *Ark Royal* and *Victorious* for a photocall of all three aircraft carriers steaming in line ahead. Three hours later, at 2.50pm on 3 December, *Hermes* secured to buoys in Grand Harbour. For *Ark's* ship's company there was the prospect of Christmas in Malta and *Victorious* was to make a fast passage home for the festive season, but for *Hermes* it was just the start of her deployment and after only a few hours moored in Grand Harbour she left for Port Said. During Tuesday 6 December she made her first southbound transit of the Suez Canal, and by that evening she was steaming south through the Gulf of Suez. After a passage of four days through the sweltering heat of the Red Sea, *Hermes* arrived in Aden Harbour on the morning of Saturday 10 December for a stay of 48 hours which, for most people, was long enough. During the visit she was opened to the public for three hours and most of those who took the opportunity to look round were from the British military bases in the colony. Before she sailed, Rear-Admiral A. A. F. Talbot, the Flag Officer Arabian Seas and Persian Gulf, together with local dignitaries, embarked in order to watch the flying operations off Aden as the ship carried out a 'Shop Window' exercise. It was of great interest because it was the first time that the new generation of naval aircraft had been seen east of Suez, and the display ended with the

Royal Marines Detachment in full battledress disembarking from two helicopters hovering over the flight deck, after which *Hermes* made a second 48-hour visit to Aden.

There were few on board who were sorry when, at 7.30am on Saturday 17 December, *Hermes* left Aden and, with the frigate *Yarmouth*, steamed south-east through the fresher and cooler breezes of the Arabian Sea bound for Colombo, where she arrived on the morning of Friday 23 December. For three days the ship's company were able to enjoy the hospitality of Colombo, and the beautiful tropical beaches of Mount Lavinia, south of the city, while on board there was the traditional Christmas dinner and a party for 300 local children. On Boxing Day *Hermes* and *Yarmouth* left Ceylon (Sri Lanka) to steam directly to Singapore Naval Base, where they arrived on the morning of New Year's Eve. The 12 days alongside No 8 berth of the naval base were the first chance for real relaxation since leaving Gibraltar in November, and with the dockyard canteen, the swimming pool at HMS *Terror*, and all the 'pleasures' of Sembawang and Nee Soon villages, with Singapore City itself only an hour's taxi ride away, the run ashore was as popular as ever. On the sports field the soccer team came up against *Bulwark* and *Belfast*, beating the latter by five goals to three.

On Thursday 12 January 1961, having hoisted the flag of the Flag Officer, Second in Command, Far East Station (FO2 FES), Rear-Admiral Michael Le Fanu, it was time to leave behind the delights of HMS *Terror's* swimming pool and head for the rougher waters of the South China Sea and the US Navy's exercise areas at Subic Bay in the Philippines. For five days, together with the frigates *Rocket* and *Yarmouth* and the destroyer HMAS *Voyager*, she exercised with US Navy units in extremely heavy seas, which proved to be some of the roughest weather of the commission. However, the discomfort was soon forgotten on 18 January when *Hermes* was secured alongside the US Navy's Naval Stores Pier at the Subic Bay base where the ship's company could enjoy two days of generous American hospitality, and the 'delights' of Olongapo Village. This was followed by a ten-day visit to Hong Kong where, with blue uniforms making an appearance again, it made a welcome change from the tropical heat and humidity. On 1 February *Hermes* left Hong Kong to return to the area off the east coast of Malaya where flying practice was resumed, but six days later the carrier secured alongside Singapore's naval base once again to carry out maintenance. Whilst *Hermes* was alongside the aircraft operated from RAF Tengah in the north-west of Singapore Island, and on 9 February one of 890 Squadron's Sea Vixens ditched into the sea south-east of Singapore. Fortunately the crew were able to eject safely and they were rescued by a helicopter of 814 Squadron and HMS *Belfast*. During the stay in Singapore the ship received a visit from Admiral of the Fleet Lord Mountbatten, the Chief of the Defence Staff, and Admiral Le Fanu struck his flag and returned to the

The frigate *Rocket* prepares to carry out a jackstay transfer with *Hermes* during heavy weather at Subic Bay. *(Terry McKee)*

A US Navy Tracker lands on during exercises off the Philippines. *(Terry McKee)*

Hermes alongside the North Arm of Hong Kong Dockyard. In the foreground land reclamation work is being carried out and today the whole of what used to be the dockyard has been reclaimed from the sea.

(Terry McKee)

Belfast. Finally, on the morning of Saturday 18 February, *Hermes* left Singapore and set course for Trincomalee.

After steaming north through the Strait of Malacca and into the Indian Ocean, *Hermes* arrived in the picturesque natural harbour of Trincomalee at 10am on Friday 24 February and she secured to No 4 buoy where, during the Second World War, her predecessor had moored. However, by 1961 the once busy harbour had become a vast expanse of tropical blue water surrounded by the dilapidated wartime naval base, and one naval officer graphically described it as, 'Scapa Flow in Technicolor'. That afternoon the Ceylonese Defence Minister paid a visit to the ship, but on a more sombre note a rating who was swimming at nearby Sandy Point was drowned. Next day the body of L/Airman Hurditch was recovered off Saval Point, and his funeral took place on 26 February at the British Military Cemetery. Finally, early on the morning of Monday 27 February, *Hermes* left Trincomalee to take part in 'Exercise Jet 61' before making her way back to the UK. As well as Royal Naval units there were ships from Australia, Ceylon, India, Pakistan and New Zealand, including the Australian aircraft carrier HMAS *Melbourne* and the ill-fated destroyer *Voyager*, as well as the frigates *Queenborough* and *Quickmatch*. Along with *Hermes* the Royal Navy was represented by HMS *Belfast* (Flag Rear-Admiral Le Fanu), and the 8th Destroyer Squadron. During the exercise RFA *Fort Dunvegan* represented a large merchantman and the *Belfast* a commerce raider, but she was soon hunted down by aircraft from *Hermes* and *Melbourne*. Eleven days later, at the conclusion of the exercise, when *Hermes* was in a position Lat 09°/Long 81°, off the coast of Ceylon and over the spot where her predecessor had been sunk 19 years before, a remembrance service was held on the flight deck.

The ceremony took place at 8am on Friday 10 March, and after the religious service Captain Tibbits committed a wreath to the sea. Next day, with the ship en route to Aden, there was a much more relaxed atmosphere on board for a belated Crossing the Line Ceremony on the flight deck. *Hermes* had actually crossed the equator a number of times during 'Exercise Jet 61', but such frivolities could not take place at the time and the passage across the Arabian Sea provided the ideal opportunity. Three days later, on 15 March, *Hermes* rendezvoused with *Victorious*, which had arrived in the area from the UK via South Africa, and the two carriers undertook an air defence exercise, 'Sea Sheikh', which also included air support for the Army in the Aden Protectorate. On 17 March *Hermes* put into Aden for three days where there was a last chance for some duty-free shopping before she sailed for Suez. She made her northbound transit of the Suez Canal on 24 March, and three days later she arrived in Malta's Grand Harbour.

During her eight days in Malta some maintenance was carried out, then on Tuesday 4 April, in company with RFA *Fort Duquesne* and HMS *Surprise* (C-in-C Mediterranean's dispatch vessel), *Hermes* left Grand Harbour to recover her squadrons from Hal Far and set course for Naples. On the following afternoon she passed the smoking volcano Mount Etna, and on the morning of 8 April she anchored in the Bay of Naples. From there members of the ship's company took trips to Capri, Pompeii and Sorrento, and 890 Squadron's football team beat a local side from Ischia, 2-0. After leaving Naples on 14 April *Hermes* called at Gibraltar two days later where she met her half-sister *Centaur*, whose football team beat *Hermes* by 9-0. After just 24 hours alongside *Hermes* left Gibraltar for home and en route she rendezvoused with the

At anchor in the picturesque setting of Trincomalee Harbour.

(Terry McKee)

cruiser HMS *Lion,* for manoeuvres before the two ships went their separate ways; *Lion* proceeded into the Mediterranean and *Hermes*, after flying off the squadrons to their respective bases, set course for Portsmouth. On the afternoon of Tuesday 18 April *Hermes* anchored at Spithead, where her first visitors were the officers of Customs and Excise, but 24 hours later she weighed anchor to steam up harbour. At Middle Slip Jetty hundreds of relatives and friends waited to greet the ship and she finally secured alongside at 4pm, having been away from home for 173 days, and having steamed 33,000 miles. The Far East cruise was over.

During her stay of five and a half weeks in Portsmouth the ship's company were able to enjoy a well-earned leave, and on 11 May it was announced that *Hermes* would leave home waters at the end of June to visit the United States and Canada. It was a trip which was eagerly anticipated by the ship's company, with *Hermes* being the second of the Royal Navy's aircraft carriers to visit America during 1961*, and calls at Norfolk, Virginia, Boston, and Halifax, Nova Scotia, were on the schedule. Before that, however, there were other duties much closer to home to carry out, and

when *Hermes* left Portsmouth at just after midday on Monday 29 May the first task was to land on all her aircraft. Almost immediately the squadrons started dress rehearsals for their part in the forthcoming Paris Air Show, during which the whole of *Hermes*' air group had to reach an exact spot over the French capital at a precise moment from somewhere in the Channel and without colliding with any other aircraft which were doing the same thing. There were also rehearsals with the frigates *Puma, Rhyl* and *Tenby* for a series of 'Shop Window' displays which were going to take place in early June. The last day of May saw the carrier anchored at Spithead, and next day the displays began. Each morning started with *Hermes* and the three frigates rendezvousing in the vicinity of the Nab Tower, and shortly afterwards the carrier and *Rhyl* would close RFA *Tideflow* for a demonstration of replenishment at sea. Every afternoon the submarine *Turpin* would dive alongside *Hermes* for a short demonstration before resurfacing, which was followed by the frigates firing anti-aircraft and anti-submarine weapons. The final demonstrations were flying displays by *Hermes*' aircraft and helicopters. There were a variety of guests on board the carrier, ranging from senior military officers to sea cadets and journalists, and on 3 June the Lord Mayor of London was the guest of honour. The displays were carried out over

*The other was HMS *Ark Royal* which visited New York for five days in February.

nine days between 1 and 9 June, with only one incident when a Sea Vixen's starboard wing tank caught fire and the plane took off in a cloud of fire and thick black smoke. Fortunately, the pilot, Lt-Cdr Anderton, managed to land the aircraft ashore safely, but several of the flight deck personnel suffered minor burns.

With the last of the 'Shop Window' displays having been completed, *Hermes* set course down the Channel for Falmouth, where she anchored the following morning. Not only was shore leave granted to liberty men, but that afternoon the carrier was opened to visitors from RNAS Culdrose, who were not deterred by the long boat ride out to the ship. Next evening *Hermes* weighed anchor and, in company with HMS *Rhyl*, she set course for the east coast of Scotland, off Lossiemouth, to take part in 'Exercise Fairwind VI', which also involved the destroyers *Battleaxe*, *Diamond* and *Duchess* and the Dutch destroyer *Gronigan*. The final stage of the exercise saw a simulated nuclear attack, with *Hermes* passing through the 'fallout' which proved a good test for the ship's prewetting system. On Thursday 22 June, however, the carrier returned to Portsmouth to prepare for her voyage to America and exercises 'Riptide' and 'Maple Royal' which were to take place off the east coast of the USA.

At 2.15pm on Friday 30 June 1961, *Hermes* left Portsmouth to embark her squadrons off the Isle of Wight and set course for Norfolk, Virginia, in company with the escorts *Chichester* and *Rhyl*. This should have been the finale of the commission but far away in the Middle East, political events were conspiring to prevent the carrier's US trip. On 19 June 1961 Britain had ended its Protectorate of the oil-rich sheikhdom of Kuwait in the Persian Gulf, and as part of the settlement with the small state it had been agreed that military aid would be forthcoming if it were necessary, and if requested by Kuwait's rulers. Of all the oil producing states with which Britain was trading, Kuwait was by far the most significant, and it was to her treaty relationship with Kuwait that Britain attached the greatest importance. On 25 June 1961, six days after the ending of the Protectorate, General Abdul Kassim, President of neighbouring Iraq, declared that Kuwait belonged to Iraq on the grounds that, under the old Ottoman Empire, it had been a province of Basra - which was indisputably Iraqi territory. The British Government took Kassim's strongly worded statement seriously, as did the ruler of Kuwait who asked for British military assistance.

As political tension in the Middle East mounted, wheels were put into motion and considerable forces were soon on their way to the area. HMS *Bulwark* was already in the Arabian Sea at the time and, as a commando carrier with 600 men of 42 Commando Royal Marines on board, she was soon off Kuwait. Having relieved *Hermes*, *Victorious* was the operational strike carrier east of Suez and she had left Singapore for Hong Kong on 26 June, but three days

later she was ordered to the Persian Gulf. Meanwhile, on board *Hermes* rumours of a change of plan were rife and during the afternoon of Saturday 1 July they were confirmed when Captain Tibbits made the following announcement to the ship's company: 'There has been a good deal of buzzing and speculating going on in the ship during the past 24 hours and I am now in a position to clear this up. The government has decided to withdraw British ships from the exercises "Riptide" and "Maple Royal" off the east coast of the United States so that they may be available for any action which may develop in Kuwait...consequently we shall be turning south instead of west as soon as replenishment is completed tonight, with the intention of entering the Mediterranean on about Tuesday...while we are all disappointed to be missing the American cruise, particularly those of us with relatives there, at least this means we shall be able to send some mail off from Gibraltar instead of waiting until we get to Norfolk.' In the event, the *Centaur* left Gibraltar on 30 June to make her way to Aden where she remained on standby for 14 days, and on the morning of 4 July *Hermes*, *Chichester* and *Rhyl* put into Gibraltar. However, they did not remain alongside for long and next day they left harbour to rendezvous with the destroyer *Crossbow* for flying exercises in the western Mediterranean, close to Gibraltar. This was followed by a week alongside the colony's South Mole and on 17 July *Hermes* and her escorts began four more days at sea. On 24 July, with political tension in the Persian Gulf having been reduced, the three ships left Gibraltar and set course for home. The trip to the United States was lost forever.

After flying the squadrons off to their shore stations the *Hermes* secured alongside Portsmouth's Middle Slip Jetty at 1.30pm on Friday 28 July, following which the ship's company commenced a 12-day break. Whilst the carrier had been exercising off Gibraltar, moves were under way to plan an alternative to the cancelled American cruise, and a visit to the Norwegian capital of Oslo was arranged instead at very short notice. In the event *Hermes* left Portsmouth with the faithful HMS *Rhyl* during the forenoon of Wednesday 9 August, and steaming via the Irish Sea and the Pentland Firth, they anchored in Oslo Harbour six days later, on 15 August. Next day, at 12.40pm, His Majesty King Olav of Norway was piped aboard and, after inspecting a guard of honour and meeting heads of departments, he toured the ship before lunching with FOAC. That afternoon, shortly before the King's departure, the customary children's party was held, and although the visit to Oslo was classed as informal, one member of the Royal Marines Detachment was heard to comment, 'If this is an informal visit I should hate to be on a formal one.' In the first two days there were 11 ceremonial guards mounted for visiting dignitaries. For two afternoons the ship was opened to visitors, but the long

On 11 March 1961, during the passage across the Indian Ocean to Aden, a belated 'Crossing the Line' ceremony was held as the ship had crossed the equator several times during 'Exercise Jet 61'. In this photograph Captain Tibbits and 'King Neptune' preside over the ritual duckings.
(Terry McKee)

Homeward-bound through the Suez Canal and a day of relaxation for most of the ship's company.
(Terry McKee)

Pre-wetting exercises during a simulated nuclear attack off the Dorset coast.

(Terry McKee)

A Scimitar mishap on the flight deck.

(Terry McKee)

boat ride deterred many and only 1,500 people came to look round. On the morning of Saturday 19 August the last foreign visit of the commission came to an end and *Hermes* left Oslo to return to Portsmouth two days later. Although the commission was drawing to a close there were still important duties to complete, and on 23 August the carrier put to sea to carry out flying trials with Sea Venoms and Sea Vixens. During the manoeuvres Captain Tibbits' successor, Captain W. D. O'Brien DSC RN, embarked by helicopter to get a 'feel' for his new command and to watch *Hermes* in action. On Friday 25 August, however, the *Hermes* returned to Portsmouth where, two days later, there were some unusual visitors to the ship in the form of performers from Billy Smart's Circus along with some of their animals including a Shetland pony, two llamas, three chimpanzees and one reluctant baby elephant. That weekend also saw Portsmouth's Navy Days and during the three afternoons she was open to the public,

40,000 people visited her.

The final duties of the commission began on Monday 28 August 1961 when, in company with the frigate *Pellew*, *Hermes* left Portsmouth for flying exercises in Lyme Bay, watched by the Flag Officer Sea Training, Vice-Admiral P. W. Gretton. On 30 August two Blackburn Buccaneer S1 strike aircraft from RAE Boscombe Down were embarked from lighters in Weymouth Bay, and *Hermes* weighed anchor and put to sea to prepare for flying operations. Next morning the first launch took place at 6.30am, and flying continued all morning, but at midday tragedy struck when one of the Buccaneers, which was being flown by Lt-Cdr Brown and Mr Dunn from RAE Boscombe Down, was launched. To the horror of those watching, the aircraft did not gain height after the launch, but crashed into the sea about 300 yards ahead of the ship in a position Lat 50° - 32.5'N/Long 03° - 13.12'W. Swift action by the Officer of the Watch enabled the carrier to avoid the stricken plane,

A dramatic series of photographs taken during the 'Shop Window' displays of early June 1961. This Sea Vixen's starboard wing tank caught fire and the plane was launched in a cloud of fire and thick black smoke. Fortunately, the pilot landed safely ashore.

(Terry McKee)

and within ten minutes the sea boat had been launched and was over the scene. Despite a thorough search by ship's divers from *Hermes* there was no trace of the Buccaneer's crew, and it was 6.15pm before the carrier was under way again with flying continuing, only this time by the Scimitars of 804 Squadron. On Saturday 2 September *Hermes* anchored at Spithead where the remaining trials Buccaneer was disembarked onto a lighter to be ferried ashore. Later that day *Hermes* steamed up harbour and secured alongside Middle Slip Jetty.

After only a weekend break in Portsmouth *Hermes* sailed again on Monday 4 September, this time with members of the Royal Aeronautical Society embarked who were treated to flying displays by the squadrons over the next 36 hours. For the next three days the aircraft carried out rehearsals for their part in the Farnborough Air Show, and although cloud and poor weather deterred many participants, for *Hermes*' air group it was business as usual and the ship's

pilots earned a good deal of admiration by arriving over Farnborough spot on time. On 10 September the aircraft left the ship to fly north for the air show, and afterwards they returned to their respective bases. Meanwhile, on the following day, *Hermes,* which had been anchored at Spithead, entered harbour to secure alongside Middle Slip Jetty at 2.15pm, following which Captain Tibbits addressed the ship's company for the last time. Shortly after arriving in Portsmouth there was some unwelcome publicity for *Hermes* when £4,200 was reported missing from a safe in the ship's pay office, and a full-scale police investigation was started. At one stage it appeared that all leave for the ship might be stopped and an officer was charged with negligence, but in the event the carrier was paid off on schedule. By the end of September most of the ship's company had departed on leave and *Hermes* had started her first long refit. The first commission was over, but already the carrier was known as the 'Happy *Hermes*'.

In late August 1961 two Blackburn Buccaneer S1 strike aircraft from RAE Boscombe Down carried out trials in *Hermes*. This aircraft, together with its pilot and observer, was subsequently lost when it crashed on launching.   (*Terry McKee*)

Chapter Seven

The Second Commission
April 1962 - March 1964

In October 1961, a few weeks after the end of the first commission, *Hermes* was dry docked in D lock, and at 11 am on Thursday 23 November Captain W. D. O'Brien DSC RN assumed command of the aircraft carrier. Captain O'Brien had entered the Navy in 1930, and for most of his career he had served in destroyers. Between 1939 and 1943 he served in HMS *Garland* and the elderly vessels *Witherington* and *Wolsey*, before being appointed to the much newer HMS *Offa*. Later in the war he commanded *Cottesmore* and in 1948 *Venus*. In 1949 he was appointed as the Executive Officer in the cruiser *Ceylon*, and after promotion in 1955 he became Captain (D) of the 8th Destroyer Squadron in HMS *Cheviot*.

During the dreary and cold winter of 1961 most of the new ship's company joined the ship, while she was still high and dry in D lock, and with unreliable heating and a flight deck which resembled a junk yard, life on board was most uncomfortable at this time. Christmas Day for those on duty was particularly depressing with the discovery of the body of a rating who had committed suicide, but in January 1962 FOAC joined the ship to hoist his flag briefly before transferring to the *Victorious*. During the early part of the year winter sports flourished ashore, and the ship's complement built up steadily as more and more men joined her. On board, the BBC recorded the radio programme 'Sporting Chance' in 4F junior rates dining hall, and on 9 March the dry dock was flooded and the carrier was afloat once again. Soon afterwards she was towed round to Middle Slip Jetty where restoring was speeded up and the flight deck was sandblasted and

Hermes undergoing sea trials in the Channel.   *(Lt-Cdr Larcombe)*

repainted. By early April steam had been raised and the first basin trials had been carried out. As the chaos of the refit was slowly cleared up parties of visitors were shown around the ship and the new FOAC, Rear-Admiral F. H. E. Hopkins, walked round and declared himself, 'pleased and surprised' at the state of the ship. Finally, on Friday 20 April the refit was complete and the ship was back 'In Routine' as recommissioning day approached.

The ceremony of Commissioning Day, which traditionally marks the beginning of a totally new phase in a ship's life, took place on Tuesday 24 April 1962 and proceedings got under way at midday when wives, sweethearts, parents and families of the ship's company arrived on board. After a buffet lunch all the guests assembled in the hangar for the simple religious ceremony which started at 2.30pm. After prayers and the Captain's address, Major-General G. D. Scott presented a silver figure of Mercury to mark the connection between the carrier and the Royal Corps of Signals, following which the chairman of Vickers Shipbuilding presented a silver bowl to the ship. Captain O'Brien assisted his wife in the cutting of the commissioning cake and, after being served afternoon tea, all the guests had left the ship by 5pm.

Originally it had been scheduled that *Hermes* would leave Portsmouth the next day to start her trials, but fog delayed her sailing and it was 10am on Thursday 26 April when she left Middle Slip Jetty and put to sea. With the ship at sea for the first time in seven months it was reassuring to find that everything was working, and over the following weeks there were many 'firsts' for the ship's company. There was the first RAS, the first fixed-wing landing and, courtesy of the engine room department, the first run ashore at Weymouth when, at the end of April, the carrier put into Portland with lubricating oil problems in the main engines. There was some light relief when an old Bentley motor car was catapulted over the bows, but mainly life was just the hard slog of exercises and manoeuvres in Lyme Bay and in the area between the Isle of Wight and Portland. Flying trials began on Tuesday 1 May and continued for three days, with Gannets, Vixens and Scimitars of 849B Flight, 892 Squadron and 803 Squadron respectively. On Tuesday 8 May *Hermes* returned to Portsmouth and two days later the FOAC, Rear-Admiral Hopkins, hoisted his flag on board while on the same day the C-in-C Portsmouth, Admiral Sir Alexander Bingley, visited the ship to look round. After eight days alongside *Hermes* sailed into the Channel once again to carry out Buccaneer trials off Devon's Berry Head and in Lyme Bay. These were followed by a quick two-day visit to Portsmouth before, at 5.15pm on Friday 25 May, *Hermes* left to embark her squadrons, together with the Wessex helicopters of 814 Squadron, and after a final fling of DLPs in Lyme Bay she set course south for Gibraltar.

The weather in the Bay of Biscay was warm and sunny

with only light winds, and on Saturday 2 June *Hermes* arrived in Gibraltar where, for many of the ship's company, it was their first 'foreign' run ashore. After 24 hours alongside, which allowed Admiral Hopkins to inspect Divisions on the flight deck, the carrier sailed for the exercise areas between Malta and Sardinia. During the passage speed was reduced on the evening of 4 June to allow the ship's MO and the sickbay staff to perform an emergency appendectomy operation on Steward Bateman, but next day work started in earnest when flying operations began. With only a short break at anchor in Marsaxlokk Bay the flying practice continued for eight days but, on the morning of 13 June, with the arrester gear not functioning correctly, *Hermes* entered Grand Harbour and secured alongside Parlatorio Wharf for a 14-day maintenance period. The last two days were spent at a buoy in French Creek, and on 27 June the carrier made an early morning departure from Grand Harbour, in company with the destroyer *Dunkirk* and the submarine *Tiptoe*, to set course for the North African coast and the exercise areas off Tobruk. During the manoeuvres the aircraft operated over the RAF's bombing range at El Adem, but on Sunday 1 July the three units set course for the Lebanese port of Beirut. *Hermes* secured alongside the city's East Mole at 9am on 5 July, and during the four-day weekend break the St George's Club opened its doors to the ship's company who enthusiastically responded by drinking the club out of beer. There was the traditional children's party and, on the official side, FOAC received the Archbishop of Jerusalem on board. The ship's official cocktail party was held on the first night, and after an impressive Beating Retreat by the Royal Marines Band a large number of the hosts and their guests ventured ashore to sample the renowned nightlife. However, according to one officer it was really, 'only for the very rich as the cost of food and entertainment was high and beyond the pockets of most of the ship's company,' and with no public transport every move had to be made by taxi, which was both expensive and terrifying. Beirut itself, however, was a remarkable city in those days, with its mixture of cultures - Arab, Armenian, Turkish and French. Traditional open-fronted shops stood side by side with modern blocks of offices and flats, and the markets were full of exotic, top-quality fruits, all grown in the fertile plains of Lebanon. Many members of the ship's company visited Baalbeck, about 70 miles inland, the site of some very well-preserved Roman temples, and a more venturesome party flew to Jerusalem. All too quickly, however, during the early evening of 9 July, some 12 hours later than the scheduled sailing time, *Hermes* left Beirut and steamed west for an area off Cyprus where, in preparation for the Operational Readiness Inspection, flying operations began in earnest.

During this period the MO and sickbay staff carried out their second emergency appendectomy, and the squadrons

With a Whirlwind helicopter flying overhead, *Hermes* enters Malta's Grand Harbour on 7 September 1962.

(*Michael Cassar*)

flew the aircraft day and night. Off Cyprus there was an exercise code-named 'Barbican II', when the squadrons supported an Army operation ashore, and Army Austers carried out deck landings on *Hermes*. These small piston-engined aircraft had a deck landing technique of their own, with what appeared to be almost a sideways approach and an alarming 'overshoot' as they came to a stop forward of the bridge. The carrier then moved west again to an area off Crete where Lieutenant Tristram of 803 (Scimitar) Squadron was returning to the ship from an 'air strike' over the island, when a bird hit the front of his canopy with a terrific bang, which shattered the windscreen and left him flying blind. After reporting his predicament he was literally talked back to the ship, and still not able to see much beyond the port side flight deck line, he was talked down to carry out a safe landing. In the event he was awarded a Queen's Commendation for valuable services in the air. As for *Hermes*, she continued her passage west carrying out flying operations off Malta and on towards Gibraltar where, in the western Mediterranean, the Operational Readiness Inspection was carried out with *Centaur* providing the opposition, and flying continued despite one unserviceable catapult. On Thursday 26 July the inspection was completed successfully, and next day *Hermes* secured alongside Gibraltar's South Mole. During this period Admiral Hopkins transferred his flag to *Centaur* and the ship's sports teams beat the *Centaur's* at cricket, hockey, swimming and water polo, although the latter had the edge at soccer.

On board *Hermes* there was the noise and discomfort of the maintenance, while ashore in the bars of Gibraltar the atmosphere was enlivened by the raucous sounds of the paso doble and the clatter of castanets. The ship was visited by Prince William of Gloucester, but at 8.15am on Thursday 9 August tropical routine temporarily came to an end when, in company with *Centaur* and an imposing number of escorts which included HM Ships *Aisne, Berwick, Brighton, Chichester, Corunna, Crossbow, Falmouth, Llandaff* and *Scarborough*, *Hermes* left Gibraltar to steam into the Atlantic Ocean to meet American and French vessels comprising the Atlantic Strike Force, off the coast of Portugal. The fleet was taking part in the NATO exercise code-named 'Riptide II', which was an air-defence and anti-submarine exercise, with the US Navy contributing their powerful aircraft carriers *Enterprise* and *Forrestal*. During the manoeuvres aircraft from all four carriers cross-operated, with the US Navy's Skyhawks and Skyraiders landing on both *Centaur* and *Hermes*. The exercise ended with the fleet anchoring in the River Tagus for two days where, with the Admirals and senior officers holding their 'wash-ups', the ship's company were able to go ashore to see something of Lisbon. After a fast passage back into the Mediterranean, with only a brief stop in Gibraltar Bay, *Hermes* and *Centaur* took part in anti-submarine exercises

with French units, including the brand new aircraft carrier *Clemenceau*, all the while battling against a full mistral gale. On Thursday 23 August, however, the period of exercising was temporarily halted when, with full ceremony, *Hermes* secured alongside the Muelle de Ribera, Mallorca. Close to the carrier's berth at Porto-Pu there were plenty of fine beaches, and a short taxi ride took liberty men into the city of Palma itself. The atmosphere with all the holidaymakers on the island helped many members of the ship's company feel that they were on the holiday stop of the Mediterranean cruise.

After leaving Palma during the forenoon of Monday 27 August *Hermes* once again set course for Malta where flying exercises with the destroyers *Corunna* and *Scorpion* were carried out in the area south-west of the island. At 9.49pm on Tuesday 4 September, when the ship was in a position Lat 35° - 12'N/Long 14° - 30'E and carrying out night flying exercises, Sea Vixen 213, which was piloted by Lt Edward Mason, with Lt Robin Lunn as the observer, came in to land heavily and struck the after part of the flight deck. Carried on by forward momentum the plane crashed into the sea off the port side. The ship was stopped immediately so that sea boats from the *Hermes* and *Scorpion* could search the area and it was not long before some wreckage, including flying helmets, was recovered, but there was no sign of the two crew members. At 11pm, with the weather deteriorating, the search was called off for the night, but at 5am next morning it was resumed, unfortunately with no success, and at 9.30am *Hermes* got under way and flying operations were resumed. Two days later the carrier secured alongside Grand Harbour's Parlatorio Wharf for a period of maintenance and the opportunity was taken to paint the ship. There was the usual burst of sports ashore, but on a more serious note, during the forenoon of Saturday 8 September, there was a memorial service on the quarterdeck for the air crew members who had been lost four days earlier.

Sailing was delayed somewhat by local industrial disputes which had held up the dockyard work on board, but on Tuesday 18 September *Hermes* left Malta to assist with the Operational Readiness Inspections of the 5th Destroyer Squadron. Once these had been completed, *Hermes* set course for the Aegean Sea with the destroyer *Dunkirk* for 'Exercise Falltrap' with Italian and US naval units. The manoeuvres took place in appalling weather with flying severely curtailed and, to everyone's relief, on 28 September course was set for Gibraltar and home. There was a moment of near disaster when, in the western Mediterranean, with most of the aircraft airborne, the after lift stuck in the lowered position. Fortunately it was righted in time for the planes to land on safely, and on the last day of September the carrier made a brief 24-hour stop in Gibraltar Bay before setting sail for Portsmouth.

On Wednesday 3 October the Scimitars were launched

Hermes steams south through the Suez Canal. *(R. W. Mason)*

The barren rocks of Aden provide a grim backdrop as *Hermes* enters harbour on 8 December 1962.

(R. W. Mason)

to their base at Lossiemouth and the Gannets to RNAS Culdrose. Next day the Sea Vixens flew off to RNAS Yeovilton and *Hermes* anchored at Spithead for Customs clearance. Finally, at just after 10am on 4 October, the carrier weighed anchor to steam up harbour and an hour later she secured alongside Middle Slip Jetty, where everyone settled down to five and a half weeks of maintenance. During the weekend of 10/11 November FOAC hosted a Taranto Night dinner on board, with Admiral of the Fleet Sir Caspar John as the guest of honour. Next day, however, saw everyone back on board and the ship ready to sail, but at the last moment a fault developed in the main engines which resulted in a 24-hour delay and, for the local men, an additional few hours at home. At 12.30pm on Tuesday 13 November 1962, *Hermes* sailed from Middle Slip Jetty to land on the helicopters of 814 Squadron. Once at sea goofing stations were soon full as the ship's company flocked to watch the last historic launch of a Swordfish aircraft from an aircraft carrier. Press and television representatives were there to film and report on the event, which went off without a hitch, as did the recovery of the squadrons which was seen on national television that evening. *Hermes* then moved round to the Irish Sea to operate off Brawdy, where the planes carried out weapons practice and shot down targets faster than they could be replaced. With gales and snowstorms disrupting flying operations, the ship moved into the lee of Ireland's south coast where a modified flying programme could be continued. Unfortunately, however, when flying guests from the ship to RNAS Brawdy, the SAR helicopter ditched into the sea with the loss of two lives, Lord Windlesham and an RAF officer. Another passenger and the helicopter's crew were rescued safely by the combined efforts of *Hermes'* own helicopters and those from Brawdy.

By 22 November the carrier had set course south for Gibraltar and after a day's flying in the warmer weather of the western Mediterranean, *Hermes* put into Gibraltar for a 48-hour visit which provided a well-earned break for the ship's company. After leaving harbour on 27 November the passage east was enlivened by 'Exercise Poker Hand' with units of the US Navy's 6th Fleet, and there was a short stop off Malta while a disabled Wessex helicopter which had been left in North Africa by *Albion* on her way to the Far East was collected, after which a fast passage was made to Port Said. This did not prevent FOAC's Divisions which took place in brilliant sunshine on Sunday 2 December, the day before *Hermes* anchored off Port Said. The carrier's southbound transit of the Suez Canal started during the early afternoon of 4 December and at 11.15 that evening she anchored in Suez Bay where, at just before midnight, FOAC transferred his flag to *Ark Royal* which was awaiting a northbound convoy on her passage home. In the early hours of 5 December *Hermes* set course for Aden where she

arrived on 8 December after a very fast passage south, to carry out a day's flying exercises. There was a setback for the SAR helicopter when it ditched close to the ship but the crew were rescued by the sea boat. Later that afternoon *Hermes* entered harbour for a two-day visit, during which there was more drama when a fire broke out in a nearby grain ship, MV *Cornish City*. The smoke could be seen for miles and the blaze had already gained a good hold when a fire-fighting party led by *Hermes'* commander went to tackle the fire, which they eventually succeeded in extinguishing.

A fast passage across the Indian Ocean was broken briefly on Saturday 15 December when, off Ceylon's (Sri Lanka) Dondra Head, a memorial service was held for those who had lost their lives when the ninth *Hermes* was sunk in April 1942, and the ashes of one of her survivors were, in accordance with his wishes, scattered on the sea over the spot where so many of his shipmates had perished. After leaving the scene *Hermes* set course for the Strait of Malacca where, on 18 December, the almost daily routine of advancing the clocks and the dog watch recreation was broken when, for two days, the squadrons carried out day and night flying exercises in conjunction with RAAF Butterworth on the Malayan mainland, and as the carrier moved down the Strait of Malacca towards Singapore the fixed-wing aircraft flew off to RAF Seletar and Tengah. Once the aircraft had gone pre-wetting trials were carried out, and at just after 8am on Friday 21 December, in a torrential tropical downpour, *Hermes* secured alongside No 8 berth at Singapore Naval Base.

The carrier's arrival at Singapore coincided with the outbreak of a rebellion in the oil-rich British Dependency of Brunei, and although the initial naval commitment was provided by the cruiser *Tiger* and the commando carrier *Albion*, hanging over the political scene was the spectre of a hostile Indonesia led by President Sukarno who was deeply suspicious of the proposed Federation of Malaysia. For *Hermes'* ship's company, however, after spending 38 of the previous 42 days at sea, the maintenance break at Singapore provided very welcome relaxation, and even the torrential rain of the north-east monsoon could not spoil the enjoyment of the swimming pool at HMS *Terror*, or the banyans on the beaches at Changi. Christmas at Singapore was celebrated quietly, with a carol service in the hangar which was attended by a large congregation, and a party for 80 orphan children from a Salvation Army Home at New Year. On Sunday 6 January 1963 the squadron ground crews rejoined the ship and next morning, in company with *Barrosa* and *Brighton*, *Hermes* sailed to land on all the aircraft. The next few days of flying were carried out in the Singapore area and mainly consisted of practice in close air support, with Army units ashore directing the aircraft. It was not long, however, before the carrier and her escorts set course for Subic Bay where they were joined by *Tiger*, from

Hermes moored at Aden with a US Navy destroyer.

(*R. W. Mason*)

which the Flag Officer, Second in Command, Far East Station (FO2 FES), Rear-Admiral Scratchard, was transferred to *Hermes*. Exercises with US Navy units, including the aircraft carrier *Ranger*, were soon under way and the squadrons were kept busy with weaponry and interception exercises as well as cross-operating with *Ranger*. There were liaison visits both ways for the aviators, and in the case of *Hermes* these included two US Navy Admirals who arrived in colourful helicopters to be entertained by FO2. Each night for the anti-submarine phase of the exercises the ship was darkened and the Wessex helicopters of 814 Squadron came into their own. On the first evening, however, one of them lost power and ditched, but fortunately the crew were rescued safely. With the ship closed up at Action Stations the ship's company were given a taste of the heat in which they would have to work in wartime conditions but, to everyone's relief, on Saturday 19 January *Hermes* secured alongside the Naval Stores Jetty at Subic Bay Naval Base where the generous hospitality of the Americans, or the dubious 'delights' of Olongapo could be enjoyed.

The stay in Subic Bay was, in fact, scheduled for the senior officers to discuss the exercise, and on Monday 21 January *Hermes* was at sea again and steaming north for Hong Kong. During the passage further exercises were carried out with the escorts, including the ill-fated HMAS *Voyager*, then on the morning of Thursday 24 January *Hermes* secured alongside the North Arm Jetty of Hong Kong Dockyard. Although this initial visit lasted for only four days it coincided with the Chinese New Year, which made for a lively run ashore in Wanchai. On 28 January, after embarking the Duke of Kent, *Hermes* left Hong Kong with the frigate *Rothesay* and other escorts to take part in 'Exercise Tussock', which involved the aircraft providing support for the Army units in the New Territories. On the last day of January, however, *Hermes* returned to North Arm Jetty for a 14-day self-maintenance period and the cooler weather saw the ship's company back in blue uniforms. On Thursday 7 February, the Duke and Duchess of Kent spent the afternoon aboard the carrier as guests of Admiral Scratchard, while the ship's company headed for the attractions of Wanchai and some well-supported and interesting bus tours of the island and the New Territories. Each afternoon the forecastle was transformed into a huge bazaar as local traders plied their wares, which ranged from miniature pagodas to made-to-measure suits which could be ready to wear in just a few hours. The staff of the ever-popular China Fleet Club were kept busy and on board the ship what seemed to be endless parties of schoolchildren enjoyed clambering up and down ladders.

The popular sojourn in Hong Kong finally came to an end during the afternoon of Thursday 14 February, when *Hermes* left Hong Kong to set course across the South China Sea to Singapore. During the passage a full-power

trial was carried out and as the stretch of white water alongside got wider and wider and the foam and spray astern crept higher, the ship really did seem to be racing across the ocean. Off Borneo the flying was resumed, with the Scimitars and Vixens making a 'show of strength' fly-past over Brunei, although one Vixen with engine problems had to divert to Labuan. The Gannets were called upon to assist in a night search for a rating who was missing from a patrol boat off Labuan, and in difficult conditions they dropped flares over the area. Happily, after 14 hours in the water, the man was rescued by a shore-based helicopter. On Friday 22 February, *Hermes* secured alongside at Singapore Naval Base for a five-day break.

Whilst alongside at Singapore the C-in-C Far East Station, Admiral Sir David Luce, inspected the ship and, as they were not taking part in the next exercise, 814 Squadron were flown ashore to Sembawang. With the break over, on Wednesday 27 February *Hermes* sailed for a Commonwealth exercise, 'Jet 63', in the Andaman Sea, which also included HM Ships *Barrosa*, *Blackpool*, *Brighton* and *Lincoln*, as well as HMAS *Voyager* and INS *Kuthar*. Although the exercise lasted for 18 days it included two weekend breaks at anchor off Langkowi, with the usual banyans, expeditions and sailing regattas. On Monday 11 March, when the fleet sailed for the final phase of the exercise, they moved away from the Langkowi area to operate close to the Nicobar Islands, where rockets and bombs disturbed the peace of at least one small island. On the conclusion of the exercise on Sunday 17 March, the aircraft were flown ashore, with the Scimitars going to RAAF Butterworth near Penang Island, and the Vixens and Gannets going to RAF Tengah and Seletar respectively. Before they landed, however, the fixed-wing aircraft joined with the RAF for a grand fly-past over Singapore Island. Next day *Hermes* secured alongside Singapore Dockyard to prepare for a five-week period of maintenance which would include dry docking.

On Tuesday 19 March Admiral Scratchard struck his flag and on the following day the carrier was shifted into the King George VI Dry Dock, with the ship's company moving into the spacious shore accommodation of HMS *Terror*. Once the ship was high and dry the interior became a cacophony of noise from windy hammers and other tools as dockyard workmen swarmed into every available nook and cranny to overhaul the ship's machinery. One of the propellers, which had a section missing, was replaced with a three-bladed type instead of the usual four, but Commander (E) was assured that it would make no difference. The ship's underwater hull and the sides were painted, as was the flight deck, and in the early hours of Friday 29 March there was an unfortunate incident when the body of an Indian workman was found in the dry dock. The unfortunate individual had clearly fallen from the ship, but a Police inquiry could shed no light on what had

Four Scimitars of 802 Squadron fly past. *Hermes* is flying the flag of the Flag Officer Aircraft Carriers. *(R. W. Mason)*

happened and it was presumed to be an accident. For the ship's company the days ashore in the ready-made comforts of the barracks provided plenty of opportunity for shopping in Singapore City, or swimming and sunbathing. A swimming gala and an athletics competition were held and the cyclists, canoeists and sailing enthusiasts were very active. On the morning of Thursday 11 April, however, this idyllic lifestyle came to an end when the ship's company re-embarked in *Hermes* and on 21 April the ship was moved back alongside No 8 berth. During the following three days stores were embarked, together with a Scimitar, which made its approach in a lighter and landed on the flight deck courtesy of a floating crane.

At 7.43am on Wednesday 24 April *Hermes* slipped her moorings and once more moved down the Johore Strait, past the fishing fences of the outer harbour and out into the open sea. That afternoon the Vixens, Scimitars and

Gannets were landed on and, after setting course for the Tioman exercise areas off the east coast of Malaya, the ship's company settled down to the post-refit work-up and flying programmes. Off Tioman the carrier rendezvoused with the cruiser *Lion*, the destroyers *Caesar* and HMAS *Voyager,* and the aircraft carrier HMAS *Melbourne* which, for the duration of the exercises, had 814 Squadron embarked. As the group steamed south to Subic Bay they met the US Navy's aircraft carrier *Yorktown* and her escorts and the submarine HMS *Andrew*. Code-named 'Sea Serpent', the exercises involved convoy escort duties and anti-submarine manoeuvres. During the exercise the MO and his staff performed their third emergency removal of an appendix and on the morning of 8 May, with the exercise concluded, the fleet of 57 SEATO ships anchored in Manila Bay. Although the shore appeared to be a long distance from the ship, once leave was piped some of the

The Wessex helicopters of 814 Squadron ranged on the flight deck during exercises in the South China Sea. *(R. W. Mason)*

more determined men managed to get ashore during the two days at anchor.

As *Hermes* left the Philippines on 10 May the helicopters of 814 Squadron rejoined the ship and there was a short exercise which enabled the flight deck personnel to relearn how to operate fixed-wing aircraft and helicopters at the same time. During the passage to Hong Kong the new FOAC, Rear-Admiral D. C. E. F. Gibson, joined the ship for a brief visit. When he addressed the ship's company he told them that they had, in the space of 12 months, flown more sorties than had been launched during the whole of the previous commission. At 1.30pm on Wednesday 15 May, the carrier entered Hong Kong Harbour for the second time in the commission to secure alongside the dockyard's North Arm, and everyone prepared to enjoy a well-earned break. This second visit to Hong Kong proved to be very different from the first, the main reason being that *Hermes* had arrived during a

heatwave, with the temperatures on several successive days being the highest ever recorded, coupled with a serious shortage of water in the colony. With water rationing having been introduced on board, the engine room department ran the ship's evaporators flat out and so were able to make a token contribution to Hong Kong's water supplies. Many friendships were renewed and several members of the ship's company were able to return the hospitality of their hosts by inviting them on board, so that on most afternoons guests were to be seen tramping the length of the flight deck. The hot weather made the visit ideal for banyans and for swimming at Repulse Bay, and every day the gangway was besieged by local traders bringing on board dinner services, camphorwood chests and other bulky purchases which had been made ashore. On Monday 27 May the visit came to an end and *Hermes* sailed for Okinawa where, with *Lion, Lincoln* and *Voyager,* she was to take part in exercises with the US Navy. This

A Scimitar of 803
Squadron about
to be launched.
*(Lt-Cdr
Larcombe)*

was to be followed by the highlight of the commission, a visit to the Japanese capital city of Tokyo.

Sadly, at just after midnight on the morning of Saturday 1 June, when the ship was about 80 miles south-west of Okinawa, while on a night sortie one of the Sea Vixens crashed into the sea. Although *Hermes* steamed to the scene at full speed and made a thorough search of the area with the assistance of her escorts and American aircraft from Okinawa, there was no sign of the two crew members, Lts John Byno and Paul Austin, who were posted as 'missing presumed dead'. At sunrise the search was resumed, but apart from a few fragments of wreckage, nothing was found and the exercises were resumed.

During operations off Okinawa a close watch had been kept on the development of typhoon 'Polly' which had been moving towards Japan, and which appeared to have every chance of arriving at Tokyo at the same time as *Hermes*. Captain O'Brien, therefore, decided to steer for the southern tip of Japan to give 'Polly' a chance to show her worst, and the carrier to escape her wrath if she approached too close. Writer Bob Mason remembers that on the days that were spent running away from the typhoon, 'The sky was as black as night and the rain lashed down continuously.' Having rendezvoused with the group's RFAs off Kyushu, *Hermes* steamed slowly north-east with *Voyager*. The swell caused by 'Polly' made the ensuing RAS and an attempted tow by *Voyager* rather more spectacular than the ship's company were used to, but that evening

there was something even more dramatic when Captain O'Brien announced over the ship's broadcast that severe corrosion had been discovered in some steam pipes of the catapult, which meant that fixed-wing aircraft could no longer be launched. In turn this meant that the ship had to return to Singapore for dockyard assistance with repairs and, therefore, the visit to Tokyo was cancelled. It seems that whilst carrying out routine maintenance on a steam pipe someone had dropped a heavy object onto the pipe and thus the corrosion had been discovered. At the time the news came as a bombshell to the ship's company, and the closest the carrier came to Japan was on the morning of Wednesday 5 June when, at 5.15am, she anchored off Osaka to wait for the cruiser *Lion* which had just completed a five-day visit to the port. It was a dull, grey morning and with clouds covering the hills, a mist over the city and with the cool air providing a change from the continual tropical heat and humidity, it was a disappointed ship's company who gazed landward that day. At 8.55am, just over three hours after her arrival and with FO2 FES having transferred his flag to *Lion*, *Hermes* set course for Singapore.

With the weather in the South China Sea looking uncertain and with a depression appearing as though it could easily turn into another typhoon, Captain O'Brien decided to take 'the pretty way', to the east of the Philippines, then through the islands and across the Sulu Sea. The passage was marred, however, by the sudden death

Hermes exercises with the cruiser *Lion* in the South China Sea.

(Lt-Cdr Larcombe)

of CPO Gordon Bartlett who died on 9 June whilst playing volleyball. That evening a simple, but impressive, burial ceremony was held on the quarterdeck. As the *Hermes* steamed south the weather grew warmer and a 'potted' sports competition was organized on the flight deck. Down below all was not well, for a small leak in the starboard stern gland had suddenly become a large leak and on 14 June, two days after her arrival in Singapore, the ship's company moved into shore accommodation while *Hermes* moved into dry dock once again. This time the docking period lasted ten days, and both the stern gland and the catapults were repaired, with the opportunity being taken to replace the original four-bladed propeller, which reduced the vibration at high speeds, and the underwater hull was repainted once again. On Monday 24 June the ship's company moved back on board and *Hermes* was moved out of dry dock as preparations were made to sail four days later. On 27 June the C-in-C FES, Vice-Admiral Sir Desmond Dreyer, addressed the ship's company and thanked them for their efforts during the six months they had been on the Far East Station. Finally, on the morning of Friday 28 June, *Hermes* left Singapore to land on the

squadrons in readiness for six days of flying operations in the Langkowi area. It was whilst the Sea Vixens were landing on that one of them 'bolted' and dived out of control into the sea, giving its crew little hope of escape. Despite a thorough search of the area there was no sign of them and only small pieces of wreckage were recovered, with Lts David Phipps and Michael Cooper being posted as 'missing believed dead'. Once flying resumed and all the aircraft had landed on, *Hermes* began her longest RAS of the commission when, for five hours, load after load of stores and provisions was transferred, ferried to the lifts and struck down into the bowels of the ship where the stores parties sweated, stacked and stowed.

The next week was busy with day and night flying operations as everyone quickly got back into sea routine once again, but at 7.17pm on Wednesday 3 July there was another fatal accident, this time on the flight deck. Whilst a Gannet was under tow an aircraft handler, NA Leslie Scott, lost his footing and fell under the wheels of the aircraft which ran over him and killed him instantly. Next day, as the ship anchored close to Singapore City to disembark those who were flying back to the UK, the body of the unfortunate rating was flown ashore to RNAS Sembawang. Following this *Hermes* returned to Langkowi Island where, on 7 July, she was due to meet *Ark Royal* which was taking over as the operational aircraft carrier east of Suez. After anchoring at 9.40am recreational leave was granted and next day, Monday 8 July, *Hermes*, *Ark Royal*, *Vampire*, *Voyager*, *Caesar* and *Duncan* sailed into the Andaman Sea to take part in 'Exercise Birdbarge', a rehearsal for the forthcoming 'Fotex 63'. On 10 July, when the manoeuvres were completed, *Hermes* and *Caesar* left the Far East Station and set course for the island of Gan and East Africa. During the passage exercise flying was continued, but on Sunday 14 July, with the ship in a position Lat 00° - 24'S/Long 74° - 65'E, the Crossing the Line ceremony was held on the flight deck, with the added bonus of a mail collection that evening as the ship passed Gan. The next few days saw more flying, but each evening during the dog watches there was a welcome break in the flying programme which enabled everyone to enjoy the sun and take some exercise on the flight deck as the ship steamed steadily westwards.

With the last evening of flying cancelled following a day of storms, at 10.30am on Saturday 20 July *Hermes* wound her way through the narrow entrance channel to her mooring in Kilindini Harbour. It was not long before the various leave parties and expeditions, including one led by the First Lieutenant to Kilimanjaro, left the ship for the mountain and the various game reserves. For some the welcome station leave meant relaxation in nearby hotels or rest houses along the coast, and there were day trips to the nearby Tsavo National Park. Back on board there were daily visits by groups of schoolchildren, and the usual busy sports programmes ashore. The final days of the visit saw the ship filling up with wood carvings, bongo drums and other local souvenirs, and it was a refreshed and rejuvenated ship's company that left Mombasa on 30 July and, with *Caesar*, set course for Aden. As the ship moved north the fresh monsoon winds kept the ship cool, but once into the Gulf of Aden the breezes vanished and the temperature rose so quickly that it was almost like stepping into an oven. Friday 2 August saw the recommencement of flying and two days later the ship anchored in Aden's outer harbour for 24 hours which, it was thought, was the final run ashore before returning to Portsmouth and shore leave

Time off in the Indian Ocean during the passage between Singapore and Gan for the 'Crossing the Line' ceremony.

(Lt-Cdr Larcombe)

was granted to allow for some last-minute shopping. At 8am on Tuesday 6 August *Hermes* weighed anchor and set course for Suez, and home – the end of the foreign leg of the commission was drawing near.

During the evening of Friday 9 August, when the ship was only 24 hours out from Suez Bay and after the hottest part of the Red Sea had been passed, there came the second 'bombshell' of the commission, when Captain O'Brien received a signal ordering him to return to Aden until the ship was relieved by *Victorious*. Suddenly, instead of heading home, *Hermes* was steaming south once more towards the Gulf of Aden. With Indonesian guerrilla incursions into Borneo becoming more frequent and serious, and heralding the start of 'Confrontation', which could easily escalate into a full-scale war, it had been decided to station two aircraft carriers, *Victorious* and *Ark Royal*, east of Suez. By 11 August the *Hermes* was off Aden where flying operations were resumed and, needless to say, rumours about the ship's movements were rife. During the afternoon of Monday 12 August a Wessex helicopter which had taken over the SAR role ditched into the sea alongside the port beam. Not only was the sea boat launched extremely quickly, but the usual SAR Whirlwind, which was in the hangar, was spread and scrambled, from hangar to airborne, in the record time of four minutes and 15 seconds. It was on the scene in time to rescue one of the crew, with the other three being picked up by the sea boat. After five days of flying *Hermes* moved into Aden Harbour, where 814 Squadron left for RAF Khormaksar to await the arrival of *Victorious* and a return to the Far East. Finally, at 9am on Sunday 18 August, came the moment for which everyone had waited, when *Hermes* left Aden and steamed north for Suez.

Entering the Gulf of Suez during the afternoon of Wednesday 21 August the air temperature became noticeably cooler, and as *Hermes* anchored there was great excitement on board as *Victorious* could be seen slowly completing her southbound transit of the Suez Canal. Captain O'Brien transmitted the signal, 'Send us *Victorious!*' to his opposite number, but it still seemed an age before, to the cheers of *Hermes*' ship's company, she anchored abeam. Next morning *Hermes* weighed anchor to begin her northbound transit of the canal, which was broken by a lunchtime 'Hands to Bathe' in the Bitter Lakes. During the afternoon there was the magic of the Gulley-Gulley Man to keep everyone amused, and by the evening the lights of Port Said were rapidly disappearing astern as the carrier made a fast passage through the Mediterranean. There was a brief pause off Malta to embark the Wessex helicopters of 819 Squadron to replace those of 814 Squadron, before the ship was under way and pounding westwards once again. Five days after leaving Port Said *Hermes* was off Cape Finisterre and at 8am on Thursday 29 August she anchored at Spithead. Just over

five hours later, at 1.20pm, she weighed anchor and in bright summer sunshine she steamed past the Isle of Wight ferry and the crowds of waving holidaymakers on Southsea seafront to secure alongside Middle Slip Jetty where, thanks to the goodwill of the Customs officers, many members of the ship's company were immediately reunited with their families.

Although it was the end of the foreign leg, it was by no means the end of the commission for *Hermes* and after only five days alongside she sailed from Portsmouth on 5 September to embark the squadrons and to practise for a major Home Fleet exercise which was to take place in the Channel. On Saturday 7 September during flying practice in Lyme Bay, there was an unfortunate accident when the Mirror Control Officer was blown over the side by a jet blast from a taxiing Vixen, but happily he survived the ordeal and, to his annoyance, whilst in the water he heard a voice on his radio saying, 'He must be all right, he's swimming.' Happily he was quickly rescued by the SAR helicopter. The exercise on Wednesday 11 September, code-named 'Unison', involved convoy protection duties, and *Hermes* flew the flag of the Chief of Defence Staff, Admiral of the Fleet Lord Mountbatten, who arrived in an RAF Belvedere. In addition there were also 120 other senior officers embarked for the exercise, but after donning foul weather gear most of them became anonymous. The exercise ended off Portland with a steam past of the participating ships and Lord Mountbatten taking the salute as *Tiger, Cavendish, Rothesay, Llandaff, Gurkha, Berwick, Decoy, Leander, Brave Borderer* and *Brave Swordsman* steamed by in line ahead. Next day, after flying off the squadrons, *Hermes* entered harbour with full ceremony to secure against North Corner Jetty.

Hermes had been scheduled to remain alongside in Portsmouth for 14 days, but with strong winds blowing, her departure was delayed by 24 hours, and she finally sailed on the morning of Friday 27 September. After embarking the squadrons she set course for the Mediterranean and the North African coast, together with *Lowestoft, Murray, Rhyl* and *Undaunted,* for exercises with USS *Independence*. She saw little of the giant American carrier, however, but visits were exchanged by the respective aircraft. On the morning of 8 October there was an expensive accident when a Scimitar of 803 Squadron reared up over its chocks, careered across the flight deck and ran into one of 892's Vixens, resulting in what was described at the time as a 'double knockout'. Fortunately nobody was injured, although the ship had to be given a two degree list to port in order to separate the combatants. Flying was continuous for ten days, but finally on the morning of Saturday 12 October the nine Sea Vixens were launched to Yeovilton and next day, after FOAC's Divisions, *Hermes* secured alongside the Muelle Pontiente at Barcelona for a well-earned break. Here coach tours were laid on for the ship's company, there was a party for local children, and the ship was opened to visitors. The Royal Marines Band was enthusiastically received ashore and a group of Flamenco dancers were just as warmly received on board.

The carrier left Barcelona on Friday 18 October and anchored at Spithead four days later, berthing alongside North Corner Jetty during the afternoon of Wednesday 23 October. This time, with essential maintenance to be carried out, *Hermes* remained at Portsmouth for over five weeks, but on the morning of Saturday 30 November she was at sea once again to land on the squadrons and to set course north through the Irish Sea for 'Exercise Limejug' in the Atlantic Ocean. With the frigate *Brighton* acting as planeguard, other units taking part were the destroyers *Cavendish* and *Decoy* and the frigates *Falmouth, Leander* and *Whitby*, but on the morning of Saturday 14 December the carrier returned to Portsmouth. At last the ship's company could relax and enjoy the Christmas and New Year festivities.

As *Hermes* lay at North Corner Jetty prior to leaving Portsmouth for the final exercise of the commission, a serious fire was discovered in 5G diesel generator room at 12.30am on the night of 16 January 1964. Fire and Emergency parties were quickly on the scene, 5F and 5G mess decks were evacuated and arrangements were made to remove all stock from the bookstall directly above the affected compartment. By 1am the City Fire Brigade was on the scene and half an hour later the fire was extinguished. Although two diesel generators were put out of action and it was suspected, '...to have been possibly caused by a deliberate act', it did not stop *Hermes* from embarking the FOAC designate, Rear-Admiral H. R. B. Janvrin, and sailing at 1pm the same day to take on borrowed aircraft off Portland. During the flying practice that followed there were runs ashore at Torquay and Weymouth, before the carrier moved into the Western

Approaches for 'Exercise Phoenix'. On the last day of January *Hermes* anchored at Spithead to prepare for her final duties and runs ashore of the commission.

After leaving the Solent on 2 February and steaming to Lyme Bay, with HMS *Dido* acting as planeguard, she carried out four days of deck landing trials with the Mk 1 Blackburn Buccaneer. These concluded on 8 February and in the following week there were further deck landing trials, this time with a Mk 2 Sea Vixen, but on Saturday 15 February she left Start Bay and set course for Copenhagen, the final 'foreign' run ashore. The four days in the Danish capital city were enjoyed by everyone, despite the fact that the harbour was almost ice-bound, and when *Hermes* left on Saturday 22 February she made a fast passage to Devonport, arriving off Plymouth Sound during the afternoon of Monday 24 February. Writer Bob Mason remembers the entrance into harbour with full ceremony: 'Some bright spark had decided it would be a good idea to tie balloons to the paying-off pennant so that it would stream from the masthead on the island, right over the flight deck and the stern. It looked really good until a strong gust of wind caught it and snapped the pennant off close to the mast, and I have an overriding memory of the paying-off pennant disappearing astern on the wind to the accompaniment of a huge impromptu cheer from the ship's company who were manning the flight deck.' *Hermes* secured alongside No 7 wharf at 3.50pm and the commission formally came to an end on Wednesday 4 March 1964 when, at midday, the C-in-C Plymouth, Vice-Admiral Sir Nigel Henderson, inspected Divisions in the hangar. At 2.45pm that afternoon Captain O'Brien left the ship and next day *Hermes* was towed into No 5 basin where destoring began. It was the end of a busy and successful commission and the start of a long refit that would keep the carrier in dockyard hands for two years.

Chapter Eight

The Third Commission
February 1966 - February 1968

Hermes' first major refit cost £10 million, and the work carried out included the strengthening of the flight deck, improving the arrester gear and extending the port catapult so that she could operate the Mark II versions of the Blackburn Buccaneer and Sea Vixen. The alterations were such that further work to allow operation of the McDonnell Douglas Phantom II aircraft, which were being purchased from the USA, would not be too difficult or costly. As it was planned that Hermes would be operating fixed-wing aircraft through to the mid-1970s, it was decided she would be fully fitted for Phantoms in 1968. In the event, however, political considerations superseded these plans. In addition to the work on the flight deck all the anti-aircraft guns were removed and replaced with Seacat surface-to-air missiles, which made Hermes the Royal Navy's first 'all-missile' ship. A new Flyco compartment was built in the island superstructure and full air-conditioning was fitted throughout the ship.

It was early 1966 before Hermes was prepared for sea, and on Tuesday 1 February the carrier's new commanding officer, Captain T. T. Lewin MVO DSC RN*, was appointed to the ship and, with everyone still living in the RN barracks, he made his first visits to the carrier two days later. Captain Lewin had joined the Navy as a Specialist Entry Cadet in January 1939. He specialized in gunnery and during the Second World War he served in the battleship Valiant and the destroyer Ashanti. It was whilst serving in the latter on Mediterranean convoys that he was awarded the DSC and three times Mentioned in Dispatches. He took part in 'Operation Pedestal', the battle to supply Malta in August 1942, Russian convoys and 'Operation Torch', the invasion of North Africa. In 1955 he commanded the destroyer Corunna, and in 1957 he was appointed as the Executive Officer to the royal yacht Britannia. This was followed by command of the frigates Urchin and Tenby, and a spell as Captain (F) Dartmouth Training Squadron. In 1964 he was appointed Director, Naval Tactical Weapons Policy Division at the Ministry of Defence, and it is from here that he was appointed to command Hermes.

As for Hermes herself, on Friday 11 February 1966 she made her first foray to sea for two years when she carried out her dockyard trials. With the main propulsion

machinery manned by dockyard personnel, but commanded by Captain Lewin, she left Devonport's No 5 wharf at 9.26am and by just after 10am she had passed the breakwater. A few minutes later a helicopter was launched from the flight deck as Hermes set course west towards the Channel Islands and a full-power trial. Her initial trials lasted for just three days and by 12.30pm on Monday 14 February the carrier was back alongside at Devonport, where deadload trials were carried out. By now the ship's company, while still living ashore in the Royal Naval barracks, was being brought up to strength and by the end of April they had moved onto the ship, which was once again lying alongside No 5 wharf.

The recommissioning ceremony took place during the forenoon of Saturday 14 May 1966, and the guests began to arrive at 10.45am with the guests of honour being the C-in-C Plymouth and the FOAC, who was in fact Rear-Admiral O'Brien, the carrier's previous commanding officer. After Captain Lewin had read the commissioning warrant there was a short religious service followed by the cutting of the cake and a buffet lunch for guests of the ship's company. Next day the ship's chaplain officiated at the baptism of five children of ship's company members on the quarterdeck, but at 3.10pm on Monday 16 May Special Sea Dutymen closed up at their stations and 20 minutes later the mooring ropes were slipped and Hermes sailed for her post-refit trials. After spending the night in Plymouth Sound she commenced the first of many full-power trials over the measured mile west of Plymouth. On 18 May, with the ship off the Lizard, the first helicopters of the commission landed on the flight deck, and over the next week more full-power trials were carried out in the Channel. During the afternoon of 24 May, when steaming at full power, a speed of 26 knots was achieved, and during the afternoon of the next day Hermes secured to C buoy in Plymouth Sound before moving up harbour on 26 May to go alongside at Devonport. During the five weeks alongside, the chaplain exceeded his previous record and on 19 June, in a 20-minute service held on the quarterdeck, he baptized eight children.

On Thursday 23 June, when Hermes sailed from Devonport again, she steamed north up the Irish Sea to the Firth of Clyde where she carried out further speed trials over the Skelmorlie measured mile. There was a brief respite on 25 June when the carrier anchored in Arran's Brodick Bay where recreational leave was granted to

*Later Admiral of the Fleet Lord Lewin KG GCB MVO DSC, C-in-C Fleet 1973-75; C-in-C Naval Home Command 1975-77; First Sea Lord 1977-79.

organized expedition parties. Next day, after Ceremonial Divisions and a march past on the flight deck, the *Hermes* sailed to begin her flying trials. These got under way on 27 June when, at 3.40pm, a Gannet made a number of touch and go runs and these were followed three-quarters of an hour later by a number of touch and go circuits performed by one of the few Fleet Air Arm Hawker Hunter jet trainers. That same day *Hermes* set course south once again, and on the last day of June she anchored in Weymouth Bay to embark the trials parties. On 3 July the squadron ground crews joined the ship and next day the carrier sailed to start landing on her aircraft. During the commission *Hermes* would carry six Buccaneer Mk II aircraft of 809 Squadron, 11 Sea Vixens of 892 Squadron, Gannet AEW 3 aircraft of 849B Flight and six Wessex helicopters of 814 Squadron. In addition she would also carry two Whirlwind SAR helicopters and a COD Gannet for air freight and passenger duties. By the evening of 5 July all the aircraft

were safely on board and, with the ship steaming between Lyme Bay and the Bristol Channel, six days of flying trials were carried out. On Wednesday 13 July, however, with the ship moored in Plymouth Sound, an MFV bearing relatives of the ship's company arrived alongside and the first Families Day was held, with a flying display off Eddystone following which *Hermes* returned to Devonport Dockyard.

After a fortnight alongside *Hermes* left Devonport to steam up Channel bound for her home port of Portsmouth, where she spent four weeks alongside Middle Slip Jetty and the ship's company were able to take their seasonal leave. On Thursday 25 August, however, *Hermes* was at sea again with flying trials having been resumed, and, in company with HMS *Lynx*, was on her way south to Gibraltar. Flying was suspended during the crossing of the Bay of Biscay, but it was resumed off Gibraltar and on 30 August the carrier went alongside the dockyard's south

Captain Lewin reads the Commissioning Warrant at the ceremony which was held on 14 May 1966.   (*Lt-Cdr Larcombe*)

The first fixed-wing launch of the commission, a Tiger Moth flown by Commander (Air). *(Lt-Cdr Larcombe)*

mole, which provided a change of scenery for her ship's company. The passage home for *Hermes* and *Lynx* began on 2 September, and after carrying out further flying exercises off Portland, at 1.45pm on Friday 9 September the carrier anchored off Spithead for her second Families Day. This time the visitors were treated to a flying display off the Isle of Wight before, at 7.30pm, *Hermes* secured alongside Portsmouth's South Railway Jetty. This time, however, after only five days alongside, *Hermes* sailed by way of the Irish Sea and Pentland Firth for the east coast of Scotland where flying exercises got under way in earnest as the carrier began her work-up. The rigorous routine of day and night flying continued without a break until 5 October when she set course for Hamburg where she secured alongside the Nieder Hafen the following morning. As part of their welcome the staff of the Edelweiss Bar on the Reeperbahn presented the ship's company with 200 beer mugs and a large barrel of beer, and on two days when the ship was opened to the public, some thousands of visitors were entertained on board. The party came to an end, however, on Monday 10 October when, with most wallets on board empty, the carrier returned to the area off the Moray Firth to begin the second phase of her work-up.

For 11 days as *Hermes* steamed off the east coast of Scotland, in company with the frigate *Blackwood* which was on planeguard duty, the Buccaneers, Vixens, Gannets

and Wessex helicopters carried out intensive flying operations while a Soviet Sonya-class minesweeper kept a close eye on proceedings. It became a persistent observer as the Mk II Buccaneers performed their first duties from an operational carrier and at times often ventured dangerously close to *Hermes* whilst flying operations were under way, but fortunately there were no accidents. There was a short break during the evening of 15 October when the carrier anchored in the Moray Firth and leave was granted to men who lived locally, but next morning the flying began again. The work-up ended on Friday 21 October when *Hermes* secured alongside the south arm of Rosyth Dockyard to begin just over two weeks of self maintenance. On Monday 7 November, with the break at an end, *Hermes* left the Firth of Forth to take part in 'Exercise Roedean' with the cruiser *Tiger,* which was on her last commission as a conventional cruiser, the frigates *Berwick, Dido, Naiad, Phoebe, Russell* and *Salisbury,* and the RFAs *Olna* and *Retainer.* Joining the exercise in the Londonderry area were the Canadian destroyers *Assinibone, Margaree, Chaudiere* and *Ottawa.* Being an anti-submarine exercise a number of boats provided the 'opposition', but with severe gales and heavy seas in the Irish Sea and Western Approaches flying was limited and enormous waves smashed the sea boat in its davits. By 16 November, however, *Hermes* had moved into the Channel where further flying was carried out in Lyme Bay with the Buccaneers undertaking more deck landing trials. On the morning of 18 November, with a crack having been discovered in one of the propellers, the squadrons were flown off to their bases and that afternoon *Hermes* moved into C lock in Portsmouth Dockyard where she remained until the New Year of 1967.

It was Monday 2 January when *Hermes* was moved out of dry dock and back alongside Middle Slip Jetty, and a few days later the Mayor and Mayoress of Tiverton in Devon visited the ship, thus beginning a long association between the town and *Hermes*. During the afternoon of Monday 16 January, with Christmas and New Year leave having well and truly ended, the carrier left Portsmouth and set course for Lyme Bay to carry out noise trials with the assistance of Buccaneers and two Hawker Hunter jets which executed touch and go circuits. Both the C-in-C Home Fleet and the C-in-C Portsmouth visited the ship then finally, on Friday 20 January, after embarking the squadrons, *Hermes* left home waters to set course for Gibraltar, the Mediterranean and the Far East.

After arriving off Gibraltar on the morning of Monday 23 January, the Governor of the colony, and the Flag Officer, Gibraltar, were embarked by helicopter to watch the day's flying programme, but sadly this got off to a tragic start. At 9.30am, when *Hermes* was in a position Lat 35° - 50'N/Long 04° - 48'W, about 45 miles south-south-west of Ceuta, Sea Vixen 314 ditched into the sea on take-off. The Wessex SAR helicopter immediately flew to the spot, but

Hermes leaving Kilindini Harbour, Mombasa, on 30 July 1963. She has Scimitars, Sea Vixens and Gannet AEWs on deck.

(Lt-Cdr Larcombe)

In Far Eastern waters during the 1966-68 commission. The aircraft ranged on the flight deck include Gannet AEWs, Wessex HAS1 helicopters, Sea Vixens and Buccaneers.
(Lt-Cdr Larcombe)

Hermes arrived back in Portsmouth Harbour on 9 September 1966, after a 'Families Day' flying display off the Isle of Wight.   *(Michael Lennon)*

At Hamburg on a dull and wet autumn day.   *(Lt-Cdr Larcombe)*

Exercising with the frigate *Arethusa* in the North Sea.

(*Lt-Cdr Larcombe*)

within a minute it too had ditched in almost the same position where the Vixen had hit the water. On board *Hermes* both engines were put full astern and the ship was manoeuvred to pick up survivors. Within seven minutes of the first accident the sea boat had been launched, but in the event the four crew members of the SAR helicopter were rescued by another Wessex helicopter. It was not long before the ship's divers were on the scene and they recovered the body of one of the stricken Vixen's crew members, Lt Betterton. It was 1.50pm before flying was resumed, and at 5.45pm the ship was stopped for the funeral service of Lt Betterton and a memorial service to Lt Smith, who had been lost that morning. The carrier arrived off Malta on Thursday 26 January for two days of flying operations off the island before entering Grand Harbour on the morning of Saturday 28 January. *Hermes* had been due to berth in Bighi Bay at 9am that morning, but her visit coincided with a political dispute between the British and Maltese Governments over the rundown of British forces on the island. The Maltese General Workers' Union also decided to take industrial action and as a result the local crew members of the Admiralty tug *Airedale* refused to handle the carrier when she entered harbour. In the event *Hermes* remained outside the harbour until the tug's crew were replaced by naval personnel, after which *Hermes* was safely secured to her buoy in Grand Harbour at 10am.

Although the visit lasted for just two days, Malta provided a welcome break for the ship's company and the political problems did nothing to mar the good relationship between the naval personnel and the local people. On Monday 30 January, *Hermes* was at sea again and carrying out intensive flying operations south of Malta. At 12.20pm on Friday 3 February, there was a second fatal flying accident when Sea Vixen 306 ditched on take-off. Within minutes both the SAR helicopter and the sea boat were on the scene and the pilot was rescued alive, although both his legs were broken. Unfortunately, the observer, Lt P. Brodie RN, did not survive, although his body was recovered. Later in the day, at 5pm, in a position Lat 35° - 46'N/Long 14° - 17'E, his body was committed to the deep. That night *Hermes* set course for Gibraltar and on 6 February, after launching the aircraft to North Front, she secured alongside the south mole to begin a two-week self-maintenance period. When the *Hermes* returned to sea she set course for Naples where she arrived two days later to secure alongside the Piscane Quay. Although the visit was for only two days, the ship's rugby team triumphed over a local side, Portenope, when, after playing for 50 minutes in both halves, the final score was 21 - 19. The fine weekend also allowed the sailing club to enjoy some sailing in the harbour and many enjoyed free coach trips to Pompeii, courtesy of the Italian Navy.

A Sea Vixen is manoeuvred on to the port catapult. Further aft are more Vixens and Buccaneers. *(Fleet Air Arm Museum)*

When *Hermes* left Naples on the last day of February she set course for the North African coast to carry out Seacat firings and yet more Buccaneer trials off Tobruk. This was a long period at sea, and there were sighs of relief when during the forenoon of 16 March she entered Grand Harbour, this time without any problems. During her stay the ship received visits from the Governor-General, Sir Maurice Dorman, and the island's Prime Minister, Dr George Borg Olivier. When she left Malta *Hermes*, together with the frigates *Lowestoft* and *Rhyl*, took part in NATO's exercise 'Dawn Clear', along with units of the US Navy's 6th Fleet, including the aircraft carrier *Shangri-La*, the cruiser *Galveston* and the destroyers *Blandy* and *Claude V. Ricketts*. Once again the flying was intensive and for most of the time *Hermes* operated with a US destroyer in the Tyrrhenian Sea, then on the conclusion of these manoeuvres she exercised off Malta for two days before setting course for Piraeus, where she anchored on the morning of Wednesday 12 April. The ship's company found the run ashore and the ouzo as good as ever, and many men took the opportunity to visit the Acropolis. The

children's party went without a hitch and on 18 April *Hermes* left Phaleron Bay to steam to Cyprus for further flying, but three days after her departure the political scene in Greece was altered when the Greek Government was overthrown in a *coup d'état* by Army generals. When steaming south from Athens to Cyprus and through the Cyclades, the carrier passed through the submerged volcanic crater of Santorini, where an advertisement was seen at the foot of a cliff beneath the town of Thira which read, '*Hermes* en Grece' whereupon Captain Lewin remarked, 'It was nice to know that our presence had not gone unnoticed!'

Whilst conducting flying operations off Cyprus the 1,000th deck landing was recorded and at just before midnight on 21 April *Hermes* anchored in Akrotiri Bay. Despite the fact that the ship was anchored a good distance from the harbour, shore leave was granted and on the official side there was a reception for the Mayor of Limassol and local guests. For the remainder of the month *Hermes* operated from Akrotiri Bay before leaving the area for Port Said and the Far East. She made her southbound

The ever-watchful Soviet Sonya-class minesweeper keeps a close eye on *Hermes* during exercises in the North Sea in October 1966.　　　　　　　　　　　　　　　　　　　　　　　　　　　　　　　　*(Lt-Cdr Larcombe)*

transit of the Suez Canal on 3 May, a month before the outbreak of the Arab-Israeli Six-Day War which closed the canal for eight years. Once she was clear of the canal *Hermes* steamed south for Aden which, by that time, was racked by a terrorist war as rival organizations battled for power and, at the same time, conducted a bombing campaign against British forces in the colony. The Government had already announced that all British forces would be withdrawn from the military base at Aden and that the colony would become independent by the end of January 1968, which led to an alarming increase in incidents of terrorism. Whereas early acts had mostly consisted of grenade throwing, mortar attacks and the use of small arms were now widespread. With this scenario, in what had never been an attractive run ashore at the best of times, the opportunities for shore leave were further reduced. In addition, *Hermes'* arrival had coincided with the evacuation of all British service families and this, together with the increasing tensions between Israel and her Arab neighbours, meant that the carrier would remain

in the area for longer than had originally been intended. After embarking the FO2 FES, Rear-Admiral E. B. Ashmore, from the homeward-bound *Victorious, Hermes* operated off Aden and Al Mukalla where the aircraft flew close to the Yemen border on missions in support of the Army and the Federal Government of the South Arabian Federation, whose senior officials were also taken to sea and treated to a demonstration of air power. Unfortunately, it would all be in vain for the Federal Government was rapidly losing what little control it had to the terrorist organizations of the NLF (National Liberation Front), and FLOSY (Front for the Liberation of South Yemen), with the former gaining a dominant position from which to assume control after independence.

On 15 May, off Aden, *Hermes* carried out flying operations with the homeward-bound *Victorious,* and it would be the last time the two carriers operated together for *Victorious* was close to the end of her 26-year operational career. Five days later, on Saturday 20 May, with *Victorious* having left for Suez, *Hermes* left Aden for

Hermes operating her aircraft in home waters.

(Lt-Cdr Larcombe)

Gan and the Far East and as King Neptune and his entourage performed at the Crossing the Line ceremony en route, everyone thought that the carrier would soon be in Singapore. However, instead of steaming east the ship was ordered to remain in the vicinity of Gan and here her aircraft exercised between the ship and the RAF airfield on the island. On Saturday 27 May, with diplomatic tensions between Israel and her neighbours rising and with war looking increasingly likely, *Hermes* was ordered to return to Aden and by the last day of May she was at anchor in the colony's outer harbour. With the political deterioration in the Middle East the British forces in Aden were faced with a wave of anti-Jewish violence in the colony and liberty men were restricted to beach leave only with the designated 'Mermaid Beach' being heavily patrolled by armed guards and with transport to the beach being escorted by armoured vehicles. Leave terminated at 6pm each day, and on board the carrier the ship's divers were kept busy making regular inspections of the underwater hull. To pass the time at anchor off the barren rocks a ship's company concert was organized, also flight deck games, a cake-

making competition, a flight deck floodlit Derby, an orchestral concert in the hangar and massed PT on the flight deck. On Saturday 3 June 1967 the Six-Day War broke out, with the swift Israeli victory taking everyone by surprise, and at the time *Hermes* was at sea off Aden with the frigates *Ashanti*, *Brighton* and *Nubian*, but by Saturday 10 June it was apparent that there would be no intervention by the Western Powers and that afternoon, in company with *Brighton*, *Hermes* set course for Gan and the Far East once again.

This time, although *Hermes* remained in the vicinity of Gan Island for four days, on standby to return to the Middle East, she was not in fact required to do so and by 17 June she and *Brighton* were heading for Singapore. On Thursday 22 June, after 66 days without unrestricted leave, the carrier finally arrived in Singapore, where she secured alongside No 8 berth in the naval base. That evening at 11.35pm, there was a report of a man overboard, but after the area had been searched by the ship's boats, no trace could be found of anyone in the water. Two days later, however, the body of Mechanician M. N. Furley was recovered in the harbour and his funeral took place on 29 June. The four and a half weeks' self-maintenance period alongside in Singapore allowed for some relaxation after the weeks spent off Aden, and many members of the ship's company were introduced to the dubious pleasures of Bugis Street. Others visited the famous Haw Par Villa, or the Tiger Balm Gardens as they were popularly known, the BBC recorded an episode of Sunday Half Hour on board the ship and a successful children's party was held. On Wednesday 19 July, the new C-in-C FES, Vice-Admiral W. D. O'Brien, hoisted his flag in *Hermes*, the ship which, only three years previously, he had commanded. Next day, in company with HMS *Minerva,* the carrier left Singapore to land on the squadrons and to take part in 'Exercise Firmstride' which involved flying operations off Singapore, and at Subic Bay with the US Navy. On 28 July, with the exercise having been concluded, *Hermes* set course for Hong Kong where, at 11am on Monday 31 July, she secured to No 1 buoy in the harbour.

As always the bars and clubs of Wanchai and Kowloon were great favourites with the ship's company, but the stay was for only seven days so a large number of activities were packed into a short space of time. For the helicopters of 826 Squadron it was a busy time too as they assisted the civil powers in an anti-terrorist operation. In 1966 President Mao Tse-tung of China had launched his Great Proletarian Cultural Revolution, the ramifications of which were felt the world over, but particularly in Hong Kong. In the city of Victoria young followers of Mao, clutching their copies of the Chairman's great works, besieged Government House chanting anti-British slogans and more of the same came from the Bank of China's loudspeakers. In the words of one local observer the situation was summed up thus: 'The worlds of Somerset Maugham and Mao Tse-tung met face to face in Hong Kong. Both were baffled.' More serious, however, were the bombs and violent rioting which had killed 15 people, including children, and wounded many more, all organized by Communist agents. Thus, at 6.35am on 4 August, Wessex helicopters of 826 Squadron operating from *Hermes* landed a force of Hong Kong police and a unit of the Welch Regiment on the rooftops of two 27-storey buildings at North Point, which were suspected of housing Communist personnel. All the 120 troops were landed on the buildings within 30 minutes of taking off, and complete surprise was achieved with a number of suspects being arrested.

As *Hermes* made her way south through the Great Bitter Lake on 3 May 1967, she met the homeward-bound Orient liner, SS *Orcades.* *(Lt-Cdr Larcombe)*

Hermes and *Victorious* in joint manoeuvres off Aden on 15 May 1967.

(Lt-Cdr Larcombe)

On 7 August, after leaving Hong Kong in company with *Galatea* and *Minerva,* the carrier returned to Subic Bay for further flying operations before putting into the US Naval Base on the morning of Saturday 12 August for a short weekend break. During that time the village of Olongapo was added to the list of dubious foreign attractions, which now included The Gut, Bugis Street and Wanchai. After leaving Subic Bay *Hermes* returned to the waters off Singapore for three days of flying after which she finally left the area on 19 August to begin a long roundabout passage home. Her return to the UK had been specially arranged in order to give the ship's company a period of home leave, thus reducing the length of continuous separation which further operational commitments east of Suez following Aden's independence would otherwise have imposed. Before steaming for home, however, *Hermes* and two frigates set course through the Sunda Strait and into the Indian Ocean to an area off the Cocos Islands to carry out further flying practice during which the Chief Administrator of the islands spent the afternoon of 22 August on board. On the last day of the exercises, Thursday 24 August, Wessex helicopter 340 ditched into the sea at 10pm in a position Lat 12° - 06'N/Long 96° - 36'E, several miles from the ship. Another helicopter, together with *Minerva,* was dispatched to rescue the aircrew and fortunately all of them were recovered safely, with the pilot being rescued by the frigate's sea boat. With the helicopter's emergency floats having inflated, the machine remained afloat and by midnight it had been hoisted onto the flight deck, allowing the carrier to set course for Western Australia.

Hermes arrived alongside No 7 berth in Fremantle Harbour at 10am on Tuesday 29 August for a six-day recreational visit. As always the visit to the Australian port was the high spot of the commission, and there were dances, a children's party for 250 underprivileged youngsters, and of course the final shopping expeditions before the voyage home. When the ship was opened to the public for just six hours over two afternoons well over 11,000 people visited the carrier, with long queues stretching right through the docks. The visit ended at 9am on Monday 4 September when *Hermes* and *Minerva* left Fremantle to make the 11,500 mile, non-stop, passage to Portsmouth. They were supported by the RFAs *Olna, Oleander* and *Reliant* and 12 days after leaving Australia they were off the Cape of Good Hope. By 27 September *Hermes* was off the Canary Islands and three days later, when she was off Berry Head in Devon, the squadrons were flown off to their respective bases. On Sunday 1 October *Hermes* anchored at Spithead, but with Customs officers doing their worst there was no shore leave that evening. Next day the carrier weighed anchor and steamed up harbour to secure alongside Middle Slip Jetty at noon.

Hermes' stay in home waters lasted for five weeks, but the ship's company had to squeeze their leave into just 29 days, for the final week was spent at sea. During the afternoon of Sunday 8 October the chaplain broke his previous records when, during a single service held on the quarterdeck, he baptized 14 babies. On 23 October there was a change of command when the new commanding officer, Captain D. G. Parker DSO DSC AFC RN, arrived on board at 10am. Shortly afterwards, at 11.45am, Captain Lewin left the ship. There is no doubt that he had been very popular with the ship's company, and one member remembers that, 'a favourite haunt for Captain Lewin was B boiler room which he often visited during the middle watch, as they made the best brew. I understand he even had his own mug there. He always said that *Hermes* was a very happy ship, the happiest he had ever commanded.'

Captain Parker had originally trained to be a chartered surveyor at West Hartlepool Technical College, but when the war broke out he joined the Royal Navy as a gunnery rating. After basic training at HMS *St Vincent* in Gosport he was selected for training as an officer and he volunteered for aircrew duties. He gained his wings flying Tiger Moths and was commissioned as a Sub-Lt RNVR, joining 772 Squadron, flying Blackburn Skuas from HMS *Landrail* in Argyll. In March 1942 he joined his first front-line squadron, 884, flying Fairey Fulmar fighters. The squadron embarked in HMS *Victorious* and sailed for the Mediterranean as part of the escort for the 'Pedestal' convoy to Malta. During 'Pedestal' he shot down an Italian aircraft off Sardinia and on the same day he shared another. Re-equipped with Seafires the squadron provided air cover for the invasion of North Africa, and in 1943 he joined 883 (Swordfish and Seafire) Squadron in the escort carrier *Stalker.* Joining 'Force V' the squadron provided fighter cover for the Salerno landings. Later that year he went to Boscombe Down to test-fly the Corsair and in 1945 he served with the British Pacific Fleet. In July 1946 he was granted a regular commission and took command of 800 Squadron flying Seafires from HMS *Triumph.* Awarded the AFC in 1952, he had his first general service appointment in the frigate *St Austell Bay.* In 1962 he had his first sea command, the destroyer *Cavendish,* and he served in *Ark Royal* as Commander (Air). *Hermes* was to be his last command before being promoted to Flag Rank.

It was at 10am on Tuesday 31 October that *Hermes* left Portsmouth to steam round the Isle of Wight to Lyme Bay where she was to recover her squadrons. At 9.30am that morning, half an hour before *Hermes* sailed, the elderly Cunard passenger liner, RMS *Queen Mary,* once the pride of the Merchant marine, left Southampton's Ocean Terminal bound for retirement on the USA's West Coast. She had been sold to the city of Long Beach, California, for £1,240,000 to serve as a maritime museum and tourist centre and, carrying 1,300 American passengers, she was just starting her final 39-day voyage via Cape Horn. A

Framed by a coconut palm, *Hermes* lies at anchor off the island of Gan in May 1967. With war in the Middle East between Israel and her Arab neighbours imminent, she was ordered to remain in the vicinity of the island.

(Lt-Cdr Larcombe)

A Buccaneer makes its final approach before landing on.
(Lt-Cdr Larcombe)

On 7 August 1967 *Hermes* left Hong Kong for exercises in Subic Bay and the Indian Ocean, before steaming on to Fremantle in Australia.
(Fleet Air Arm Museum)

On Tuesday 31 October 1967, shortly before steaming to Aden via Cape Town, *Hermes* saluted the Cunard passenger liner RMS *Queen Mary* which was on her final voyage from Southampton to retirement at Long Beach, California.

(Fleet Air Arm Museum)

number of warships, including the destroyer *Dainty,* and the frigates *Argonaut* and *Wakeful,* escorted her through the Solent while 14 helicopters led by a Whirlwind from Portland and 826 Squadron's Wessex helicopters, performed a fly-past in anchor formation. At 12.30pm, once the *Queen Mary* was clear of the Nab Channel, *Hermes* steamed past the once great liner, her flight deck lined by the ship's company who cheered ship as a final tribute and farewell from the Royal Navy. Once clear of the *Queen Mary,* however, the carrier altered course for Lyme Bay where the squadrons were safely embarked and four days of flying practice were observed by the Flag Officer, Naval Flying Training, Rear-Admiral D. W. Kirke.

During the afternoon of Saturday 4 November, *Hermes* left Lyme Bay and set course south to make her passage back to the Indian Ocean and the Gulf of Aden, once again by way of the Cape of Good Hope. By 13 November the carrier was off Ascension Island where three days of flying exercises were carried out and the Royal Marines Band

landed to entertain the residents of Georgetown by Beating Retreat in front of the Town Hall. By 22 November, however, *Hermes* was exercising off the Cape of Good Hope and on Friday 1 December she secured to buoys in Kilindini Harbour, Mombasa. Next day, having become ill a few days earlier, Captain Parker was taken ashore to hospital and five days later, on 7 December, he was flown home to the UK for treatment. In his absence, the Executive Officer, Commander J. D. Fieldhouse RN, was appointed Acting Captain to command *Hermes* at 8am on Saturday 9 December. Next day, in company with the frigate *Phoebe,* the carrier sailed from Mombasa and set course for an area between Salalah and Masirah, Muscat and Oman, where British bases remained after the withdrawal from Aden which had been completed on 28 November. *Hermes* and *Phoebe,* together with the commando carrier *Bulwark* and the escorts *Barrosa* and *Devonshire,* remained off Masirah and, for a time, the aircraft operated with those from *Eagle,* which had covered

Hermes exercising with the submarine *Talent*, which is about to submerge. (Lt-Cdr Larcombe)

the withdrawal. On Christmas Day *Hermes* and *Bulwark,* and the escorts, steamed through the Strait of Hormuz to anchor at 7am off Duhar Dibbah, close to Sharjah in the Trucial States (United Arab Emirates). The only shore leave, however, came on Boxing Day when, between 10.30am and 4.30pm, limited recreational leave was granted. Three days later, *Hermes* and *Bulwark* left for the Aden area to patrol the international waters off the former colony until they dispersed to their individual exercise areas on 3 January 1968. The duties in connection with the Aden withdrawal were over.

Both *Hermes* and *Bulwark* steamed east from Aden to Masirah where, on 5 January, *Hermes'* advance recommissioning party who had flown out from the UK to RAF Masirah, were airlifted on board courtesy of the *Bulwark's* helicopters. That weekend, with the carriers anchored off Masirah, some very limited shore leave was allowed for organized sports parties, and both units remained in the area until the forenoon of Monday 15 January when, after embarking a number of aircraft engines from RAF Masirah which were brought to the ship by *Bulwark's* LCVPs, *Hermes* weighed anchor and set course for Mombasa, where she arrived four days later. After anchoring in Kilindini Harbour at 4.30pm on Friday 19 January, the ship's company got their first run ashore for over five weeks, and at 7.45pm that evening Captain Parker returned to the ship and assumed command once again.

Following the long weekend in Mombasa *Hermes* set sail south on Tuesday 23 January for the Cape and the long passage home. As she approached the Cape of Good Hope the effects of cyclone 'Georgette' were felt, with heavy seas and gale force winds which caused speed to be reduced. In the event the severe weather delayed the carrier's entry into Cape Town Harbour, but at midday on 1 February she secured alongside the city's Duncan Dock for a four-day visit to the port. The call at Cape Town was the last foreign visit of the commission, and on Monday 5 February *Hermes* was at sea again and steaming north for home. On 12 February she rendezvoused with RFA *Tidepool* off Freetown and three days later she passed between Tenerife and Hierro in the Canary Islands. On the morning of Sunday 18 February all the serviceable fixed-wing aircraft were launched to their parent stations, and later in the day the helicopters of 826 Squadron flew off to Culdrose. Next morning *Hermes* anchored at Spithead where she was cleared by Customs, then during the afternoon she weighed anchor and with her flight deck manned, she steamed up harbour to secure alongside Pitch House Jetty at 5pm. Since leaving Portsmouth in May 1966 she had steamed 122,348 miles during which her non-stop voyage from Fremantle to Portsmouth had created a post-war record for a surface warship. More importantly, however, she had maintained her tradition of being known as 'Happy *Hermes*'.

Departing from Cape Town on 5 February 1968 on her way home, *Hermes* leaves the port with her paying-off pennant flying.

(FotoFlite)

Chapter Nine

The Fourth Commission
March 1968 - June 1970

Even before the third commission was over the future for *Hermes*, which had appeared to be secure until at least the mid-1970s, was suddenly thrown into doubt by the Government's announcement in January 1968 that the Royal Navy's aircraft carrier force was likely to be disbanded in early 1970. With the end of 'Confrontation' in the Far East and the success of the Federation of Malaysia, it had been decided to withdraw British forces from the very costly military bases in Singapore, with the intention that any air presence east of Suez would be provided by the RAF from island bases such as Gan. The plan that *Hermes* should be adapted to operate the new Phantom F4K general-purpose fighter, the replacement for the Sea Vixen, was scrapped and instead it was announced that the carrier would be withdrawn from service, at the latest, in 1971 which was four years earlier than expected. Not only was *Hermes* to be decommissioned early, but *Victorious,* which had been due to recommission in November 1967 for what was generally accepted would be her final commission, was withdrawn from service only days before the recommissioning ceremony, and large numbers of her ship's company were drafted to *Hermes* which lay in Portsmouth Dockyard undergoing maintenance prior to recommissioning.

By late March 1968, with *Victorious* having been decommissioned and most of her complement having transferred to *Hermes*, it was not long before *Hermes* was ready for sea and on Friday 17 May the recommissioning service was held in the hangar. The guest of honour was Admiral Sir John Bush, the C-in-C of the Western Fleet, and also present was the FOAC, Rear-Admiral L. D. Empson. Over 1,700 relatives and friends of the ship's company attended, as did the Mayor and Mayoress of Tiverton, and the commissioning cake was cut by Mrs Margaret Parker, the Captain's wife, ably assisted by the wife of the Master-at-Arms. By 3.30pm, after having been entertained to a buffet lunch in the hangar, all the guests were clear of the ship and four days later, at 8.30am on Tuesday 21 May, *Hermes* left Portsmouth Harbour to begin her post-refit trials. She was put through her paces for six days, steaming between the south coast of the Isle of Wight and the Scilly Isles, and at 12.50pm on Friday 24 May, Phantom F4K, VL 725, made several runs close to *Hermes* as it circled the ship for 20 minutes. On Monday 27 May, while she was at anchor in Weymouth Bay, the ground crews for 814 Squadron joined the ship, and they were

followed shortly afterwards by the eight Wessex Mk 3 anti-submarine helicopters which they were to operate. Next morning, after weighing anchor at 5am, the helicopters carried out operational trials with the submarine *Ambush* providing the opposition. On 29 May, as the carrier steamed between Lyme Bay and Start Bay, the Buccaneers and Sea Vixens of 801 and 893 Squadrons respectively, both of which were to be carried by *Hermes*, performed touch and go circuits. These trials were to be continued on the following day, but poor visibility prevented any flying and on the morning of 31 May, with the ship anchored at Spithead, the ground crews of 801, 893 and 849A (Gannet AEW3) Flight were embarked. During the afternoon, as *Hermes* steamed off the Isle of Wight, all the aircraft were safely embarked and the carrier set course for the Moray Firth to begin her work-up.

For 18 days of June *Hermes* carried out intensive flying programmes off Scotland's east coast, although a major exercise which was to have been carried out with the destroyer *Hampshire,* and the frigates *Aisne, Danae, Jaguar, Juno, Naiad* and *Zulu,* was cancelled because of thick fog, which also disrupted flying operations. The progress of the work-up was, however, closely observed by the C-in-C Western Fleet who hoisted his flag in *Hermes*, and by Soviet naval units and 'trawlers' bristling with radar aerials. On Wednesday 19 June, with the work-up completed, *Hermes* steamed south down the east coast to secure alongside Portsmouth's Middle Slip Jetty on the morning of Thursday 20 June, when a short pre-deployment leave was granted to the ship's company.

During the stay in Portsmouth BBC film crews came on board to interview Vice-Admiral Sir Richard Smeeton as part of a documentary film about the Fleet Air Arm, then on Tuesday 9 July, with both watches having completed their one week's leave, *Hermes* sailed from Portsmouth. Although she was bound for the Far East, before leaving home waters she took part in exercises in the Western Approaches with the destroyers *Cavalier* and *Diamond* and the frigates *Galatea* and *Lincoln*. After embarking her Air Group off the Isle of Wight she steamed west to Portland and Plymouth where the exercises were to start. During the forenoon of 14 July one of her helicopters attempted to transfer a Medical Officer to *Cavalier* to attend an injured man, but due to heavy seas the attempt had to be abandoned and the destroyer returned to Devonport. During the afternoon of 17 July, with the carrier having

Hermes at sea in northern waters during her final commission as a conventional fixed-wing aircraft carrier. *(Derek Coombes)*

returned to Lyme Bay, she came as close as she would ever get to the new Phantom aircraft when one of the planes from Boscombe Down made a number of touch and go circuits on the flight deck. That evening, with the exercises over, *Hermes* and *Diamond* set course for Cape Town and a fast passage to the Far East.

During the evening of Monday 22 July *Hermes* passed the African port of Dakar and three days later, at 9am, the carrier crossed the equator. For operational reasons, however, the Crossing the Line ceremony did not take place until the morning of Friday 26 July when *Hermes* was almost due east of Ascension Island. Finally, 14 days after leaving Lyme Bay, the carrier secured alongside J berth of Cape Town's Duncan Dock at 8.30am on the last day of July. With the Suez Canal closed to shipping, the South African city and the nearby base at Simonstown were receiving regular visits from British warships, and *Hermes* was the 114th unit of the Royal Navy to visit a South African port since the closure. The people of Cape Town were always pleased to see British warships and when the

carrier opened her gangways to the public during the weekend of 3 August, some 7,200 people were entertained on board. The visit came to an end on Monday 5 August when *Hermes* left Cape Town to set course across the Indian Ocean bound for the Strait of Malacca where she was to carry out her first exercises with the Far East Fleet. The 12-day passage took her south of Madagascar and Reunion, with a day's flying off Gan on 14 August. She finally arrived off Penang four days later, when she rendezvoused with the destroyers *Fife* and *Glamorgan,* the frigates *Euryalus* and *Grenville* and the Australian units *Parramatta* and *Vendetta* for a ten-day anti-submarine exercise during which *Amphion, Onslaught* and *Rorqual* provided the underwater opposition, and RAAF Meteors and Sabres from Butterworth did battle with *Hermes'* Air Group. The exercise, which completed the carrier's work-up, took the force into the Andaman Sea and for a short period they anchored off Langkowi Island, although there were no banyans on this occasion. On Friday 23 August there were no fewer than four Admirals on board *Hermes,*

With a Wessex helicopter over the flight deck, *Hermes* steams past Southsea seafront on 5 April 1976.

(Don Smith)

Hermes receives a tumultuous welcome when she returns from the South Atlantic in July 1982.　　*(Don Smith)*

A four-ship RAS with a County-class destroyer.

(Derek Coombes)

with the C-in-C FES, Vice-Admiral O'Brien, visiting his old ship by helicopter along with his second in command, Rear-Admiral A. T. F. G. Griffin. Just over an hour later, at 1.15pm, four Buccaneers of 803 Squadron arrived on board after an epic flight from Lossiemouth, via Gan. On board one of them was a totally unexpected 'observer', the First Sea Lord, Admiral Sir Michael Le Fanu, who had flown out from the UK to visit the Far Eastern Fleet. Later that evening the FOAC, Rear-Admiral M. H. Fell, arrived on board to carry out his Operational Readiness Inspection and to hoist his flag in *Hermes* for just a few days. It was said that 4U flat was extremely crowded that night.

With the exercise and inspection over, *Hermes* set course for Singapore where, at 9am on Friday 30 August, she arrived alongside No 13 berth in the naval base to begin a 17-day dockyard assisted maintenance period. At midnight on Saturday 31 August, with the restructuring of Flag ranks, the post of Flag Officer, Aircraft Carriers, was dissolved and Admiral Fell became the first Flag Officer, Carriers and Amphibious Ships (FOCAS). On Monday 16

September, with the maintenance period completed and with Rear-Admiral Griffin having taken over from Admiral Fell, the carrier left Singapore to rendezvous with *Glamorgan, Defender, Diamond, Diana, Euryalus, Grenville, Puma, Parramatta, Vendetta* and RFA *Olna* for exercises in the South China Sea. On 22 September the force set course for the Balabac Strait, steaming across the Sulu Sea and through the Sibutu Channel and into the Celebes Sea, where they rendezvoused with an amphibious force which included *Albion, Intrepid, Triumph, Caprice* and RFA *Tidespring*. The whole task force then made its way to the Bismarck Sea where, off the Admiralty Islands at midnight on 30 September, 'Exercise Coral Sands' began. The opposition was provided by a US Navy force and the Australian carrier *Sydney*, which was acting in the capacity of a commando carrier. Initially aircraft from *Hermes* carried out sorties to probe the 'enemy' radar defences and these were followed by bombing raids on Townshend Island off the coast of Queensland. The exercise was completed during the evening of Sunday 13 October and *Hermes*' task force formed up for the passage to Sydney where they arrived the following morning. *Hermes* herself passed Sydney Heads at 9.10am and 20 minutes later she secured alongside the Oil Wharf at Garden Island Naval Base.

During the carrier's 17-day stay in Sydney the city extended its usual legendary hospitality to the ship's company and most mess decks were soon decorated with boomerangs and toy koalas. So numerous were the party invitations from ashore that the ship's company were hard-pressed to keep up with them, and a few tears were shed when, at 10am on the last day of October, *Hermes* left Sydney Harbour and set course for Jervis Bay where the squadrons were recovered from RNAS Nowra. The first five days of November were spent operating from Jervis Bay with Australian Navy STF Trackers and A4 Skyhawks landing on board during the manoeuvres. When *Hermes* left Australian waters she carried out a full-power trial as she steamed up the coast, and her final link with the country came on 7 November when a sick rating was flown to hospital in Townsville. On Monday 11 November, with the ship in the Sulu Sea, non-diversion flying exercises were carried out, but next day she set course for Okinawa and her next exercise programme which was to be with the US Navy once again. On 15 November, after arriving in the exercise areas south of Okinawa, intensive flying operations got under way and this period spent operating in the Pacific Ocean will probably be remembered for the number of accidents which took place. The first came during the afternoon of 19 November when the ejector seat of a Sea Vixen was fired accidentally, causing spinal injuries to the plane's unfortunate observer. A few days later, during flying exercises on Friday 22 November, Gannet 260 ditched close to the port side of the ship during recovery at 9.15pm. Fortunately the planeguard escort, HMS *Diana*, was quickly on the scene and all three crew members were rescued safely. That weekend *Hermes* anchored off Okinawa Shima, and shore leave to the US Naval Base was granted to the off-duty watch. During the evening, however, a rating died in an accident ashore and early on the morning of 25 November *Hermes* sailed for the second phase of the exercise. At 8am that morning, when the ship was in a position Lat 26° - 14'N/Long 128° - 15'E, the first launch of the day took place with a Gannet of 849A Flight. Unfortunately, the aircraft ditched into the sea on take-off, and after the carrier had taken evasive action the sea boat was quickly launched. Despite an intensive search only one body was recovered, with no sign of the other two crew members or the wrecked aircraft. The search continued all day until 6pm when, sadly, it had to be discontinued. Next day, with a heavy swell running, there were no flying operations and on Wednesday 27 November *Hermes* set course for Hong Kong.

At noon on Friday 29 November the carrier secured alongside the North Arm of Hong Kong Dockyard, for what was to be the Royal Navy's last visit by a traditional fixed-wing aircraft carrier to the colony. The visit was marked by the 'Hermes Harriers', a three-man running team who, spurred on by a record set by a team from HMS *Eagle*, decided to set a new Peak Race record. Setting off at 6am on the chosen day the three runners pounded up the steep and narrow road, and by the time they had reached Jardine's Corner, which was just over half way, they had already chopped over a minute and a half off *Eagle's* time. Higher still they went, until they emerged through the mists enveloping the Peak to reach View Point in 22 minutes, 48 seconds - almost three minutes faster than *Eagle's* record. Another, more popular, highlight of the stay was the visit of five local actresses to the ship, but on Saturday 7 December *Hermes* left the colony to set course for Singapore where, over the Christmas and New Year break, the carrier would undergo a self-maintenance period. Before entering the dockyard, however, she carried out two days of manoeuvres off the island to assist with HMS *Glamorgan's* sea inspection. Following the exercises her aircraft flew off to RAF Changi and at 11am on 14 December *Hermes* secured alongside at the naval base. In anticipation of the four weeks that the carrier would spend alongside during the holiday period, a number of ship's company wives had booked a flight out to Singapore with British Eagle Aviation, and £10,000 had been paid to charter a Britannia airliner. Unfortunately, however, the company was in financial trouble and in early November it had gone into voluntary liquidation, with unsecured creditors unlikely to receive more than a few shillings in the pound. After strenuous efforts by the Admiralty and RAF Transport Command, most of the wives were able to obtain 'Indulgence' passages with the RAF at a cost of £14 each and they arrived in Singapore on 15 December, the day after the carrier docked.

After carrying out successful basin trials, *Hermes* left Singapore at 9am on Friday 13 December 1968 to embark all her fixed- and rotary-wing aircraft then, with HMS *Danae*, she set course through the Strait of Malacca for an area off Penang. Once in the exercise areas, she and *Danae* rendezvoused with the commando carrier *Albion*, the destroyers *Decoy*, *Diamond* and *Duchess*, the frigates *Ajax*, *Aurora*, *Blackpool* and *Cleopatra* and HMAS *Derwent* for the annual 'FOTEX 69' exercise. During Wednesday 29 January 1969, the C-in-C, FES spent the day aboard *Hermes*, whose aircraft cross-operated with RAF and RAAF fighters from Tengah and Butterworth respectively. For the ships' companies, on Saturday 1 February, there was a short break at Langkowi Island, with the usual beach parties, but next day the fleet was at sea again for phase two of the exercise, with *Hermes* operating in the rear of the main body and providing air support. The exercise ended with a full-scale 'invasion' of Penang by amphibious forces from *Albion*, and on Saturday 8 February *Hermes* secured

An immaculate 'Procedure Alpha' entry into harbour whilst east of Suez. *(Derek Coombes)*

alongside Singapore Naval Base so that senior officers could attend the 'FOTEX' critique in *Terror's* cinema, and so that FO2, FES, could transfer his staff and flag ashore, having been on board *Hermes* since September 1968. This time, however, the stopover in Singapore lasted for only four days and at 2.30pm on Wednesday 12 February, in company with *Ajax, Aurora, Grenville* and the RFAs *Olna* and *Regent*, *Hermes* sailed for Australia's west coast on her second visit to the country.

After passing through the Sunda Strait, and keeping a close eye on a nearby cyclone, the force exercised in the Timor Sea before they went their separate ways; *Grenville* to Geralton, *Ajax* and *Reliant* to Bunbury, *Aurora* and *Olna* to Albany and *Hermes* to Fremantle, where she secured alongside Victoria Quay at 10am on 18 February. On the second day of the visit a ship's dance was held, which was attended by over a thousand guests who easily outnumbered the ship's company. During the weekend of 22/23 February, when the ship was opened to the public, nearly 12,000 people were welcomed over the gangways and a few days later a successful children's party was held on board. The visit came to an end on the morning of Thursday 27 February, when *Hermes* left the port to rendezvous with *Aurora* and *Grenville* for exercises off the West Australian coast. Grenville, however, had to withdraw from the manoeuvres suffering from condenseritis, and she was ordered to steam ahead for Cape Town. *Hermes* began her passage to Cape Town on 1 March, although five days later, in the early hours of 6 March, she too suffered machinery problems when steam was lost in A boiler room, which resulted in a turbo-alternator and the steering gear losing power. After a voyage of 11 days, *Hermes* finally secured alongside at Cape Town at 8.45am on Wednesday 12 March, and here the ship's company had the final run ashore of the deployment. Finally, on Tuesday 18 March, in company with RFA *Olna,* the carrier left Cape Town and set course for home, with 814 Squadron carrying out deck landing practice on the RFA during the passage north. On Sunday 30 March the Buccaneers were launched to Lossiemouth, and next day the Sea Vixens took off for Yeovilton, 849A Flight returned to Brawdy and 814 Squadron to Culdrose*. At 6am on Tuesday 1 April *Hermes* anchored at Spithead for Customs clearance, but by midday she had weighed anchor and half an hour later she was secured alongside Middle Slip Jetty where she received an enthusiastic welcome from thousands of relatives, friends and well-wishers. For 40 members of the ship's company there was the pleasure of seeing their children for the first time, while for 14 other men there were forthcoming marriages to look forward to. One couple, PO Stephen Wright and his wife, were about to purchase a house courtesy of a raffle on board in which PO Wright

had won a £700 motor car. As he felt a house was more important he planned to sell the car and use the money as a deposit.

Hermes now faced a five-month dockyard assisted refit and there would also be a change of command, for during the passage home Captain Parker had been promoted to Rear-Admiral. In the immediate future, however, on 1 May, the ship was moved into D lock for dry docking, and the ship's company moved onto the former carrier *Centaur,* which was being used as an accommodation ship at Portsmouth. A few weeks later, on Wednesday 2 July, Captain P. M. Austin RN took command of both *Hermes* and *Centaur*. Captain Austin had entered the Navy in the mid-1930s and during the Second World War he served in destroyers and in the cruiser *Cornwall*. After qualifying as a pilot he served in 807 and 736 Squadrons, and in 1953 he commanded 850 Squadron in HMAS *Sydney* during operations off Korea. Following that appointment he served in HM Ships *Bulwark* and *Eagle,* with his first command, between 1963 and 1965, being HMS *Lynx*. After a spell in command of RNAS Brawdy and on the staff of the NATO Supreme Allied Commander, Atlantic, he was appointed to *Hermes*.

During the refit *Hermes* was repainted throughout and her main propulsion machinery was completely overhauled so that when the ship's company moved back on board from *Centaur* on Wednesday 30 July, she looked almost a new ship. The next day *Hermes* was moved out of dry dock and back alongside Middle Slip Jetty and on Thursday 21 August, with the refit over, Rear-Admiral Fell inspected the ship. Eight days later there was a rededication service on board which was attended by Rear-Admiral Fell and a large number of relatives and friends as the occasion was combined with a Families Day. The last weekend in August and the public holiday on 1 September saw Navy Days in Portsmouth with *Hermes, Bulwark* and *Blake* providing the main attractions. Over the three days more than 25,000 people visited *Hermes*, with almost half that number arriving on the last day, causing huge queues through the dockyard. Finally, however, it was time to set sail once again and at 4.30pm on Tuesday 2 September, *Hermes* left Portsmouth with full ceremony to head for Portland where she would carry out her post-refit trials. After eight days in the area of Weymouth Bay *Hermes* returned to Portsmouth where she spent another week alongside before returning to Portland for further trials. At 10.45am on Monday 22 September, when the carrier was off Berry Head, two Phantom F4Ks overflew the ship and the following day two Hawker Hunter jets performed a number of touch and go circuits. During the evening of 24 September, after spending eight hours anchored at Spithead, *Hermes* left for a fast passage via the Pentland Firth to the east coast of Scotland where, on 27 September, all the squadrons joined the ship. During the intensive flying operations the ship

*814 Squadron was subsequently awarded the Boyd Trophy for its magnificent work during 1968.

An aerial view as *Hermes* enters harbour with her flight deck fully manned. *(Derek Coombes)*

The ship's pop group, 'Tickett', perform in the junior rates' dining hall. *(Jan Davey)*

Operating with *Eagle* off Gibraltar in autumn 1968.

(Fleet Air Arm Museum)

was visited by the C-in-C Western Fleet, who took time off to add the 'flavouring' to the ship's Christmas pudding mixture. The submarine *Ocelot* did its best to 'sink' the carrier, the frigate *Eastbourne* faithfully carried out planeguard duties and two USAF Phantoms 'attacked' the ship. On Friday 10 October there was a long weekend break at Rosyth for a 'Meet the Navy' visit, during which a full programme of sports activities was arranged and hundreds of young people from schools and youth organizations were given guided tours of the carrier. A party of sailors even managed to visit the ship's mascot, a Golden Eagle called Hermes, at Edinburgh Zoo, although the bird, which had been adopted in 1966, appeared unmoved by the honour. By Tuesday 14 October *Hermes* was back at sea again and during the next round of exercises the SAR helicopter was able to recover HMS *Bacchante's* Wasp helicopter which had crashed in boggy ground on a mountainside at Cape Wrath. After the Wasp had been hoisted out of the peat bog, mechanics removed the undercarriage so that the main body of the aircraft could be taken the four miles to a waiting lorry for transportation to Lossiemouth. Afterwards the SAR helicopter returned to pick up the remainder of the aircraft and the maintenance

personnel, before the helicopter then passed a tow line from *Hermes* to RFA *Olwen* for a towing exercise. During the evening of Thursday 23 October there was a flying accident when Gannet 263 ditched on take-off, but fortunately the planeguard escort *Diamond* was soon on the scene, as was the carrier's sea boat, and the three aircrew members were all rescued. Finally, on Tuesday 28 October, with the work-up having been completed and the squadrons flown off, *Hermes* set course down the North Sea to Portsmouth. After passing the Wash at midnight on 29 October, the ship was worked up to full power and just over 15 hours later, at 3.30pm, she was secured alongside Middle Slip Jetty to begin a dockyard assisted maintenance period.

During the afternoon of 1 November there was a 'spy' scare when two East German nationals were apprehended at the foot of the gangway, clearly having strayed from the area of the dockyard which was open to the public for access to HMS *Victory*. However, with the cold war at its height nobody was taking any chances and they were handed over to the dockyard police. On 3 November television film crews were on board to film a 14-year-old English and Welsh diving champion taking some spectacular plunges from the flight deck into the water,

Leaving Cape Town on 18 March 1969.   *(Derek Coombes)*

accompanied on one occasion by the ship's divers who jumped in feet first. Six days later came a very popular event when Thames Television's outside broadcast teams, complete with chorus girls and the presenter, the late Hughie Green, descended on the ship to record the amateur talent show, Opportunity Knocks, which over the years 'discovered' a number of entertainers who went on to become household names. During the day, whilst the hopeful contestants rehearsed in the hangar, the chorus girls toured the ship looking for photo-opportunities such as scrubbing the decks, sitting in the Captain's chair, swinging aloft on a jackstay and taking part in a not-too-serious tug-of-war. That evening, at 6pm, the show itself was broadcast live from the hangar.

On Thursday 13 November, with the maintenance completed, *Hermes* left Portsmouth to embark the squadrons and to steam west for flying exercises in St George's Channel. At 10.40pm on Sunday 16 November, after receiving an urgent request for assistance, *Hermes* altered course to head for a position Lat 51° - 45'N/Long 06°, to assist in the search for a crew member who had been washed overboard from a French trawler. For six hours *Hermes*, and her escort *Cleopatra*, searched the

stormy seas, but no trace of the man could be found and next morning flying began again. A few days later, on 24 November, *Hermes*, *Eagle*, *Cleopatra* and *Charybdis* took part in 'Exercise Decamp' in the eastern Atlantic which was watched over by the Chief of the Defence Staff, Marshal of the Royal Air Force, Sir Charles Elworthy. For *Hermes* the exercise began at 6am when three Buccaneers were launched to find *Eagle* and they were followed by further sorties which were sent out to 'destroy' the larger carrier. Meanwhile, on board *Eagle*, her squadrons were carrying out similar missions to find and 'destroy' *Hermes*. Next day the two carriers rendezvoused and flew sorties to find and 'destroy' five RFAs which were steaming south to Gibraltar. The exercise ended during the evening of Thursday 27 November and next morning, with *Eagle* leading the column, the four warships steamed in formation to enter Gibraltar Dockyard, where *Hermes* secured alongside at 9.15am. Both *Hermes* and *Eagle* left Gibraltar during the forenoon of 2 December and *Hermes* set course for home. Next day the Sea Vixens were flown off to Yeovilton and on 4 December the Buccaneers and Wessex helicopters were launched for Lossiemouth and Culdrose. Having flown off all her aircraft, on the morning of 5 December *Hermes*

The North Sea washes down the cable deck during exercises in autumn 1969.   *(Jan Davey)*

Hermes enters Gibraltar on 27 November 1969.   *(Michael Lennon)*

Off Gibraltar in January 1970.

herself anchored at Spithead and by 10.15am she was secured alongside Middle Slip Jetty for Christmas and New Year leave.

The final fixed-wing deployment for *Hermes* began on Tuesday 13 January 1970, when she left Portsmouth bound for Lyme Bay to land on the squadrons. With *Danae* acting as planeguard, there were six days of flying while *Hermes* steamed between Portland and St George's Channel, then during the afternoon of 20 January the two ships set course for Gibraltar. Three days later, having passed through the Strait of Gibraltar, they rendezvoused with *Ajax* and *Charybdis* for manoeuvres off the colony. There followed a 48-hour weekend break in the port, but on the following Monday *Hermes* was back at sea and flying her aircraft each day from dawn to dusk. At 8am on Thursday 29 January the crew of a Buccaneer had a lucky escape when their aircraft crashed into the sea. The plane was on the port catapult and, at the moment of launch, with its engines roaring at full power, the hold-back bridle fell onto the flight deck. Without catapult assistance and unable to stop, the Buccaneer launched itself over the bow and into the sea, but not before its crew had fired their new rocket-powered ejector seats, which threw them to safety. *Hermes* was stopped immediately and the sea boat was lowered to

recover the wreckage of the plane, all of which was of great interest to a Soviet trawler which sailed in close down the port side to watch proceedings.

After another weekend break at Gibraltar there were more exercises with *Danae* and *Dundas* in the western Mediterranean, where 814 Squadron's mission was to search out and 'destroy' the nuclear-powered submarine *Warspite*, which proved to be an elusive opponent. On 11 February, after a third weekend break at Gibraltar, *Hermes* and *Danae* steamed east for Malta and after five days of manoeuvres south of the island, they entered Grand Harbour on 18 February. For *Hermes* the 14-day visit to Malta was an opportunity to carry out maintenance, but it also provided a chance for the sports teams to play inter-ship matches. The carrier sailed again on 6 March for flying operations between Sardinia and North Africa, with the SAR helicopter acting as planeguard. Next day, at just after 5pm, in a position Lat 09° - 19'E/Long 37° - 49'N, some 30 miles north of the Tunisian coast and close to the island of La Galite, the SAR helicopter recovered a lifebuoy from a missing yacht, *Mercedes 893,* which it was presumed had been lost, with its occupants, during a storm in the area. Continuing westwards *Hermes* carried out Seacat firings and during the afternoon of 15 March she passed through

Entering Malta's Grand Harbour on 18 February 1970, and...

...tugs nudge her to a berth in Bighi Bay.

(Michael Cassar)

Hermes alongside at Devonport in March 1984 whilst undergoing her final refit before being laid up at Portsmouth. *(Don Smith)*

INS *Viraat* anchored off Mumbai for the International Fleet Review which celebrated the 50th anniversary of the Indian Republic.

(Mike Critchley/Maritime Books)

the Strait of Gibraltar into the Atlantic Ocean to take part in 'Exercise Oceanex', which also involved US, French and Portuguese Navy units, all under the watchful eye of a Soviet destroyer which attached itself to *Hermes*. By 20 March both *Hermes* and her Krupny-class shadow were back in the western Mediterranean, and on 24 March the carrier secured to No 1 buoy in the Rade de Villefranche for a six-day visit to the French holiday resort. Here the casino proved a great attraction, and on the evening of 28 March the town put on a dance for the ship's company. The ship itself was opened to visitors and almost 3,000 local people got more than they had anticipated when the boats which had been chartered to ferry them between the ship and the shore stopped running. Eventually, however, the ship's boats managed to get everyone ashore by 9pm that evening. After leaving Villefranche on 30 March *Hermes* carried out flying operations off Iles de Hyrès before making her way back to Malta by way of the Tyrrhenian Sea, the island of Stromboli, which she circled twice, and the Strait of Messina. Once off Malta flying exercises were resumed and it was not long before she attracted another Soviet shadow, this time in the form of a Mirka-class frigate. On 12 April, when *Hermes* was about 100 miles north-west of Tripoli, she encountered the Soviet helicopter cruiser *Leningrad*, together with an escort of three destroyers and two frigates, which were followed closely by a Sverdlov-class cruiser, in all a formidable Soviet force. Finally, at 10am on 14 April, *Hermes* secured alongside Grand Harbour's Parlatorio Wharf to begin a three-week self-maintenance period.

When *Hermes* left Malta again on Monday 4 May she immediately acquired another Soviet shadow, this time a Kotlin-class destroyer which stayed dangerously close to the carrier and on one occasion, when flying operations were under way, Captain Austin warned the vessel to keep clear of his ship. After leaving the Malta area *Hermes* and her shadow set course for Istanbul, and it was not until she approached the Dardanelles that the Russian destroyer finally left the carrier to make her way to Istanbul alone. Although the visit to the Turkish capital lasted for only four days it was long enough for the ship's company to stock up on suede and leather coats, and what seemed to be limitless supplies of Turkish Delight. After leaving the Dardanelles,

however, it was not long before the Kotlin-class destroyer joined her for the passage to Cyprus and once again she stayed close to *Hermes* until the carrier anchored off Limassol during the early hours of Sunday 24 May. The eight days off the Cypriot port were marked by extremely long boat journeys to and from the ship, and the arrest of a Cypriot civilian who had managed to get on board and hide himself in the island superstructure. After sailing on 1 June *Hermes* rendezvoused with the frigate *Yarmouth* and her Kotlin-class shadow, which was soon joined by the cruiser *Oktyabrskaya Revolutsiya*. Both Soviet ships followed *Hermes* to the area off Malta and into the Ionian Sea where the two British units joined US and Italian ships, including USS *Forrestal*, the Italian helicopter cruiser *Andrea Doria*, the destroyer *Impavido* and the frigate *Canapo*, for 'Exercise Dawn Patrol'. The exercise was concluded off the coast of Greece on 15 June and after *Hermes* was detached for the return passage to Portsmouth, her Soviet shadow finally left her. During the return voyage one of the helicopters gave assistance to the small coaster, MV *Earner*, which had run into difficulties with machinery problems in heavy weather. In the event a salvage team and equipment were lowered onto the vessel, but this did not delay *Hermes* and on 18 June she anchored briefly in Gibraltar Bay. Next day, as the carrier steamed up the coast of Portugal, all the fixed-wing aircraft were flown off to their bases, and after passing Ushant on 21 June the helicopters of 814 Squadron were flown off to Culdrose. At 3.30pm on Monday 22 June, after embarking families at Spithead, *Hermes* secured alongside Portsmouth's Middle Slip Jetty. It was the end of the commission and, it seemed, the end of her career as a fixed-wing aircraft carrier.

In the immediate future, however, she was to be decommissioned and on the day that the Ensign was lowered Captain Austin entertained four of his predecessors, Captain Tibbits, Admiral Sir William O'Brien, Rear-Admiral Parker and Captain Fieldhouse, on board. Three days later tugs towed *Hermes* to Pitch House Jetty where destoring began and most of her ship's company were drafted to other ships. It appeared that there were three options for her future and she would either be sold to a foreign navy, sold for scrap or, possibly, be converted to a commando carrier.

Chapter Ten

The Commando Carrier
July 1970 – April 1976

Following her return to Portsmouth in June 1970 *Hermes* faced an uncertain future for it was not known whether she would ever again be recommissioned. However, after being destored and paid off there was a glimmer of hope for her indicated by the fact that a small care and maintenance party was left aboard in order to carry out essential work on the carrier. Fortunately, although the Government had decided to strip the Fleet Air Arm of its fixed-wing aircraft carriers, there were no plans to scale down the commitment to amphibious warfare and it was decided that in 1973 *Hermes* would replace her half-sister *Albion* as a commando carrier. It was also confirmed that the conversion work would be carried out by Devonport Dockyard, and in October 1970 she was towed from Portsmouth down Channel to Devonport to prepare for her transformation.

As a commando carrier, and as successor to HMS *Albion, Hermes'* principal role would be to carry a Royal Marines Commando with the ability to land men at short notice in support of NATO operations, while her secondary role would be providing anti-submarine support for the fleet. She would be equipped with Wessex V and Sea King helicopters and the conversion work began in

March 1971. It was a major undertaking for Devonport Dockyard, lasting two years and costing over £12 million, being the biggest dockyard contract since the modernization of *Ark Royal,* which had also been completed at Devonport, in 1969. The work involved the removal of the steam catapults and arrester wires as well as the distinctive Type 984 CDS radar with its huge 'searchlight' antenna. The latter was replaced with the Type 965 long-range air search radar, with its 'bedstead' antenna which was placed on its own purpose-built mast above the bridge. Other radar aerials fitted included Types 993 and 978, all of which gave the ship a greater ability to detect aircraft and missiles. Down below, the hangar was adapted to take heavy transport and light armoured vehicles, as well as the Wessex and Sea King helicopters. New mess decks were constructed which were more spacious and comfortable than those of her predecessors. The air-conditioning system was improved and a complex of storage compartments for the commando stores was built in the after section of the ship. This meant that assault routes would differ from those in *Albion* and *Bulwark,* with 'sticks' of troops making their way to the flight deck by way of the after lift. In order to house the four landing craft which *Hermes* would carry new sponsons were built,

Hermes alongside at Devonport in March 1973. Her conversion to a commando carrier is almost complete.
(Maritime Photo Library)

and on the port side this meant cutting away a section of the angled flight deck in order to make room for the davits. The galleys, bakery and laundry were all completely modernized in order that they could cope with the additional complement and in the main machinery spaces the remote-control systems were updated and an automatic feed system was installed in the ship's main boilers. This allowed the whole ship's company to take shelter in the 'citadel' if it ever became necessary to steam through a nuclear fallout cloud. Finally, her flight deck was strengthened in order that she could operate the British Aerospace Sea Harrier which at that time was still under development.

Despite industrial problems in the dockyard, by early 1973 most of the work had been completed and on Monday 26 February *Hermes'* new commanding officer, Captain C. R. P. C. Branson RN, was appointed to the ship. Captain Branson had entered the Royal Navy as a cadet during the Second World War, and in 1941 he served in the elderly light cruiser *Dragon* in the Far East. During this time she escorted troop convoys to the beleaguered garrison at Singapore, and after the fall of the island to the Japanese she joined Dutch Admiral Helfrich's Western Striking Force based on Tanjong Priok. It was only her slow speed which prevented her from taking part, and almost certainly being sunk, in the Battle of the Java Sea. On the last day of February 1942 *Dragon*, together with *Danae*, HMAS *Hobart* and the destroyers *Scout* and *Tenedos*, was ordered to search for a Japanese invasion force off Muntok Island. However, as the convoy was escorted by five Japanese heavy cruisers and destroyers, it is fortunate that they were not located. Later in the war Captain Branson specialized in submarines, and in 1944 he returned to the Far East in HMS/m *Sea Rover*. In the early 1950s he served as the First Lieutenant of the destroyer *Defender*, and as the Commanding Officer of HMS *Roebuck*. In the early 1960s he was the Executive Officer of the aircraft carrier *Victorious*, followed by command of the shore establishment HMS *Rooke* at Gibraltar, and the Leander-class frigate *Phoebe*. His appointment to *Hermes* came after a spell as the Naval Attaché in Paris.

Once converted *Hermes* was capable of operating any kind of helicopter or VTOL aircraft such as the Harrier. When operating in her dual role she carried an amphibious force, and the helicopters and landing craft needed to put it ashore, as well as a number of Sea King anti-submarine helicopters. She was officially designated as a 'Landing Platform Helicopter' (LPH), but was more commonly known as a commando ship. When operating in the LPH role with Wessex V helicopters embarked, *Hermes* could take on board at very short notice a full Commando Group, which included a Royal Marines Commando Detachment. This force could be landed and be fighting as a comprehensive unit within two hours, before the ship had even appeared over the horizon, and the force could then be supported for a considerable time. On occasions *Hermes* could operate entirely as an anti-submarine ship, in which case only Sea King helicopters were embarked. Like her half-sister, HMS *Bulwark*, and the assault ships *Fearless* and *Intrepid*, which carried heavy transport and military equipment, *Hermes* afforded NATO peace-keeping forces the capacity to intervene swiftly and effectively in a wide range of situations. Her ship's company now consisted of 980 officers and men and, when operating in the LPH role, she would have one of four Royal Marines Commandos embarked, together with a Commando Battery of the Royal Artillery and a Commando Troop, Royal Engineers, whose organization included a flight of Sioux helicopters.

In early May 1973, with her ship's company having been brought up to full strength, *Hermes* put to sea under her own steam for the first time in three years to carry out her post-refit trials. Although they were completed successfully there was one genuine emergency when 250 gallons of Avcat was spilled in the hangar, but fortunately, after the ship went to 'Emergency Stations', the incident was dealt with efficiently and no lasting damage was done. Meanwhile, at Culdrose, 814 Squadron, which had been disbanded in July 1970, was recommissioned with four anti-submarine Sea King helicopters for service in the new commando carrier. A few weeks later, on 19 July, Tiverton Borough Council, which had adopted the ship in 1968, conferred the Freedom of the Borough on the officers and men of *Hermes*, 'in recognition of the glorious achievements of the Royal Navy both in peace and war and in appreciation of the close and cordial association between HMS *Hermes* and this town.' The association had begun in 1959 when Tiverton's Sea Cadets unit was renamed TS *Hermes*, to coincide with the ship's first commissioning. The friendship grew until the carrier had been formally adopted and the freedom ceremony, appropriately, was attended by Vice-Admiral Sir Terence Lewin who at the time was the Vice-Chief of Naval Staff, and 200 members of the ship's company marched through the streets with bayonets fixed. As the last platoon passed the saluting base, aircraft from RNAS Yeovilton and Wessex helicopters of 707 Squadron roared above in a fly-past over the town. The ceremony concluded with the formal presentation of a scroll and an engraved casket.

The ship's recommissioning ceremony took place on Saturday 18 August 1973, and the guest of honour was Lady Mary Soames, whose mother, Lady Churchill, had launched the ship 20 years earlier. Principal guests included four of the five officers who had commanded the carrier since her first commissioning in 1959 - Captain D. S. Tibbits, who was by then a Principal Elder Brother of Trinity House; Admiral Sir William O'Brien; Vice-Admiral Sir Terence Lewin, who was about to become C-in-C Fleet, and Rear-Admiral P. M. Austin, Flag Officer Naval Air

With her conversion over *Hermes* steams out of Devonport to sea. Here she is passing The Hoe and steaming into Plymouth Sound.

(Keith Wood)

Command. More than 2,000 relatives and friends of the ship's company packed into the colourfully decorated hangar where Captain Branson read the Commissioning Warrant, the Ensign was hoisted and the masthead pendant was broken. This was followed by a short religious service which included the Act of Dedication, the ancient Gaelic Blessing and the Naval Prayer. During the ceremony Lady Soames was presented with a vase bearing the ship's badge before she cut the magnificent commissioning cake, which was lavishly decorated with *Hermes* and Squadron badges. That evening a dance was held in HMS *Drake,* which was attended by some 700 officers, ratings, wives, parents and friends. In all it had been a successful and memorable day.

During the period that *Hermes* remained alongside at Devonport Dockyard she was again in the news when 700 schoolchildren took part in a sponsored walk round the flight deck, raising £2,500 for disabled children's charities. On 20 August the commando carrier's four landing craft, together with the Royal Marines Detachment, made an 11-hour journey from Devonport to Poole to take part in the Freedom of the Borough celebrations. Fortunately, with a calm sea the passage there was smooth, but on the way back a choppy sea made for a very uncomfortable journey. On 17 September, however, it was down to work in earnest when *Hermes*, flying the flag of Rear-Admiral R. D. Lygo (FOCAS), sailed for 'Exercise Swift Move'. The exercise was designed to work the ship up in her anti-submarine role, and for this purpose she carried 16 Sea Kings from 814, 819 and 824 Squadrons, and four Wessex Vs from the resident 845 Squadron. The helicopters flew in excess of 900 hours during the three-week exercise, but perhaps the most excitement was caused by a Soviet Kanin-class destroyer, 252, which suffered a fire on board while shadowing *Hermes* and in order to prevent an explosion fired off a torpedo from its starboard torpedo tubes. Fortunately this did not hit any of the ships involved in the exercise and for a time the Royal Navy turned the tables on their Russian follower by closely watching the efforts to extinguish the blaze. RO Keith Wood remembers that *Hermes* contacted the destroyer by radio to ask if she required any assistance - not surprisingly the offer was refused. The exercise ended in Oslo on 11 October when *Hermes* steamed into the Norwegian capital for a four-day visit, during which the exercise wash-up was held. The Royal Marines Detachment were kept busy on the first day in the city when they paraded five Guards of Honour, one being a Royal Guard for King Olav who visited the ship in his capacity as an Honorary Admiral of the Royal Navy. During the stay the ship's football team played a local side from the NATO base near Oslo, but unfortunately nobody mentioned that they were also a Norwegian league team and *Hermes* lost the match by 13 goals. Happily the beer that flowed freely afterwards eased the pain somewhat.

On returning to Devonport *Hermes*' role was changed to

that of LPH and for the first time she embarked 45 Commando Royal Marines. This part of the work-up, in November 1973, was carried out off the Western Isles with 845 Squadron landing the 800 men on the Isle of Skye. To everyone's relief Christmas and New Year were spent alongside at Devonport where leave was taken by the ship's company. When *Hermes* was ready for sea again in late January 1974, sailing was delayed for 24 hours by strong winds and in the event she left harbour at the same time as *Bulwark,* sailing north for Rosyth to embark 45 Commando and to prepare for 'Exercise Clockwork 74', an important NATO exercise designed to protect the Alliance's northern flank by preventing a Soviet occupation of Norway which, in a war with the West, would allow free access to and from Murmansk by her nuclear submarine fleet. Winter training in Norway by NATO forces was considered to be very important, but when *Hermes* arrived at Rosyth to embark the Commando Group, gale force winds were sweeping the area and it was thought that 'Clockwork' might have to be abandoned. After dragging her anchors in the Firth of Forth and spending an anxious night manoeuvring in the confined waters west of the Forth Bridge, *Hermes* was finally able to put to sea and set course with the other units for northern Norway where 45 Commando were to be landed by air in an area between Narvik and the North Cape. Once again severe gale force winds, which at times were blowing at speeds in excess of 63 knots, threatened the exercise, but the powers that be considered it too important to abandon and so, in atrocious weather conditions, the Royal Marines were successfully landed.

Meanwhile, however, the severe gales and blinding snowstorms were taking their toll on shipping from the Bay of Biscay to the Arctic Circle. During the afternoon of Friday 8 February, the 1,100-ton Hull-based trawler *Gaul,* which had been designed and built to operate in northern latitudes in all weathers, was reported missing, together with her 36-man crew north of the Arctic Circle. Despite the Force 12 gales and blinding snow blizzards, a full-scale air and sea search was set in motion and *Hermes* and her escorts steamed north to search an area off northern Norway which lay within the Arctic Circle. Keith Wood remembers the incident thus: 'We were ordered to head north from the coast of Norway to search for the trawler *Gaul.* With us was our escort HMS *Nubian* and an RFA, which I think was *Retainer.* As we steamed northwards the rough seas became mountainous, and I remember that *Nubian* and the RFA were ordered back towards the coast. The flight deck and all the weather decks were placed out of bounds, but this did not include us as we had been issued with Arctic clothing and we had to continue using the signal deck. The ship was being buffeted by enormous waves and at one point I heard both propellers racing as they came right out of the water. One morning I went up to the bridge and saw the huge waves crashing over the bows and rolling right aft down the flight deck and over the stern. We steamed right round Bear Island in this appalling weather, but after the search was called off we steamed south to calmer waters. When the severe weather had eased it was discovered that 30 feet of the flight deck walkways had been broken away on both sides of the ship, together with some of the metal storage lockers. On one of the sponsons it was found that one of the sea boats was missing after having been swept from its davits. It was clear from the ferocity of the seas that *Gaul* would have stood little chance of surviving the storm.'

Although an orange marker buoy was spotted off Bear Island, when *Hermes* moved in for a closer examination it was found that it did not come from the missing trawler. Despite the atrocious conditions, with snow being driven by hurricane-force winds, low cloud and poor visibility, over 25 vessels joined in the search for the trawler, including Soviet naval vessels. By Friday 15 February, however, with no trace having been found of the *Gaul* or her 36-man crew, the search was called off. It was clear that the trawler had foundered in the hurricane-force winds and mountainous seas which were raging at the time, and that no one could have survived such conditions. For *Hermes* a return to calmer waters meant that some repairs could be made before 45 Commando was re-embarked and the commando carrier returned to Portsmouth to carry out a dockyard assisted maintenance period.

Hermes' next deployment, to the Mediterranean, was made by way of Hamburg, a port she had last visited during October 1966, so for many it was an introduction to the dubious delights of the Reeperbahn. After arriving in Malta in early April *Hermes* spent three weeks undergoing maintenance as well as her Harbour Inspection by Rear-Admiral A. D. Cassidi, FOCAS, before sailing on 22 April with 41 Commando embarked to take part in a series of NATO exercises. As a work-up to the main exercise, 'Dawn Patrol', a small-scale exercise code-named 'Double Base 2/74', involving units from Greece, Italy, Turkey and the United States, took place off Cyprus. Three days later *Hermes* anchored off Dhekelia in perfect weather conditions to carry out a helicopter landing of the marines and their vehicles into the Troulli training area where, for three days, they were engaged in a fast moving exercise which involved a night march, a commando attack and a helicopter withdrawal back to the ship. Then, on 28 April, three days after first sighting Cyprus, *Hermes* sailed to join the rest of the NATO task force off Greece to begin the main exercise of the deployment which ranged from Kalamata Bay and Kyparissia in southern Greece to Cape Teulada in Sardinia, via the Strait of Messina.

After re-embarking 41 Commando following their 'invasion' of Sardinia, *Hermes* steamed west out of the Mediterranean to make a transatlantic crossing, bound for New Brunswick, Canada, where the marines were landed to take part in 'Exercise Black Swan'. Whilst they were ashore *Hermes* herself exercised off the east coast of the USA and visited Halifax, Nova Scotia. Once 41 Commando were back on board, together with 845 Squadron and Canadian HS 50 (Sea King) helicopters, *Hermes* left Canadian waters for the warmer weather off Bermuda to take part in the annual Canadian 'Exercise Marcot', and a short visit to the island of Bermuda itself. This was followed by the highlight of the deployment, a five-day visit to New York which coincided with the 4th July Independence Day celebrations. Misty weather on arrival soon gave way to sunshine and on 'Open to Visitors' day more than 3,000 people queued in sweltering heat to board the carrier while the New York Police assisted with security precautions. As always the ship's company enjoyed very generous hospitality along with plenty of sporting events, and they even found the shop prices not too exorbitant. The fact that 41 Commando were ashore was realized only too clearly by two New York 'muggers' who selected as a likely victim a 'tourist' who happened to be a fit young commando. On this occasion the attackers were well and truly 'floored'. Visitors to the ship included two stars of Broadway stage productions, Lynn Redgrave and Jim Dale, who supervised the ship's prize draw for a Mini motor car. Perhaps the most popular visitors were two beauty queens, Miss New York and from Bristol in the UK, Miss Avon County, who was visiting the city as part of her prize. Also joining *Hermes* for this visit was the Royal Marines band from *Ark Royal* who impressed everyone with their displays, including open-air performances in Rockerfeller Plaza.

After leaving New York *Hermes* steamed east once again, bound for Malta where 41 Commando were to be disembarked before the ship herself returned to the UK. However, after entering the Mediterranean world politics dictated a change in her itinerary when, on 20 July, Turkish troops invaded the north-east coast of Cyprus ostensibly to protect the minority Turkish-Cypriot population following the overthrow of the President, Archbishop Makarios, by Greek Cypriot troops. The situation escalated from a local to an international crisis when Greece mobilized its Army and Moscow, always a traditional ally of Greece, put its troops on alert. As well as having two Sovereign Base Areas at Akrotiri and Dhekelia, Britain, as the former colonial power, had strong ties with and interests in Cyprus, in addition to which the island was of course very popular with British holidaymakers and ex-patriots looking for a place in the sun. That evening, after receiving orders from London, Captain Branson announced to the ship's company that *Hermes* was being diverted to Cyprus where he would take charge of a naval task group which included HM Ships *Andromeda*, *Devonshire* and *Rhyl*, and RFA *Olna*, which would be stationed off the island. Meanwhile,

Wessex helicopters ranged on the newly arranged flight deck.

(Keith Wood)

Hermes in her LPH role in the Firth of Forth.   *(John Proverbs)*

ashore, some 4,500 civilian refugees, including British, American, French, German, Italian and Russian nationals, had been caught up in the fighting as the Turkish Army advanced rapidly towards Nicosia. In the capital itself sniper fire was soon making the city a very dangerous place and the British High Commission quickly organized a convoy escorted by the British Army's Ferret armoured cars, under United Nations command, to make the 35-mile journey to the base at Dhekelia. As well as *Hermes* and her group the US Navy sent the helicopter carrier *Inchon* and a number of other warships to stand off the south coast of the island. However, although the organized evacuations were getting most refugees to safety, on the north-east coast of Cyprus fighting around Kyrenia was bitter and at least two elderly Britons were killed in the battle. This fighting caused more than 1,500 refugees to make for the beaches of Kyrenia where they hoped to find refuge and, possibly evacuation. Meanwhile, British armoured vehicles were escorting more people to the area and as they waited on the exposed beaches in the hot Mediterranean sun the lack of food and fresh water rapidly made itself felt, but fortunately help was on the way. As soon as *Hermes* arrived

off the south coast of Cyprus, 41 Commando was deployed ashore to reinforce the Sovereign Base Areas and the commando carrier remained in the area to provide support for them. However, as soon as the plight of the refugees at Kyrenia was known, Captain Branson ordered his force to steam round to the north coast in order to evacuate the hapless civilians from the war zone. Keith Woods remembers the events: 'Not knowing what the reaction of the Turkish forces would be to our arrival, as we neared the coast the LCVPs and Wessex helicopters had large Union Flags painted on them and were ordered to "Action Stations". Captain Branson gave us regular briefings over the tannoy as to what was happening, and at one point as we closed the island I watched Turkish aircraft bombing a hillside village. It seemed very unreal and was almost like watching a war film and I had to remind myself that this was in earnest.'

Originally it had been planned to evacuate the refugees using the ship's boats and the LCVPs, and all boats' crews were issued with white overalls which was to be the rig for the operation. However, after all the preparation of getting the boats ready the weather deteriorated and even more

Black smoke belches from the Russian Kanin-class destroyer 252's funnel as she suffers a serious fire whilst shadowing *Hermes* during 'Exercise Swift Move' on 7 October 1973. *(Keith Wood)*

worrying for Captain Branson, reports came in that the beach designated for the evacuation had been mined. In the event it was decided to use the Wessex helicopters of 845 Squadron to carry out the main evacuation, with the LCVPs providing a back-up service. Keith Wood takes up the story again: 'We were ordered to approach Kyrenia beach where all European nationals had been directed for evacuation and as we closed the beach our helicopters and LCVPs made numerous trips to evacuate the people there. The helicopters brought the injured first and I can remember that those who were suffering from gunshot and shrapnel wounds were taken straight to the sickbay. Preparations were made for the evacuees to be billeted in the commando mess decks, but there were so many that alternative bunks had to be found in any available spaces. We eventually received over 900 people from ashore and there were some enormous queues for the dining hall and the NAAFI. They remained on board overnight whilst we ferried them round to the base at Akrotiri and we Communications staff sent hundreds of telegrams by morse code to inform their friends and relatives that they were

safe. I distinctly remember one of these telegrams just said, "Thank God for the British Navy", which was sent to the relatives of some American refugees.'

In all *Andromeda* evacuated 195 people, *Devonshire* came away with 197 evacuees, *Rhyl* 55 and *Olna* 188, but *Hermes* with her 20 troop-carrying helicopters rescued an impressive 919 people. After disembarking the refugees at Akrotiri, where they were taken to the RAF base, *Hermes* was ordered to re-embark 41 Commando by LCVP and return them to Malta which was achieved without incident. While they disembarked in Grand Harbour, the ship's company were given a few hours' leave in order to buy any last-minute presents before *Hermes* left for Devonport. For their part in the evacuation Rear-Admiral Cassidi sent the following signal to the units: 'Your well-conducted operation has been widely acclaimed and reflects the highest traditions of naval service and support for those in danger. I am delighted by the way all concerned rose to the occasion during such an anxious period. Well done.'

During her six weeks alongside in Devonport summer leave was given and the ship took her place in Plymouth's

Navy Days, before it was down to work again to begin 'Exercise Northern Merger' in the area off Denmark. The two-week exercise, which was staged in the latter half of September, was an important NATO event set in the eastern Atlantic and North Sea, culminating in an amphibious phase in the Jutland area of Denmark. Commodore D. T. Smith, Commodore Amphibious Forces, flew his Broad Pendant in *Hermes* and originally it had been intended that 40 Commando would provide the major part of the landing force. With their deployment in Cyprus, however, they were replaced at short notice by 1 Amphibious Combat Group, Royal Netherlands Marine Corps, popularly known on board as the 'Cloggies', whose original contribution was to have been one company under the command of 40 Commando. Before steaming north there was a brief visit to Rotterdam where the 'Cloggies' were embarked and it reflected well on the ship's company that they were able to settle quickly into the ship's routine with very few problems. *Hermes* and *Fearless* started the exercise with a rehearsal landing on to the Barry Buddon training area in Scotland on 18/19 September, when the 15 hours ashore proved to be a useful prelude to the main landing. This was followed by a six-day opposed transit in gradually deteriorating weather conditions, after which the main amphibious landing took place at the Oksbol training area on the Jutland Peninsular of Denmark. Poor weather conditions considerably hampered operations, and this was aggravated by shallow coastal waters and a very real mine threat, a leftover from the Second World War. In the event both *Hermes* and *Fearless* had to operate further off shore than had been planned, which slowed down the build-up ashore. The land phase, which was controlled by the Danish Army, lasted for three days and they provided a good 'enemy'. Meanwhile, at sea more than 150 ships were exercised in anti-submarine warfare, minelaying and countermeasures, control of merchant shipping and anti-aircraft warfare. After the exercise the participating forces gathered in Copenhagen for the wash-up and to sample the city's lager, but after six days there were few on board who had any money left. After leaving Denmark there was a brief pause to fly off the 'Cloggies' before the commando ship returned to Devonport to carry out maintenance.

When she left Plymouth Sound again *Hermes* had on board the Royal Marines of 42 Commando and this time her destination was the Lulworth Cove area of Dorset where she joined 'Exercise County Fair'. This time the amphibious landings involved a great deal of LCVP work while the units were landed and resupplied for two days as they assaulted the Purbeck Hills. Once the landing exercise was over *Hermes* carried out various manoeuvres in the Channel before the next phase of the trip which was a visit to Cherbourg before returning to Portsmouth. On Friday 8 November 1974, whilst the ship was in Portsmouth, there was a change of command when Captain D. R. Reffell RN

took over from Captain Branson. Captain Reffell had entered the Navy during the Second World War and in the years between 1946 and 1963 he served in various ships on the Home, Mediterranean, West Indies and Far East Stations. After commanding the Leander-class frigate *Sirius* in 1966, and after a spell on the Naval Staff at the Admiralty, he was appointed to *Hermes*. With very little time to settle down to his new command it was not long before the commando carrier was at sea again, and this time it was to exercise in her anti-submarine role with the Sea Kings of 824 Squadron and two helicopters from 819 Squadron embarked. The exercises, which took the form of a Joint Maritime Course (JMC), saw *Hermes* back off the coast of Scotland and then in the English Channel where an unusual helicopter landing took place. Just completing his Commando Operational Flying Training was HRH Lt The Prince of Wales, who carried out deck landing practice on board prior to his joining 845 Squadron and *Hermes* in 1975. Following this the commando carrier returned to Devonport for an extended docking period, during which there were many changes to the ship's personnel affecting both officers and ratings.

During the docking period at Devonport Christmas and New Year leave was taken and the BBC broadcaster and popular disc jockey, Jimmy Saville, visited the ship in December to record an episode in his series 'Saville's Travels', which was broadcast nationwide on Sunday 22 December. After what was a busy docking period *Hermes* left Devonport on 26 February 1975 to undergo sea trials, but a few days later she returned for adjustments to her machinery. The return to Devonport, however, was for only four days, which amounted to a long weekend alongside before, on Monday 10 March, flying the Broad Pendant of Commodore D. T. Smith, *Hermes* sailed for her next deployment, this time to the Caribbean and Canada for 'Westlant 42'. Embarked for the deployment were 42 Commando and 845 Squadron, the latter with its new pilot, HRH Lt The Prince of Wales. Also under Commodore Smith's command were four frigates and, once they reached the Caribbean, four US and four Dutch units. The first major exercise, 'Rum Punch', began on 29 March when the US Navy's 39th Marine Amphibious Unit was embarked and several different types of American helicopter began operating from *Hermes*, including the Bell HUI (Huey). During the exercise 42 Commando, together with units of the US and Netherlands Marine Corps, were landed on a remote Caribbean island where, according to their version of events, they did not spend their time sunbathing, but were engaged in some gruelling exercises. This was followed by a visit to Willemstad on the Dutch island of Curacao and then 'Exercise Van Gogh' with Dutch forces that concluded with a visit to Oranjestad on Curacao's neighbouring island of Aruba. In more ways than one, however, Fort Lauderdale was the hottest place visited during the deployment and as well as the generous hospitality offered there were visits to Cape Kennedy and Disneyworld, both of which were much appreciated. *Hermes*' arrival in the port received a large amount of publicity, with 845 Squadron staging a fly-past with the Stars and Stripes, the Union Flag, the White Ensign and 42 Commando's flags flying below them. As always in the USA the hospitality was overwhelming and for most members of the ship's company it was the most memorable run ashore of the deployment.

After leaving Florida *Hermes* steamed north through heavy seas and strong winds for Canada, where 845 Squadron flew ashore to Gagetown, New Brunswick, and 42 Commando deployed to St John, to make their way overland to Gagetown. *Hermes* herself went into the Canadian Navy Yard at Halifax, Nova Scotia, where she underwent two weeks' maintenance. It was said that after

the visit the Dick Turpin Bar in Halifax would never be the same again. After recovering 845 Squadron at sea, and going alongside in St John, New Brunswick, to embark 42 Commando, the commando carrier made the 200-mile passage up the St Lawrence River for official visits to Montreal and, on her return passage, to Quebec. Although it was the ship's first passage along the St Lawrence River, her predecessor HMS *Albion* had steamed as far as Quebec in 1972, and some of the bridges between that city and Montreal were a tight squeeze for *Hermes*, but the masthead came through it intact. During the visit to Montreal coach trips were arranged to the Niagara Falls and for the passage back down to Quebec the British High Commissioner and his staff were embarked. As *Hermes* steamed downriver the VIPs, and the residents of the area, were treated to a flying display by 845 Squadron. After her eventful passage of the river *Hermes* arrived in Quebec on the morning of

Hoses are played onto the Russian destroyer's torpedo tubes in order to prevent an explosion. *(Keith Wood)*

Hermes at Bermuda during a WESTLANT deployment.   *(Keith Wood)*

Wednesday 11 June and berthed at Wolfe's Cove, beneath the Heights of Abraham. The visit to Quebec was noted for the infamous incident in which *Hermes* was 'impounded' by a writ issued by the Federal Court of Canada. It all started when two members of the ship's company, a sick berth attendant and a marine, were involved in a brawl with a local man. The individual concerned took a private civil action against the pair and a Federal Registrar issued a writ 'impounding' *Hermes* until charges against the two members of the ship's company had been heard. However, after taking legal advice, Captain Reffell learned that a writ brought by a Federal Court 'could not be served on a sovereign ship of HM Forces.' Under various agreements such matters could only be handled by the respective governments involved and, on Monday 16 June, as scheduled, *Hermes* left Quebec to return to Devonport. The two errant members of the ship's company were not so lucky as they had been remanded to the city's prison until their case was heard. In the event the story ended happily when they were acquitted of all charges.

During the eastbound transatlantic crossing various sponsored events took place on the flight deck, including a 'village fete' which raised £1,500 in all for the Riding for the Disabled Association. In those days that was a large sum of money and it reflected the enthusiasm and dedication of the ship's company. *Hermes* arrived back in Plymouth Sound on the morning of Thursday 26 June, when 845 Squadron were flown off to Culdrose and 45 Commando was disembarked. It was the end of the Prince of Wales' association with the ship, and he paid a farewell visit at Devonport to present two crystal decanters, each engraved with the words, 'Red Dragon at Sea - February to June 1975', his own crest and the ship's badge. For *Hermes* a nine-week maintenance period lay ahead, during which summer leave was taken and the ship herself took part in Navy Days.

It was on Monday 1 September 1975 that *Hermes* left Devonport to embark 814 Squadron and set course for Gibraltar where a strong contingent from the ship's company took part in the 'Rock Race', a course of three miles which climbs from sea level to 1,200 feet. From Gibraltar she steamed east to Malta where 41 Commando was embarked and the ship took part in the biggest amphibious landings on NATO's southern flank for ten years. The exercise, code-named 'Deep Express', included a task force of 30 ships, including *Hermes* and *Bulwark* as

Replenishment at sea with a US Navy fleet auxiliary and destroyer.
(Keith Wood)

board for a party. They had been due to attend RFA *Olwen,* but her arrival in Malta was delayed and *Hermes'* ship's company agreed, at short notice, to honour the *Olwen's* invitation. The day's programme included trips round Grand Harbour in landing craft, a cartoon film show in the hangar and a splendid tea. On a less happy note, however, on Tuesday 14 October helicopters from 814 Squadron helped to search for survivors from an air accident. The tragedy happened when an RAF Vulcan bomber from No 9 Squadron at RAF Waddington near Lincoln was on a training flight to RAF Luqa in Malta. The aircraft got into difficulties over Malta and the pilot tried to make an emergency landing, but he had to abandon the attempt when the plane's undercarriage fell off. Soon after this the Vulcan exploded in a ball of flame and much of the wreckage fell onto the village of Zabbar, a mile south-east of Valletta. Sadly one young woman in the village was killed and 15 people were injured when burning debris fell on a busy street, but fortunately it just missed a local primary school. Both pilots were able to bale out from the plane and they were picked up from the sea by one of 814 Squadron's helicopters, but five other crew members were killed outright.

The visit to Malta was followed by a brief return to Devonport to take on board the Sea Kings of 819, 826 and 737 Squadrons in readiness for the ASW role. *Hermes* then steamed north to take part in exercises 'Moby Dick' and 'Ocean Safari' in the North Atlantic and Denmark Strait, where the BBC presenter Richard Baker visited the ship in his capacity as a Lt-Commander RNR. He spent two weeks at sea with the fleet and on board *Hermes* he made his first-ever live broadcast during a NATO exercise. At just after sunset on 17 November, in near gale strength winds, high seas and sub-zero temperatures, whilst *Hermes* was just south of the Arctic Circle, a Sea King helicopter ditched and sank close to the ship. Rescue operations began immediately and one of the aircrew members was recovered by the SAR helicopter. The three other crew members were rescued by the sea boat which was called away, 'at the very limits of safe operating'. Despite the considerable risks to his own safety and that of his crew, the coxswain, Ldg Seaman Jefferies, handled the boat with great courage and skill, which resulted in a wholly successful rescue operation. The entire crew were commended for their efficiency in such difficult conditions, and in particular Ldg Seaman Jefferies for his high standards of leadership and seamanship.

well as *Intrepid* and the RFAs *Sir Tristram, Sir Percival, Sir Galahad, Sir Geraint* and *Bacchus,* with the destroyer *Antrim* and the frigate *Ashanti* forming part of the escort. Unusually, Rear-Admiral J. H. F. Eberle, FOCAS, who commanded the force, flew his flag in the USS *Daniels* and it was believed to be the first time that a British Admiral had flown his flag in a US ship during a major NATO exercise. The main amphibious landing took place at Saros Bay in Turkey and among the VIPs watching parts of the exercise were NATO's Supreme Allied Commander Europe, General Alexander Haig, and Frank Judd, the Defence Minister for the Navy. After the exercise the ships visited various ports in the area, with *Hermes* steaming through the Dardanelles and Sea of Marmara to Istanbul. This was followed by a 13-day maintenance period at Malta, where some 100 wives flew out to the island to join their husbands. During the visit 30 youngsters from a local children's home on the outskirts of Valletta were invited on

Landing exercises, and here a Wessex helicopter is lifting Landrovers ashore. *(Keith Wood)*

Meanwhile, back on shore, the Fleet Air Arm received some hopeful news when it was announced that the Navy was to operate sea-going versions of the Harrier fighter, reconnaissance and strike aircraft which would be flown initially from *Hermes* and later from the new 'through deck' cruisers (HM Ships *Invincible, Illustrious* and *Ark Royal*). It was apparent that some seven years after being stripped of her fixed-wing flying capability, *Hermes* would once again operate such aircraft, thereby breathing new life into the Fleet Air Arm. For *Hermes* the final exercise of 1975 was followed by Christmas and New Year leave at Devonport, together with maintenance.

Hermes left Devonport again on Monday 12 January 1976, a cold but clear day, and headed north for Arbroath where she embarked 45 Commando Group, together with all their Arctic equipment. Supporting 45 Commando,

Hermes took the role of the 'enemy' in the month-long NATO exercise, 'Atlantic Express', in northern Norway. As well as the Royal Marines she had on board the 16 Wessex V helicopters of 845 Squadron, four Sea Kings of 814 Squadron, and a company of the Netherlands Marine Corps. After steaming to Narvik, *Hermes* and 45 Commando took the role of 'Orange' force alongside Norwegian units and after disembarking her troops the ship sailed on exercise, with a visit to the port of Harstad. This was followed on 4 February by a visit to Cherbourg for five days and then to Portsmouth for eight days, where many were able to take a weekend break. On Wednesday 18 February, however, *Hermes* headed north once again to take part in various exercises, and for Arctic training the weather could not have been 'better', as it was the coldest winter in the region since 1912, with special protective clothing being required for those on flight deck duties. Short visits to Harstad and Narvik offered some relaxation, giving members of the ship's company a chance to do some skiing although beer at one pound a pint was a cheaper option. The last phase of the exercise on 10 March, code-named 'Atlas Express', involved 45 Commando Brigade in an amphibious assault in northern Norway and, finally, on 22 March, the Commandos disembarked at Rosyth. Then with the band of the Royal Marines on board, together with the Flag Officer Naval Air Command, *Hermes* sailed for a short, but very popular, visit to Copenhagen.

When she arrived at Spithead on 2 April from her trip to Denmark, over 150 VIPs and guests were embarked for the first of two 'Shop Window' sea days when, supported by HMS *Lowestoft* and RFA *Olna,* the commando carrier played host during two action-packed days when the displays ranged from small-arms fire to the operation of Sea Harriers from the flight deck, and from replenishment

exercises to rockets, bombs and Buccaneer and Phantom aircraft roaring overhead. Guests over the two days included MPs, naval attaches, senior officers, and a variety of cadets and press, radio and television reporters. The displays also included the firing of mortars and 4.5-inch guns, a hovercraft demonstration, an amphibious assault which kept the helicopter and LCVP crews busy, and a fly-past by an RAF Nimrod aircraft. With the sea days over *Hermes* embarked 70 sons of ship's company members and headed for Plymouth Sound where, on Thursday 8 April as a 'farewell' to the carrier as a commando ship, some 2,000 relatives and friends were embarked for a day at sea during which they were entertained by the Royal Marines Band and by flying displays. Later that day, with the ship alongside in Devonport, Easter leave began for the ship's company and *Hermes* commenced a six-month refit from which she would emerge with the prime role of anti-submarine warfare.

Evacuees being escorted by the Army to the beaches of Kyrenia during the Turkish invasion of Cyprus.   *(Keith Wood)*

Hermes in May 1975, carrying out a vertical replenishment with RFA *Regent*.

(George Mortimore/Action Photos)

Chapter Eleven

A Return To The Fixed-Wing Role
May 1976 – March 1980

Although the primary function of *Hermes* was to be that of anti-submarine warfare, she would retain her role of commando carrier as a secondary job and little was required to be carried out in the way of conversion work during her eight months in dockyard hands which accounted for most of 1976. In September that year, with the long hot summer having been spent in No 10 dry dock, the carrier was moved back alongside the sea wall as the autumn approached and the much needed rain arrived. On Tuesday 21 September her new commanding officer, Captain R. G. A. Fitch RN, joined the ship. Captain Fitch had graduated from the Royal Naval College, Dartmouth, in 1946 and during the 20 years which followed he spent a great deal of time at sea, perhaps most notably in the destroyer *Consort* during the Korean War. After qualifying as a navigator in 1956 he served as the Navigating Officer of the assault ship *Narvik* which acted as the headquarters ship for the 1957 series of British nuclear weapons tests in the Pacific Ocean. After serving in the destroyer *Camperdown* and the aircraft carrier *Victorious* he was promoted to Commander in 1966

and was appointed to command the frigate *Berwick* which was in the middle of a General Service Commission, joining the ship in July that year at Hong Kong. This command was followed by a spell on the staff of the Flag Officer, Second in Command, Far East Station, and a period at the Ministry of Defence in London. In 1973 he took command of the Leander-class frigate *Apollo,* and after 12 months on the staff of the First Sea Lord he was appointed to *Hermes*. It was an appropriate appointment for during his period at the Ministry of Defence he fought hard to promote the development of the Sea Harrier for the Fleet Air Arm and his period in command of *Hermes* would see the carrier take the first tentative steps towards operating these aircraft.

Just nine days after taking command of *Hermes,* on Thursday 30 September 1976, Captain Fitch and 120 officers and men, which included the Royal Marines Detachment, travelled to Tiverton to exercise their right, for the first time since the Freedom of the Borough had been conferred on them in 1973, to march through the town with band playing, Colour flying, swords drawn and bayonets fixed. During a civic lunch at the Town Hall Captain Fitch described the new primary role of anti-submarine warfare which *Hermes* would be taking on, with a secondary amphibious capability. The Colour was paraded by Lt B. Heston who, like his guard, AB M. Clarke and RO T. Weekes, was a Tivertonian. The Lady Mayoress took the salute in the town's Fore Street and following the parade Captain Fitch joined in a mayoral procession to the 900-year old St Peter's Church, where the ship's commission was re-dedicated during an inter-denominational service. Fifty younger members of the ship's company were invited to a meal at the East Devon Technical College, where

Hermes in her anti-submarine role during the late 1970s.   *(Derek Coombes)*

An anti-submarine Sea King, with its dipping sonar, leaves *Hermes*. Note the two Sea Harriers at the after end of the flight deck.
(Derek Coombes)

local girls organized a disco. Captain and Mrs Fitch visited a special *Hermes* display at the town's museum and later they were entertained to dinner by the Mayoress and her councillors. Despite the fact that it had been very wet and windy it had been a memorable day.

The refit was finally completed on Friday 10 December and the First Sea Lord, Admiral Sir Edward Ashmore, inspected the ship. Three days later on 13 December, *Hermes* left Devonport for her post-refit trials, but a week later she was back alongside and Christmas and New Year leave began. In January 1977 a further two weeks of sea trials were held in the Portland area and with a reduced ship's company there were less people on board to run and clean the ship, with a resultant increase in drudgery all round. For many who remembered her LPH days there was a certain amount of nostalgia, not for the dining hall queues, but for the 800-strong 'cleaning parties' who regularly used to take passage. During the trials the Sea

Kings of 814 Squadron operated from the ship, together with four Wessex V helicopters of 845 Squadron. In February 1977 *Hermes* operated in the Channel and South Western Approaches where, with four Harriers embarked, she was scheduled to carry out proving trials for the aircraft. In the event, however, the trials were curtailed because high winds, swell and poor visibility were affecting the tolerances to which the trials team wanted to work. From the South Western Approaches the carrier headed for the Moray Firth via the Irish Sea, but after two days an easterly gale caused problems and so she headed south in a beam sea to operate in calmer waters in the southern part of the North Sea. The trials were vitally important for the Royal Navy for the Sea Harrier was due to be accepted for service with the Fleet Air Arm in 1979, with the first fully operational squadron planned for embarkation in *Hermes* during 1980. With the Harrier trials completed *Hermes* paid a visit to Portsmouth which proved popular with most of the ship's company.

When the carrier put to sea again she carried out a mini work-up in the Portland area which concentrated on her anti-submarine role with the 12 Sea Kings of 814 Squadron, with each aircraft having the capacity of a frigate to find, monitor and, if necessary, destroy submarines. The requirement for the anti-submarine role would come at a time of direct tension between East and West, and *Hermes* would operate to keep the seas around Britain free of submarines to allow for the passage of seaborne reinforcements to Europe and the passage of imports into Britain. In a time of real global tension *Hermes* would operate in the eastern Atlantic, deploying her considerable potential where it was most needed. It was a new concept for the Navy, who had never before possessed such a capability to operate against submarines with such intensity from one ship. As she was also retaining her capability as a commando ship she still had the accommodation for a Commando Group, over and above her CVS complement. She also had the largest hangar in the Navy for holding Sea King and Wessex helicopters as well as commando transport, with a special brow for assisting the rapid embarkation of vehicles. She also retained her four LCVPs and an Amphibious Operations Officer, Assault Supply Officer and Officer Commanding Royal Marines, otherwise popularly known as 'Major Boots', 'Minor Boots' and 'Action Man' respectively. During the work-up both roles were practised and it was clear that *Hermes* was both the best anti-submarine and commando ship that the fleet possessed. By mid-March the intensive period of activity off Portland and the South Western Approaches had been completed and, despite gale force winds, 51 sorties were flown totalling some 15 hours of daytime and 31 hours of night flying, all in the space of five days.

Following her successful work-up *Hermes,* in company with HMS *Glamorgan* and RFA *Olwen,* steamed south to Gibraltar where a record number of men turned out for the 'Rock Race'. The winner, LAM Hetherington, completed the run in just under 22 minutes, and the Royal Marines Detachment, led by Lt Grant, took the departmental prize. Back on board 50 children from Hermes House at St Christopher's School in the colony were given an intensive tour of the ship which included the bridge and operations room, the flight deck and hangars, and one of the main engine rooms. To round off the visit they were entertained to tea in the Junior Rates' Dining Hall. After leaving Gibraltar *Hermes* and *Glamorgan* exercised off the south coast of France with French units, the main purpose of which was a tactical firing of Exocet missiles, all of which was observed by Admiral J. Tardy, the French C-in-C Mediterranean. Not to be outdone, *Hermes* joined in the firings with her Seacat missiles, which quickly shot down the pilotless target aircraft. Once the exercises were over *Glamorgan* paid a visit to the French island of Levante, near

Toulon, which is both the site of a military test range and a nudist colony, while *Hermes* put into Toulon itself where the ship's company were invited on tours of the French aircraft carrier *Foch* which were much appreciated. The handicapped children at the Renee Sabron Hospital in Toulon had particular cause to remember the visit, for the ship's volunteer band, together with 'Quadrangle', a pop group from a PO's mess, went to the hospital to play a two-hour programme of music for the children.

By the end of March both *Hermes* and *Glamorgan* were at Malta where the carrier spent two weeks undergoing self-maintenance. In early April an inter-ship Sports Day was held with the helicopters from *Hermes* flying in competitors from *Glamorgan, Hermione, Olwen* and *Regent.* The event was a great fun day, with FOCAS, Rear-Admiral W. D. M. Staveley, awarding the prizes and without doubt the most popular was the fancy dress prize which went to two members of the Stores Department who had disguised themselves as a pantomime horse. The availability of international passenger flights meant that some wives and girlfriends of ship's company members were able to fly out to Malta for the Easter break which was encompassed by the maintenance period. By mid-April, however, *Hermes* was ready for sea again and for three days between 20 and 22 April she exercised off Malta watched by the First Sea Lord and ex-*Hermes* captain, Admiral Sir Terence Lewin. During a lull in the exercises, on the evening of Thursday 21 April, a horse race meeting was held in the hangar and next day there was a fancy dress and kite flying competition, although the latter suffered from a distinct lack of even a slight breeze. The fancy dress competition saw Admiral Lewin totally 'outranked' by an 'Admiral of the World', alias Ldg Steward Griffiths, who was able to offer some 'words of wisdom' to *Hermes'* former commanding officer.

The final exercises of the Mediterranean deployment took place in the Tyrrhenian Sea where the ship reverted to her LPH role and carried out an amphibious assault with 41 Commando. This was followed by a visit to Naples where FOCAS was embarked and whilst the senior officers planned for the NATO exercise 'Dawn Patrol 77', the ship's company enjoyed trips to Pompeii and Rome. As a prelude to 'Dawn Patrol' *Hermes* took part in 'Exercise Determined Defenders' and both operations kept the helicopter crews extremely busy. Finally, with the exercises over, 41 Commando were picked up from their assault exercises on Sardinia and the carrier set course for Gibraltar and home, finally arriving in Devonport on Wednesday 25 May. Once alongside a delayed Easter leave could be taken and the ship herself started a four-week dockyard assisted maintenance period.

When *Hermes* sailed from Devonport again on Friday 17 June she had on board 70 sons of ship's company members, whose ages ranged from eight to 17 years, and she set course for Torbay where she anchored later in the

Dressed overall and with her ship's company manning the flight deck, *Hermes* looks very smart for the Queen's Silver Jubilee Fleet Review at Spithead.

(Derek Coombes)

day. In the sheltered waters off the south Devon resort of Torquay the ship's company prepared the carrier for the next big event in her career, the Queen's Silver Jubilee Review of the Fleet at Spithead. On Saturday 18 June the gangways were opened to visitors from the three holiday towns in Torbay, and on the following day visitors from Tiverton were shown round. Six days later *Hermes* left for Spithead to take her place next to HMS *Ark Royal* for the fleet review. On the day after her arrival a Families Day was held on board between 1.30pm and 6.30pm, although as she was at anchor, a minimum age of six years was set for children. The Fleet Review of 1977 was the first to be held at Spithead since the Queen's Coronation Review of 1953, and for the first time the memory of the battleship had finally been laid to rest. The fleet which assembled in 1977 had its origins in the 1966 decision to abandon plans for a new class of fleet aircraft carriers. The sole representative of these leviathans was *Ark Royal,* flying the flag of the C-in-C Fleet, Admiral Sir Henry Leach, but she had only another

18 months to serve before being withdrawn from service. It was *Hermes* in her dual anti-submarine and amphibious assault role, with the capability of operating Sea Harrier aircraft, that represented the future for the Fleet Air Arm, and she was flying the flag of FOCAS, Rear-Admiral W. D. M. Staveley. There were 180 ships anchored at Spithead for the Review, most of them representing the Royal Navy, while 20 were foreign and Commonwealth warships, and during the week of the Review hundreds of pleasure craft, among them even tiny canoes, arrived to see the ships at anchor. Monday 27 June was taken up with final rehearsals for the big day and the ship's company manned and cheered ship yet again, while RFA *Engadine* assumed the role of the royal yacht. Overhead 154 aircraft rehearsed their fly-past in an 'ER' and anchor formation, and shortly afterwards the pride of Britain's merchant fleet, the liner *QE2,* passed the review lines as she steamed out of the Solent on a voyage from Southampton to Cherbourg and New York.

A pilot's-eye view of the Silver Jubilee Fleet Review during the helicopter fly-past. *Hermes* is to the right of the photograph and *Ark Royal* is on the left. Also in the picture is the Australian aircraft carrier *Melbourne*.　　　*(Derek Coombes)*

Although everyone had hoped for a warm, sunny day, Tuesday 28 June dawned distinctly chilly and blustery, with a wind that at times reached 16 knots, but at least the threatened rain held off. The Review got under way with a 21-gun salute from seven warships as *Britannia,* led by the Trinity House Vessel *Patricia,* left Portsmouth Harbour. Unfortunately, the cold weather kept many of the expected sightseers away from Southsea seafront, but for two hours the royal yacht, dressed overall, cruised at eight knots down the 15-mile circuit of warships, while 30,000 sailors snapped to attention on deck, raised their caps and cheered as *Britannia* passed by. Because of the weather conditions the Fleet Air Arm fly-past had to be significantly reduced, and only 90 helicopters took part. On board *Hermes* there was a somewhat unusual reunion when five former commanding officers, Rear-Admiral Branson, Admiral Sir William O'Brien, Vice-Admiral Austin, Rear-Admiral Parker and Captain Reffell, joined Captain Fitch for a photo-call on the flight deck. The only former CO missing

was Captain Tibbits who was in Bermuda. At the end of the Review came the signal which many had been hoping for which read: 'In celebration of my Silver Jubilee and with the Royal and Commonwealth ships assembled at Spithead, Splice the Main Brace - Elizabeth R.'

Next day, as the ships left Spithead, *Hermes* weighed anchor and headed for the southern side of the Isle of Wight where she and *Ark Royal* led a steam past of 61 warships to acknowledge the retirement of the Chief of the Defence Staff, Admiral of the Fleet Sir Edward Ashmore, who was embarked in the destroyer HMS *Birmingham.* Once this duty had been performed *Hermes* set course for Plymouth where she embarked 42 Commando for an amphibious exercise, code-named 'Forest Venture', which involved landing them at exercise areas in the vicinity of the Kyle of Lochlash, on Scotland's west coast. This was followed closely on 4 July with an ASW exercise, 'Highwood', in the eastern Atlantic Ocean before 40 Commando was embarked for the second phase of 'Forest

Heavy weather in the Atlantic...

Venture' eight days later. During the exercise *Hermes* passed close enough to the isolated White Rock lighthouse, nine miles south-west of Land's End, to allow Admiral Staveley to visit in his capacity as a Younger Brother of Trinity House. As she steamed along the south coast towards Plymouth Sound 40 Commando and their vehicles were airlifted ashore to be landed on Dartmoor, whilst one of 814 Squadron's Sea Kings helped the Padstow lifeboat to rescue two people from their yacht, *Calcutta Princess,* which was in danger of sinking off the coast of north Cornwall. The end of the exercises came on Tuesday 19 July when, with the ship at anchor in Plymouth Sound, families were embarked for the passage up harbour where *Hermes* secured alongside at Devonport for a six-week maintenance period and summer leave.

The last week alongside was extremely busy with *Hermes* and *Ark Royal* heading Navy Days at Devonport, and on Wednesday 31 August *Hermes* left the port to rendezvous with HM Ships *Arrow, Antrim, Diomede* and *Kent,* and the RFAs *Resurgent* and *Tidereach,* before setting course west-south-west bound for Bermuda. It was not long before blue uniforms had disappeared into mothballed kit bags after whites were donned in the rising temperatures. On Sunday 4 September a sports competition was held on the flight deck with competitors being flown over from the accompanying ships. The fancy dress competition was won by the Royal Marines Detachment with a 'trot past' of the 'Royal Seaborne Cavalry' led by C/Sgt Cummings disguised as a 'Corporal of Sea Horse'. The ship's entry into Bermuda was held up by severe weather, but by 9 September *Hermes* had anchored and two of the LCVPs were soon ferrying sports teams and liaison officers ashore. No sooner were the teams into their respective games, however, than they received a recall which stated that because of an approaching hurricane named 'Clara' the ship was sailing at 5pm. Eventually, after riding out the storm for a day, *Hermes* returned to Bermuda for another 24 hours, the whole visit having been curtailed somewhat. After leaving her anchorage *Hermes* rendezvoused with her escorts for a 'Shop Window' display for the Government of

...lifts *Hermes* up and washes down the flight deck.

(Derek Coombes)

Bermuda, with her VIP guests including the Governor of the island, Sir Peter Ramsbotham. During the forenoon they toured the ship and watched a flying display, manoeuvres, firings and a five-ship replenishment at sea. After the guests had left the ship, *Hermes,* together with *Antrim, Tidereach* and *Resurgent,* headed south-west for Mayport, Florida, where they received a special welcome from the Jacksonville High School Band and some pretty majorettes on 14 September. Mayport will probably be remembered for two major tours, to Disneyworld and to NASA's space centre at Cape Canaveral, both of which were very popular.

After leaving Mayport, and on passage to Norfolk, Virginia, Harrier aircraft from the US Marine Attack Squadron (No 452), based at Cherry Point, North Carolina, operated from the ship and the Royal Marines Detachment were flown ashore to Camp Lejeune in North Carolina, to exercise with the US Marine Corps on their 'Environmental Combat Range', where they spent a day on field firing exercises, complete with steel helmets and flak jackets. On the following day, 24 September, *Hermes,* which was now wearing the flag of the Flag Officer First Flotilla, and the rest of her force, arrived in the US Naval Base at Norfolk, Virginia. For the Royal Marines Detachment there were the usual rounds of ceremonial guard duties, and between sports matches they managed to fit in a day's field firing and amphibious landings on the US Marine Corps' Little Creek beach exercise area. On sailing from Norfolk *Hermes'* group and US Navy units took part in 'Exercise Combined Effort', an anti-submarine exercise, on their two-week transatlantic crossing. This was followed by a four-day visit to Lisbon where *Hermes* anchored in the River Tagus just downriver from the Tagus Bridge and the Statue of Christ. The anchorage in mid-river meant that a boat routine was worked between the ship and the shore, but after 14 days at sea this was a minor inconvenience for most liberty men. The call at Lisbon was followed by another two weeks at sea for 'Exercise Ocean Safari', which ended on 28 October when *Hermes* steamed up Channel to spend a week alongside in Portsmouth for the post-exercise discussions, when no less than 41 Admirals visited the ship.

Before leaving Portsmouth on 7 November, the Junior Band of the Royal Marines was embarked for a five-day visit to Copenhagen where they performed at official functions and at the ship's open day which drew large crowds. It was the first time these talented young musicians had performed in public overseas and, according to the British Ambassador, they were very much appreciated. Finally, however, on Friday 18 November, having steamed over 48,000 miles during the year, with some 141 days having been spent at sea, *Hermes* arrived back in Devonport to carry out maintenance and for the ship's company to take their seasonal leave.

It was on Tuesday 17 January 1978 that *Hermes* left Devonport to embark 814 Squadron before steaming south for the warmer waters of the western Mediterranean where she carried out a short trials programme and work-up and made two visits to Gibraltar where she survived FOCAS's Harbour Inspection. During this period she also embarked six senior managers from Vickers Shipbuilders who were closely associated with the fitting out of the new light fleet carrier HMS *Invincible* (which was still, at that time, described as a through-deck cruiser) on the River Tyne. The team was led by Mr T. E. Blacklock, the outfitting manager, who had been on board *Hermes* when she was launched in 1953 and during her sea trials six years later. He had actually been Vickers' ship manager on board until the carrier was handed over to the Royal Navy, and now he and his team were spending their time in what was described as 'big ship familiarization', so they could transfer their ideas to *Invincible*. During her period in the western Mediterranean *Hermes,* together with *Antrim, Devonshire, Kent, Arrow, Yarmouth,* the submarines *Churchill* and *Oracle,* RNNS/m *Tiggerhaai,* and the RFAs *Olmeda, Olna* and *Resource,* took part in 'Exercise Spring Train', which was headed by HMS *Blake* wearing the flag of Flag Officer First Flotilla, Rear-Admiral Squire. During the exercise the First Sea Lord, Admiral Sir Terence Lewin, paid a visit to his old ship, and after arriving by Sea King from *Blake* he visited many sections of the carrier and met members of the ship's company. The exercise ended on 27 January, but a combination of strong winds and poor visibility prevented the carrier from berthing at Gibraltar in the forenoon and she was forced to spend an extra five hours at sea off the Rock, before returning to make a successful berthing alongside the south mole. The wind and rain associated with the depression swept north over the UK and that weekend it caused the postponement of many FA Cup ties.

Despite the fact that the break in Gibraltar lasted for only a long weekend it was time enough to stage a 'Rock Race' with the winner beating by 24 seconds his own time that he had set in March 1977. On the morning of Tuesday 31 January, *Hermes* and the 'Spring Train' force sailed from Gibraltar to continue their three-week weapons training exercise. *Hermes, Churchill* and RFAs *Olna* and *Resurgent* then experienced an extremely rough transatlantic crossing to Bermuda with a mid-Atlantic rendezvous with the frigate *Phoebe* for another WESTLANT deployment which took them to the Caribbean for 'Exercise Safe Pass', following which *Hermes* underwent a three-week assisted maintenance period in Mayport which, with its beaches, sunshine and, of course, Disneyworld, was a very popular destination. After leaving the Florida port *Hermes* returned to Bermuda and while there a change of command took place in the latter half of April.

On Saturday 22 April 1978, Captain D. C. Jenkin RN

(Derek Coombes)

Sea Harrier trials in November 1978. One of the aircraft shows off its landing versatility.

A Sea Harrier about to be launched with a short take-off.

(Derek Coombes)

relieved Captain Fitch in command of the carrier. Captain Jenkin had entered the Navy at the Royal Naval College, Dartmouth, in 1942 at the age of 13 and in 1953 he qualified in gunnery. In 1961 he commanded the frigate *Palliser* and in 1964 the destroyer *Cambrian,* followed by the Leander-class frigate *Galatea*. It was after a spell at the Ministry of Defence that he was appointed to *Hermes*. Soon after taking over command of the carrier Captain Jenkin put to sea for the transatlantic passage home with a NATO force during which 'Exercise Open Gate' took place. There was a brief stop at Gibraltar, but in early May *Hermes* arrived back in Devonport to undergo a three-month refit and dry docking.

The refit ended on Tuesday 15 August when *Hermes* sailed with 814 Squadron and a detachment of 707 Squadron for a short shakedown cruise and a 'Sons at Sea' weekend from Friday 18 to Sunday 20 August. The 72 boys, whose ages ranged from eight to 16 years, were embarked by LCVP outside Plymouth breakwater and taken to three mess decks where they were accommodated according to age, with two Leading Hands acting as 'Sea Daddies'. During their 36 hours at sea a programme of events was arranged with guided tours of the ship,

including machinery spaces. Wherever possible they ate their meals with their fathers and during the Saturday evening they had a film show in the hangar. Finally, on the morning of 20 August, after cleaning up their mess decks and having breakfast, they disembarked by LCVP for their journeys back home after what had been an exciting weekend. After dropping the boys off, 40 Commando was embarked and *Hermes* steamed round into the Bristol Channel to airlift the Royal Marines onto the exercise ranges at Castlemartin, Pembrokeshire, in an exercise code-named 'Noon Whisper'. Events were made somewhat more interesting when Sea King 272 of 814 Squadron, which was being flown by Lt Keith Dudley, ditched into the sea a mile south of Lundy Island. The aircraft was returning to the ship from Plymouth, and in addition to the four crew members it was carrying three passengers and the incoming mail. When the aircraft was over the Bristol Channel it suffered a major gearbox oil leak, but the pilot was able to make a controlled descent into the water where it landed upright and, with the assistance of floatation bags and a calm sea, it remained that way. Rescue operations were soon under way and the seven occupants were picked up safe and sound by another Sea King from *Hermes* and by

The Harrier trials off Scotland were carried out in wet and windy weather as can be seen in this photograph as one of the aircraft takes off.

(Derek Coombes)

the SAR helicopter from RAF Chivenor. Once *Hermes* arrived on the scene operations to recover the helicopter began, and with the assistance of the ship's divers and two of the landing craft, this was successfully accomplished. First of all lifting gear was fitted, then one of the main rotor blades was removed and the others were lashed into place, before the helicopter itself was lifted slowly onto the carrier's flight deck. To everyone's credit the incident was handled without suffering any casualties and, in addition, not a single letter in the consignment of mail got wet.

Once the helicopter was back on board, *Hermes* returned to the Pembrokeshire coast where 40 Commando was re-embarked and preparations were made to sail for the major NATO exercise, 'Northern Wedding'. However, just as she was getting under way there came a pipe over the tannoy from the bridge to the effect that a civilian yacht had come alongside, and that she was carrying some 'interesting' passengers. Not much notice was taken at first

until a roar of approval on the flight deck signalled the fact that two young women on board the yacht had decided to indulge in some topless sunbathing. Within a minute there was a veritable stampede onto the flight and weather decks and the ship took on a substantial list as over 1,000 men crowded to the port side of the ship. Unfortunately for everyone the popular attraction had soon been left behind as *Hermes* set course for the Dutch port of Den Helder, stopping first at Spithead to drop off the stricken Sea King 272. After anchoring off Texel Island the LCVPs were kept busy ferrying liberty men to and from shore and transporting a unit of 'Cloggies' out to the ship. As soon as the operation was completed *Hermes* set course for the Shetlands and 'Exercise Northern Wedding'. The first phase involved the landing of the Dutch Marines by LCVP and 40 Commando by helicopter onto Shetland Island, before the ship sailed to the Iceland-Faroes gap to carry out anti-submarine operations with a US Navy task group.

Refuelling the frigate *Falmouth*...

...and a replenishment with *Yarmouth*.

(Derek Coombes)

Phase two of the exercise started with all the marines being re-embarked and the landing of 2,500 US Marines, then on 17 September *Hermes* and the US group sailed through some atrocious snowstorms to Arendal in southern Norway for 'Exercise Black Bear', which brought on some green faces and caused some damage to the ship, including a sea boat which was smashed into three pieces. However, once the marines had been disembarked to assault the Norwegian shores, *Hermes* sailed to Copenhagen for a greatly looked forward to and, after 35 days at sea, a much needed run ashore. A reception on the first day was followed by a 'British Week' fashion show in the hangar on the second day, as well as two days of playing host to visitors. Many members of the ship's company enjoyed trips to the Carlsberg Brewery, particularly as free samples were being given away, and before *Hermes* left Danish waters a Sea Day was arranged for government ministers and officials.

After leaving Copenhagen on 25 September *Hermes* returned to Arendal to pick up 40 Commando and then headed for Devonport for a short stay of only a week. Four days after leaving Denmark the ship secured to C buoy in Plymouth Sound and that afternoon about 300 family members were embarked for the trip up harbour. After being served tea on board, the families assembled on the flight deck for a very informal entry into Devonport where she secured alongside. The few days at Devonport were busy ones with Ceremonial Divisions being inspected by the Flag Officer Plymouth, to mark the ship's change of base port to Portsmouth, the ship's boxing team left their mark on the port by winning six of the ten weights in the Plymouth Command Novice Boxing Championships, and there was also a visit to the ship by an ex-Royal Marine who, in 1942, had survived the sinking of the ninth *Hermes*. After leaving Plymouth Sound there were more anti-submarine exercises, a visit to Hamburg and then, on 7 November, while she was in the Moray Firth area, *Hermes* became a fixed-wing carrier once again. Ten days of trials with the new Sea Harrier were carried out, and Monday 13 November saw a landmark event when one of five aircraft landed on the flight deck and was struck down into the hangar. This aircraft was followed by four more and, for the first time in eight years, the flight deck looked 'just like the old days'. On 14 November, in near gale-force conditions, one of the Sea Harriers showed its versatility by landing over the bow of the carrier as she steamed downwind. Even the old stagers who remembered the 1960s had to agree that Buccaneers and Vixens could not do that. The ten days of trials were a great success, with more than 80 sorties being flown, including seven by a Sea Harrier which arrived on board direct from RNAS Yeovilton. In the event 35 of the aircraft were ordered which, initially, would equip three front-line squadrons and a training squadron and, although nobody knew it at the time, the move ensured that both *Hermes* and the Sea Harrier would be involved in Britain's last colonial war which was only three and a half years away. On completion of the trials *Hermes* was able to return to Portsmouth for Christmas and New Year leave.

During the Christmas break there was a fire on board the ship which caused some damage to a mess deck, but it did not stop the carrier from sailing as scheduled in the following month. It was on Friday 12 January 1979, a cold and grey winter morning, when *Hermes* sailed again for a four-day shakedown and trials cruise off Portland and after having been successfully inspected by FOST, she commenced what was officially known as 'Continuation Operational Sea Training'. Basically this meant that *Hermes* was acting as the Dartmouth Training Ship and for seven weeks she would have on board 150 midshipmen, 14 flight officers and ten instructor officers under training, as well as 45 marine engineering apprentices, together with all their training staff. By 26 January *Hermes* was heading south for Gibraltar where during the week of 29 January the inevitable 'Rock Race' took place, only this time with a difference. Saddened by a newspaper report about an eight-month-old baby girl who had been orphaned by a terrible road traffic accident which claimed the lives of her parents, the 16-man bosun's party, led by Lt Constable, undertook a sponsored run up the Rock carrying the ship's bell which weighed one hundredweight. Their magnificent effort raised £1,000 which was put in trust for the little girl. On leaving Gibraltar the carrier steamed back out into the Atlantic again to exercise with the American nuclear-powered submarine USS *Skipjack* before returning to Gibraltar for another brief visit before sailing east for Naples. During the passage the Flag Officer Third Flotilla (FOF3), which was the new title for FOCAS, was embarked for the Operational Readiness Inspection, and five days after leaving Gibraltar *Hermes* arrived in Naples for a six-day visit during which many took advantage of coach tours to Rome, Pompeii and even Vesuvius.

Within two days of leaving Naples *Hermes* arrived in Phaleron Bay outside the Greek port of Piraeus for an official visit to Athens, where receptions were held for Greek VIPs and the ship was opened to the public. After saying goodbye to Greece on the last day of February the carrier steamed south to the Egyptian coast to watch part of the Soviet Navy's fleet, including the carriers *Kiev* and *Minsk,* on exercise. Both sides took plenty of photographs of each other and Soviet helicopters made close passes over *Hermes,* one of them even dropping a Red Star badge on the flight deck. This was just a brief interlude, however, and the carrier was soon homeward bound, with only a brief 24-hour stop at Gibraltar, and on Saturday 10 March, with the ship off Falmouth, all the men under training were either flown ashore or disembarked by LCVP. However, there was no respite for *Hermes* herself and as soon as the men were ashore the carrier continued her passage to the colder climes of northern Norway.

The Arctic exercise which took place over 12 days between 12 and 23 March, code-named 'Cold Winter', involved the embarkation of the 3rd Commando Brigade HQ, part of the Brigade Air Squadron, 59 Independent Commando Squadron, elements of 42 Commando Royal Marines, and an amphibious combat group of the Netherlands Marine Corps. This massive operation was carried out by air and by landing craft, with one of the last arrivals being a Gazelle helicopter which was airlifted on board by a Sea King. *Hermes* then steamed to the fjords north of the Lofoten Islands where she landed most of the embarked force and picked up 45 Commando, disembarking them by air or LCVP near Narvik two days later. For 200 members of the ship's company the highlight of the short visit to Narvik was a skiing trip outside the town. As *Hermes* steamed south again, through severe gales which were sweeping the North Sea, two of 814 Squadron's Sea King helicopters went to the aid of the Grimsby-based trawler *Angol,* which was in difficulties in the stormy conditions. After receiving a distress call via Humber Radio the two helicopters were sent to the area where one of them, piloted by Lt-Cdr Keith Hindle, the squadron's commanding officer, winched up two of the four crew members from a small rubber dinghy since the trawler's wildly swaying masts prevented their recovery from the deck. The other two decided to remain on board to await the arrival of the MV *Martinique,* which was about seven miles away. A third Sea King kept a safety watch while the remaining trawlermen were transferred to the rescue vessel.

Following the successful conclusion of 'Cold Winter' *Hermes* anchored at Plymouth to disembark her commando force before returning to Portsmouth on Thursday 29 March. Unfortunately, however, bad weather prevented families from meeting the ship at Spithead and accompanying her up harbour. During the eight and a half week maintenance period spent alongside, 180 officers and men from the carrier travelled to Tiverton where large

Hermes at sea in her LPH role.

(Derek Coombes)

Leaving Portsmouth on a cold and grey Tuesday 15 January 1980, as seen from the tug *Agile*.   (*Michael Lennon*)

crowds turned out to give the contingent an enthusiastic welcome as they marched through the town. The Mayor, accompanied by Captain Jenkin, took the salute and four Sea King helicopters carried out a roof-top fly-past as a dramatic finale to the parade. Afterwards, in the town hall, a large cake which had been baked in *Hermes* was ceremoniously cut and the pieces sent out to old people's and children's homes in the area. Meanwhile sports teams from the ship's company prepared to take on Tiverton at football, rugby, hockey and squash, but before the games got under way two Sea Kings landed on the town's rugby field where they were 'opened for public inspection' before giving a mini air display. Despite heavy rain it was a memorable day for all concerned.

Back on board *Hermes* preparations were under way for the next deployment and on Thursday 31 May the ship left Portsmouth to embark 814 Squadron before sailing south for Gibraltar where she carried out a full programme of exercises which were interspersed by visits to Gibraltar and Villefranche. While at the latter port two Sea Kings of 814 Squadron flew to Cambrai for an international meeting of aircraft squadrons with 'Tiger' emblems. During the deployment the main exercise, code-named 'Highwood', involved embarking additional helicopters from 819, 824

and 845 Squadrons whilst the ship was off Falmouth. In command of the exercise, and flying his flag in *Hermes,* was Rear-Admiral D. J. Halifax. On conclusion of the exercise on Friday 13 July in the Firth of Forth, *Hermes* headed back to Portland via the Pentland Firth. On 16 July the carrier sailed west for a transatlantic crossing and 'Exercise Mayflower' which included a visit from the C-in-C Fleet, Admiral Sir James Eberle. The passage also included a fund-raising fete on the flight deck, with attractions which included a fancy dress competition, a tug-of-war, Morris dancing, a competition to see who could kick a football fastest and numerous fun-fair stalls. In all the events raised £750 in aid of the Sailors' Children's Society, Hull.

It was on 27 July that *Hermes* arrived at Mayport, Florida, this time for a three-week stay since she was undergoing an assisted maintenance period at the American port, and the ship's company got to feel quite at home there. With *Hermes* flying the flag of the Flag Officer Third Flotilla, Rear-Admiral P. G. M. Herbert, the full Royal Marines Band was also on board and they left the ship at Mayport to make a tour of the eastern states. The first performances were two well-attended concerts in Atlanta, Georgia, followed by appearances at Hampton, Virginia, which were rehearsals for a joint concert with the

US Continental Army Band. The next stop was Philadelphia to play for the ships of the US Navy's 1st Frigate Squadron, and to fulfil public concert engagements. Then, after sightseeing and Beating Retreat at Penn's Landing, the band returned to Hampton for a marching display before the highlight of the tour, the joint concert before an audience of 3,000. The ship's company enjoyed the usual tours to Disneyworld and Cape Canaveral, along with the generous hospitality of the people of Mayport. After leaving the port on 21 August she joined in anti-submarine exercises with the US Navy before docking at Norfolk, Virginia, on the last day of the month for a ten-day visit.

When *Hermes* left Norfolk, Rear-Admiral Herbert was acting in his NATO appointment as 'Commander ASW Group Two' and on passage across the Atlantic Ocean the ship exercised with US and Canadian units as a work-up to the main NATO exercise, 'Ocean Safari', which was to follow. The exercise actually involved a total of 70 vessels, 200 aircraft and 17,000 men, and it was designed to demonstrate and improve NATO's capability of providing maritime support to Europe in time of crisis or war. Taking place over a wide area of the North Atlantic and Norwegian Sea, *Hermes* headed an anti-submarine warfare group while the Sea King helicopters of 814 and 824 Squadrons and two Wessex V helicopters of 846 Squadron were in the air continuously. It was thought at the time that during the 24-day period between leaving Norfolk and arriving at Bergen in Norway, the carrier had set a record for continuous hours at 'Flying Stations'. From Bergen *Hermes* sailed to Portsmouth where she was met at Spithead by 1,500 wives, children and friends for passage into the harbour. This break at Portsmouth was only brief, however, and she was soon back at sea for Sea Harrier trials in Carmarthen Bay and the Bristol Channel and in addition to the trials Harrier, which was equipped with Blue Fox radar equipment, she operated two aircraft from 700A Squadron for deck familiarization. On 2 November, with the trials successfully completed, she returned to Portsmouth for Christmas leave and maintenance.

It had been originally planned that the end of 1979 would see *Hermes* starting a long refit which would include the addition of a 'ski jump' ramp for Sea Harrier aircraft, but industrial problems in the dockyard had affected the work schedule and the start of the refit was postponed until the end of March 1980. In September 1979, when it had become clear that *Hermes* would be spending additional weeks at sea, a drafting officer had flown out to Norfolk, Virginia, with drafting proposals covering this extra sea time, and about 150 ratings who had expected to leave the ship before the end of 1979 had their sea service extended, but only 20 had to complete more than 30 months at sea. Of the 33 men who expressed a strong wish to leave the ship, only five had to remain on board for the extra months

prior to the refit. During the Christmas period some 40 members of the ship's company, including a choir formed by Lt-Cdr Crawford, toured hospitals and old people's homes in Tiverton singing carols and delivering Christmas hampers, all of which had been bought with the proceeds of voluntary events which had been held on board. On Monday 10 December 1979 there was a change of command when Captain D. J. Mackenzie took over from Captain Jenkin. Captain Mackenzie had entered the Royal Navy during the Second World War and throughout the post-war years he served in HM Ships *Brinkley, Barrington, Hardy, Lincoln* and *Hermione,* with his first command being HMML 6011. After being promoted to Captain in 1972 he commanded HMS *Phoenix,* the NBCD School, and in 1974 he was appointed Captain F8 in HMS *Ajax.* In January 1979 he took command of HMS *Blake* for her final 12 months of service, and it was from that ship that he came to *Hermes.*

As a result of the carrier's extension of operational service, rather than seeing her sitting in the dockyard awaiting her refit, it was decided that she would be better employed carrying out a 'training cruise' to the United States. For the voyage her 'pupils' were made up of 80 Dartmouth midshipmen, including HRH Prince Andrew, 50 apprentices and 150 junior ratings, all of whom would be completing the seamanship phase of their training. Others who embarked for training at sea included 24 members of the RNAS, ten MoD civilians and 18 members of the Royal Tank Regiment. There were also 36 schoolboys on board whose ages ranged from 12 to 16 years, all of whom were sons or close relatives of ship's company members. All the boys had the written permission of their parents and their head teachers, but when the news became public it led to questions in Parliament and accusations that the Navy was, 'resorting to cheap labour to keep its ships afloat.' Fortunately, this was not the case and the resultant publicity did nothing to spoil the opportunity for the youngsters to sample naval life at sea, and in addition to the boys there were no fewer than 35 'schoolies' on board to ensure that their education was not neglected. When the carrier sailed from Portsmouth on Tuesday 15 January 1980, however, there were problems with the main propulsion machinery and for the first two days of trials only one propeller shaft was available. Fortunately, the problem in one of the main boilers was soon rectified and *Hermes* was able to carry out trials and manoeuvres in home waters. On Friday 22 February, after embarking the last 19 trainees, who were midshipman HRH Prince Andrew and the other members of his class, *Hermes* set course for the warmer waters of the Caribbean.

For the trainees on board the transatlantic passage was hard work as well as fun as *Hermes* exercised with HMS *Birmingham* and the two accompanying RFAs, *Lyness* and *Tidespring.* Contributing to the carrier's busy world were the Sea Kings of 820 Squadron and a flight of Wessex Vs of 846 Squadron and, for official events at the different ports, the Royal Marines Band of the Flag Officer Third Flotilla. The first port of call was Port of Spain in Trinidad where trainees entertained children of St Dominic's Home to a tea party on board, and the Royal Marines Band Beat Retreat in the town centre. After her departure for an exercise with Dutch marines, FOF3 joined the ship and this was followed by a five-day visit to Willemstad, Curacao, with a banyan day at Cannouan Island in the Grenadines. On a visit to New Orleans the Royal Marines Band, led by Colour Sergeant Bob Baker, and a Royal Naval Colour Party and Platoon from *Hermes* were invited to take part in the famous Mardi Gras celebrations. True to form the Navy got a wonderful reception as they proudly led the colourful procession through the Southern city on no fewer than four occasions. The huge crowds that gathered greeted the band's rendition of 'The Stars and Stripes Forever' and 'Colonel Bogey' enthusiastically as they marched in a style which contrasted dramatically with the frenzy of the other participants. The next visit was to Pensacola and whilst the ship was on passage from that port to Fort Lauderdale, America's version of the Sea Harrier, the AV-8A, completed a successful week-long evaluation of a new landing system which had been installed in *Hermes*. The aircraft, with a team from the USN Test Centre at Patuxent Rover, embarked in *Hermes* where they tested the 'Horizontal Approach Path Indicator', a visual approach aid which was designed to assist the operation of the Sea Harrier. The US Marine Corps completed 55 approaches by day and night, and they enabled the system to be installed in their own landing aids.

From Fort Lauderdale *Hermes* steamed to Bermuda which was the final visit before she made the return passage across the Atlantic, pausing briefly off the coast of Cornwall to fly off the helicopters and stopping in Plymouth Sound to disembark the trainees. Finally, on Thursday 20 March the carrier arrived at Spithead where she was met by families and friends and, not so popularly, by Customs officials, for the passage up harbour. It was the end of another phase in the carrier's career and four days later the refit began.

Chapter Twelve

Western Atlantic And War In The South Atlantic
April 1980 - April 1984

ermes remained in dockyard hands at Portsmouth for over a year, during which time the most noticeable alteration to her profile was the 12° 'ski jump' ramp, or her 'nose job' as it was popularly known, which was fitted at the forward end of the flight deck to enhance the payload of the Sea Harriers that she would operate when she recommissioned in 1981. In all the refit cost some £30 million and it also included the fitting of new communications systems which gave *Hermes* one of the most modern systems afloat, new machinery, refurbishment of the accommodation spaces, landing aids for the fixed-wing squadron and repairs to her keel. Although she would carry a Sea Harrier squadron, *Hermes'* primary role remained that of anti-submarine warfare for which she would continue to operate her Sea King ASW helicopters. At the same time she retained her LPH role and with a Commando Group embarked the Sea Harriers' role would be to counter long-range air and surface threats. On Monday 3 November 1980 the carrier's new commanding officer, Captain L. E. Middleton RN, was appointed to the ship. Captain Middleton was an experienced Fleet Air Arm officer, having qualified as a

pilot in 1952 and having served in HM Ships *Centaur, Eagle, Victorious, Ark Royal* and the frigate *Mounts Bay.* In 1966-67 he commanded 809 Buccaneer Squadron in *Hermes* and in 1970 he commanded the frigate *Whitby.* In 1973 he was appointed Captain of the 2nd Frigate Squadron in the elderly frigate *Undaunted,* and in 1974 he commanded the much newer Leander-class frigate *Apollo.* In 1975 he served on the staff of FOCAS and after a spell as the Director, Naval Air Warfare, he was appointed to *Hermes.*

In March 1981, with the ship still very much in refit in No 3 basin, the ship's company moved back on board and on Tuesday 12 May 1981, with all the major work having been completed, the carrier left Portsmouth for her post-refit trials. As she steamed out of harbour she passed her half-sister *Bulwark* which was being destored prior to being laid up, and the new light fleet carrier *Invincible* which had been commissioned in July 1980. In fact, in the long term, the commissioning of the new light fleet carriers signalled the end of the line for *Hermes,* for it was planned to decommission her as soon as the second ship of the new class, HMS *Illustrious,* was operational in 1983. However,

Undergoing 'plastic surgery' at Portsmouth Dockyard.
(Fleet Air Arm Museum)

these plans would change as time went by. Following nine days of trials in the Channel between the Isle of Wight and Plymouth, *Hermes* returned to Portsmouth where rectification of defects was carried out. It was just over two weeks later, on Tuesday 9 June, that the carrier's rededication ceremony took place in the hangar with the Chief of the Defence Staff, and former commanding officer of *Hermes,* Admiral of the Fleet Sir Terence Lewin, taking the salute of the Honour Guard. Taking pride of place on a partially raised lift behind the guard was a Sea Harrier of 800 Squadron, and a rededication cake in the shape of *Hermes* was cut by Mrs Pamela Middleton, wife of the commanding officer, who was ably assisted by the aptly named youngest member of the ship's company, JMEM Young.

With the ceremonial over it was back to work again for the ship's company and *Hermes* left Portsmouth to undergo further trials off Portland and finally, in July, came the flying trials for the Wessex helicopters of 707 Squadron and the Sea Kings of 812 Squadron, while the Sea Harriers of 800 Squadron carried out intensive day and night flying from the newly fitted 'ski jump'. When she returned to Portsmouth on 24 July a Families Day was held on board, before pre-deployment leave was given and the ship herself took part in the summer Navy Days at Portsmouth. Despite her 'nose job', which everyone agreed was not her most becoming feature, *Hermes* took the starring role and, as always, her flying displays drew large crowds with everyone keen to see the Harrier which was still very much a novelty. Finally, however, with leave over and the newly formed E Company, 41 Commando, Royal Marines, having been embarked, *Hermes* left Portsmouth on Wednesday 2 September to embark the Sea Harriers of 800 Squadron, the Sea Kings of 812 Squadron and the Wessex helicopters of 707 Squadron, before setting course north for exercises in the eastern Atlantic. As the ship approached the remote island of Rockall, the Royal Marines Detachment, together with four officers from E Company, landed on the lonely outcrop of rock to crack open a bottle of champagne and leave a Union Flag flying. After leaving the area *Hermes* rendezvoused with the giant aircraft carrier USS *Forrestal* and her escorts to carry out exercises south of Iceland, before she and the US carrier set course south for the warmer climes of Florida and a WESTLANT deployment. Shortly before disembarking E Company to Camp Lejeune, an inter-ship sports meeting was held with beer, hot dogs and ice cream for sale on the flight deck, along with some unusual activities such as football and deck cricket, all of which got some strange looks from *Forrestal* and her task group. However, the fun and games were brought to an end by joint exercises with aircraft from the US Naval Station at Cecil Field, which attacked the ship's splash target, and before *Hermes* berthed alongside at Mayport to begin an assisted maintenance period, the

Harriers flew ashore to Cecil Field. As always the period spent at Mayport was extremely popular, with a liaison team arranging many tours and visits to attractions such as Cape Canaveral, Daytona Beach, Disneyworld, Everglades National Park, Fort Lauderdale, Miami Beach, Silver Springs and, of course, the miles of beautiful beaches around Jacksonville. An 'Exped Centre' was also set up which enabled would-be adventurers to indulge in all sorts of activities from windsurfing to snorkelling. The four LCVPs made a 40-mile trip down the St John's River where they used an ex-US naval base as their home while they explored different parts of the river. During the visit two Harriers of 800 Squadron put on some impressive displays for the aero-engine manufacturer Pratt & Witney.

On 20 October, with the maintenance completed, *Hermes* left Mayport and set course for Norfolk, Virginia, and during the passage the aircraft rejoined the ship, as did a US Marine Corps Harrier AV-8A for trials on the carrier's 'ski jump' ramp. One night, whilst the ship was alongside in Norfolk, two members of the ship's company who were returning to the ship in the early hours of the morning experienced at first-hand America's lax gun laws, when they were shot at within yards of the ship. On board, the gangway staff, thinking that perhaps they had drunk one too many Budweiser beers, told them to go and get some sleep. Shortly afterwards, however, a third man arrived back at the ship and he too complained that somebody had been shooting at him. Before anyone could take any action the gunman himself appeared at the top of the gangway and insisted that he be shown round the ship, but fortunately the local police were soon on the scene and the 'visitor' was forcibly removed and taken into custody. Whilst at Norfolk, E Company were re-embarked and FOF3, Vice-Admiral J. M. H. Cox, joined the ship and hoisted his flag.

After leaving Norfolk *Hermes* exercised with two large US Navy battle groups, one headed by the carrier *John F. Kennedy* and the other by the even bigger, nuclear-powered *Dwight D. Eisenhower.* During the ensuing 'battles' *Hermes* acted in her ASW role, with the Sea Harriers of 800 Squadron carrying out interception and attack exercises. Once the manoeuvres were completed *Hermes* set course for Tortola in the British Virgin Islands where, on Beef Island, E Company and banyan parties were landed. Although the recreation parties had been ferried ashore by the LCVPs, a sudden increase in wind speeds meant that they had to be evacuated by air. After leaving the Virgin Islands *Hermes* steamed north to Bermuda where she stopped for four days before heading home through 56-knot winds and mountainous seas to arrive back in Portsmouth on Thursday 3 December 1981, in plenty of time for Christmas.

Whilst *Hermes* was in the USA and Caribbean, Margaret Thatcher's Conservative Government was showing that it had no more regard for the role of the Fleet Air Arm than

On 20 January 1981 *Hermes* made her first public appearance with her partially completed 'nose job'. Here the tugs *Dalmation, Foxhound* and *Setter* manoeuvre her from No 3 basin.

(Michael Lennon)

Guided by the tug *Bustler,* on 12 May 1981 *Hermes* goes to sea for the first time with her new 'ski jump' ramp.

(Michael Lennon)

had the 1960s Government of Harold Wilson, as they negotiated with the Australian Government for the sale of the new HMS *Invincible*. In addition to these negotiations they had, as part of the 1981 Defence Review, announced their intention on economic grounds, to withdraw the ice patrol ship HMS *Endurance* at the end of her 1981-82 deployment in the South Atlantic. Unfortunately, in South American countries, and in particular in Argentina, the impending withdrawal of *Endurance* was construed not as an inevitable economy, but as a deliberate political gesture which signalled the end of Britain's interest in the South

Atlantic, namely the Falkland Islands and South Georgia, two territories to which Argentina had long-standing claims of sovereignty. For *Hermes*, however, the proposed sale of *Invincible* for some £175 million to the Australian Navy in 1983 meant a possible extension of service in the Royal Navy, for it had been decided that she would run on until 1985 when the third Invincible-class carrier, *Ark Royal*, would join the fleet. Meanwhile, as *Hermes'* ship's company enjoyed their Christmas and New Year leave, two events took place which were hardly reported in the British press. The first concerned the Government of Argentina when, on 22 December 1981, General Leopold Galtieri succeeded Roberto Viola as the President of Argentina, at the same time retaining his position as the C-in-C of the Argentine Army. The second was that the British Government made it clear to the Argentine Government that they were prepared to discuss sovereignty of the Falkland Islands with them, albeit in the form of a leaseback of the islands by Britain. Taken together with the withdrawal of *Endurance* it is clear that in Argentina it was thought that Britain was no longer interested in its South Atlantic possessions and with a hardline military government in power in Buenos Aires it was apparent that there could be problems, although nobody apparently foresaw war.

The New Year of 1982 saw the carrier involved in anti-submarine exercises in the South Western Approaches, in company with *Invincible* and the submarines *Odin* and *Onyx*, which ended with a five-day visit to Lisbon. After leaving the River Tagus *Hermes* steamed north to Plymouth Sound where, during the following three days, she embarked 40 Commando Royal Marines. The temporary reversion to her LPH role was not always popular with the ship's company because it meant long queues for the dining hall and for the NAAFI, and by the time the embarkation was completed on this occasion the carrier had 29 helicopters, five Sea Harriers, 72 vehicles, 70 trailers, a battery of 105mm guns and, including the ship's company, a total of 2,511 men on board. Once everything had been safely stowed, *Hermes* left Plymouth Sound on Wednesday 17 February to steam out into the Channel where, on the following day, 'heliborne attack' was mounted on the 'enemy' at Tregantle Ranges as part of 'Exercise Quickdash'. Despite the fact that the commando transport occupied approximately a third of the flight deck, the Sea Harriers of 800 Squadron were still able to fly sorties, but with the Commando Group ashore the Harriers and the Sea Kings of 826 Squadron also left the ship. *Hermes* then returned to Plymouth Sound for a weekend break, but on the following Monday, 22 February, she returned to sea to re-embark 40 Commando. Next day, in a little over seven hours, they and all their transport were flown ashore to the Lulworth Cove area of Dorset, returning to *Hermes* on 24 February by LCVP and helicopter. That evening, with just under three-quarters of an hour's notice, they were again flown ashore to Bovington Training area, to be followed on the next day by their stores. From Bovington the Commando Group made a tactical withdrawal to positions at Lulworth Ranges where, on 26 February, they were once again re-embarked in *Hermes* to be returned to Plymouth. It had been an arduous exercise, but it had proved beyond doubt that the carrier was still capable of fulfilling her amphibious duties with efficiency. She then went on to perform more anti-submarine exercises in the South Western Approaches in company with HM Ships *Antrim, Ariadne, Coventry,*

Glamorgan and *Lowestoft,* together with the submarine *Spartan,* then on Friday 19 March she entered Portsmouth Dockyard to begin a dockyard assisted maintenance period.

Meanwhile, in the period between January and March 1982 the diplomatic situation between Britain and Argentina had been steadily deteriorating and in mid-March a number of intelligence reports had been received in London, one of which indicated that the Argentine junta was frustrated at what it saw as a lack of progress in diplomatic talks regarding sovereignty of the Falkland Islands and that, in view of the unpredictability of General Galtieri and some senior members of his armed forces, an invasion of the islands could not be ruled out, and it was well known that the Argentine Army studied and admired *coup de main* operations of all sorts. As early as December 1981, Constantino Davidoff, a scrap metal dealer from Buenos Aires, had left the city in an Argentine ice-breaker, *Almirante Irizar,* to inspect scrap metal on South Georgia. Although Davidoff had an option dating from 1979 to purchase this scrap he had shown little interest in it over the years. Not only did he and naval personnel from *Almirante Irizar* land illegally at South Georgia, but also a subsequent protest by the British Government was rejected by the Argentine Ministry of Foreign Affairs. A few weeks later, on 25 January 1982, when HMS *Endurance* put into the Argentine port of Ushuaia, her commanding officer reported that he and his ship's company had received a cold reception, and that he had heard that there had been an order not to fraternize with the British. A few weeks later, on 23 February, Davidoff called at the British Embassy in Buenos Aires and, after apologizing for problems caused by his previous visit, asked for instructions on how to receive clearance for another visit to South Georgia. However, before receiving such advice or permission, on 9 March he set out for the island in the Argentine naval support vessel, *Bahia Buen Suceso.* Suddenly, on 20 March, when the Argentine ship arrived in Grytviken Harbour, South Georgia, and a sizeable party of civilian and military personnel had landed and raised the Argentine flag, fired shots and defaced notices which warned against unauthorized landings, the British press took notice and the dispute became headlines in British newspapers. In view of the fact that this was the second violation of the territory by Davidoff he was ordered off the island, and *Endurance* was sent to South Georgia to enforce the eviction. Next day, although the Argentine flag had been lowered, Davidoff's party of 50 or 60, most of whom were in civilian clothing, showed no signs of leaving and further gunshots had been heard and reindeer had been killed. Despite the fact that the Argentine Foreign Ministry denied any knowledge of Davidoff's activities, in *Endurance* a signal from Argentine Naval Headquarters in Buenos Aires congratulating the *Bahia Buen Suceso* had been intercepted and it was clear evidence that Davidoff's

At sea with the frigate *Broadsword*.

(Ian Currow)

Here resembling a grey steel cliff *Hermes* looks every inch a fighting machine as she leaves Portsmouth for the South Atlantic on 5 April 1982. *(Michael Lennon)*

operation had been undertaken with the full knowledge and assistance of the Argentine Navy. Although *Bahia Buen Suceso* left South Georgia, at least ten men were left behind at nearby Leith and by 23 March it was clear that what had begun as a minor local problem in a dispute which had rumbled on for many years was now a major international confrontation.

For two days it appeared that the Argentine nationals in South Georgia would be evacuated peacefully from the island and that the furore would die down, but on 25 March it became apparent that Argentine warships had sailed to prevent HMS *Endurance* from evicting the Argentines at Leith and that a second Argentine naval supply ship, *Bahia Paraiso,* had arrived at Leith and, flying the flag of the Argentine Senior Officer, Antarctic Squadron, she was building up supplies for the illegal landing party. During the day diplomatic exchanges between London and Buenos Aires became more urgent, and with the Argentine Navy taking a hard line, two of their frigates, both armed with Exocet missiles, were deployed between South Georgia and the Falkland Islands. By Saturday 27 March there were reports of intense naval activity at Puerto Belgrano, including the embarkation of marines, the sailing of various ships and a submarine, but even at this stage no one suspected that the Falkland Islands were about to be invaded. However, by 29 March

the Prime Minister and Foreign Secretary, Lord Carrington, were becoming concerned about the situation and they decided to send a nuclear-powered submarine to support *Endurance* off South Georgia and later that day, with reports that five Argentine warships had been dispatched to the area and all Argentine naval leave had been stopped, the C-in-C Fleet, Admiral Sir John Fieldhouse, ordered the Flag Officer First Flotilla (FOF1), Rear-Admiral J. F. (Sandy) Woodward, to prepare a suitable group of ships from Gibraltar and be ready to proceed to the South Atlantic if required. As it happened Admiral Woodward was directing 'Exercise Springtrain' at Gibraltar in which HM Ships *Antrim, Arrow, Brilliant, Glamorgan, Glasgow* and *Plymouth* were taking part, as well as the RFAs *Appleleaf* and *Tidespring,* and this force was put on standby to head south when required. During the days that followed there were more disturbing intelligence reports from the South Atlantic regarding Argentine naval movements. In Argentina itself there had been violent demonstrations in the streets of Buenos Aires against the junta's economic policies, and in response to British press reports of the dispatch of warships to the South Atlantic the Argentine Foreign Minister was quoted as telling reporters that his country would not give way to threats of force and that the group on South Georgia was actually on Argentine soil. It was clear that far from wanting to defuse

On the flight deck Harriers and Sea Kings were crammed into every available space.

(Fleet Air Arm Museum)

the situation, Argentina was being deliberately provocative and the dispute was being used to distract attention from the junta's domestic political problems. During the evening of 31 March intelligence was received in London to the effect that, in the early hours of 2 April, Argentine forces were set to invade the Falkland Islands. There were just 36 hours in which to try to head off what would be an act of unprovoked aggression by the Argentine Government.

During the evening of 1 April, with General Galtieri refusing to accept telephone calls from US President Ronald Reagan, the Governor of the Falkland Islands was warned that an Argentine naval task force would be assembling off Port Stanley the following morning and he quickly deployed his small Royal Marines garrison of 61 men (Naval Party 8901). The first Argentine landing took place at 4.30am local time at Mullet Creek, when 50 elite 'Buzo Tactico' marine commandos attacked the empty Royal Marines' barracks at Moody Brook. Fortunately the marines had been deployed into the island's main town, Port Stanley, and in the event they were able to hold off a large Argentine force until the arrival of the main invasion force, and as they were equipped with artillery the Governor decided to surrender. On South Georgia, Lt

Keith Mills RM and his small Detachment put up a magnificent defence against an overwhelming Argentine force and they damaged a corvette and helicopter with anti-tank rockets and killed four Argentine soldiers before being forced to surrender. Meanwhile, back home the nation was understandably shocked by this invasion of British territory and when, during the evening of Wednesday 2 April, the Prime Minister gave Admiral Leach authority to form a Naval Task Force which would sail to the South Atlantic with the objective of retaking the Falkland Islands and South Georgia, the country's support was overwhelming.

The end of March 1982 saw *Hermes* in Portsmouth Dockyard with her island superstructure covered in scaffolding and at extended notice for steam. Many members of the ship's company were on leave and her main engines had been opened up for maintenance. In short, under normal circumstances it would take three weeks to get her ready for sea, but in the early hours of 2 April when *Hermes* was ordered to four hours' notice for steam, she had just 72 hours to prepare for sea as the signal was given for 'Operation Corporate', the code name for the liberation of the Falkland Islands and South Georgia. The maintenance period was swiftly curtailed and as both the dockyard and the ship's company redoubled their efforts to make good the defects, work continued day and night. Some dockyard workmen had been recalled from leave and some gave up their planned Easter holidays, for as well as rectifying operational defects, there was a massive storing task to carry out on both *Hermes* and *Invincible*. Ironically the work was started on the same day that many of the dockyard workers had been issued with redundancy notices under the first stage of the defence cuts which would see the Naval Dockyards lose 15 per cent of their workforces. By the morning of 5 April *Hermes'* air group was at wartime strength with the Sea Harriers of 800 and 899 Squadrons embarked, along with the ASW Sea Kings of 826 Squadron and the LPH Sea Kings of 845 Squadron. In addition she had embarked A Company, 40 Commando, Royal Marines, and she was literally crammed with men, aircraft, and all the machinery of war.

At 10am on 5 April, from the flagstaff of Semaphore Tower there flew a crimson flag barred with white, which warned traffic in the harbour to, 'Clear the Channel, big ship in movement'. A few minutes later the carrier *Invincible* slipped her moorings and manoeuvred into the harbour to face the Narrows before beginning her slow but inexorable passage to Spithead and the Channel. On her 'ski jump' ramp, looking like some sort of space age figurehead, sat Sea Harrier 713, with its winged fist emblem emblazoned on its tail fin. More Harriers were lashed down on either side of the flight deck, along with Sea King helicopters, one of which was piloted by Prince Andrew. About 30 minutes later the tug *Bustler* led *Hermes* into sight from North Corner Jetty and she proved an awe-inspiring sight, looking like a grey steel cliff and far more weathered than the trim *Invincible*. She looked every inch a fighting machine ready to justify her existence. At her masthead the signal flags spelled out 'Goodbye', and along the sides of her flight deck the ship's company stood to attention facing the shore, as her flight deck speakers played the unofficial anthem - Rod Stewart's 'Sailing'. On the flight deck Harriers and Sea Kings were crammed into every available space, whilst down below the ship was filled to capacity with an almost endless stream of men, with every berth taken and makeshift camp beds set up in any spare corner of every passageway.

Meanwhile, ashore an emotional wave of patriotism and pride was sweeping the country and thousands of people travelled to Portsmouth and Gosport that day to bid farewell to the two big ships of the Task Force. From the Hard to South Parade Pier and beyond thousands of people packed every vantage point as they lined docks, jetties, walls, beaches, parks and, of course, the famous Round Tower, to wave banners, Union Flags of all sizes and goodwill messages. There were all sorts of conflicting emotions; sadness, inevitable apprehension, as well as pride and patriotism, as Portsmouth once again said farewell to a

battle fleet which was sailing to war, for no one on board had any illusions about the task ahead. As the cacophony of cheers, car horns and sirens faded into the background, Captain Middleton signalled: 'The commanding officer, officers and ship's company of HMS *Hermes* would like to pass to the City of Portsmouth, the Naval Base and Royal Dockyard their heartfelt thanks for the magnificent co-operation and goodwill that sped them on their way so expeditiously. They would also like to thank the families and friends of the ship for their support and their encouraging and warm messages and telegrams.' Perhaps the occasion is best summed up by the wife of one ship's company member who said, 'I hope the Falklanders get their islands back... and we get our men back.'

Down below in the engine and boiler rooms the Engine Room Department was still working hard to ensure that one of the boiler rooms was brought back to a fully operational state, for the carrier had actually sailed with one boiler room and one propeller shaft still out of action. Once clear of Portsmouth Harbour and Spithead, *Hermes*, *Invincible* and RFA *Pearleaf* steamed to the area of the South Western Approaches to wait for other ships of the Task Force, including the assault ship *Fearless**, before heading south. On board *Hermes* the aircraft and the marines competed for valuable flight deck space as intensive flying training and physical exercise routines began in earnest and continued relentlessly as the carrier steamed south. On Monday 12 April a Total Exclusion Zone came into force around the Falkland Islands and three days later, just north of Ascension Island, *Hermes* rendezvoused with the destroyer *Glamorgan* and the Task Force Commander, Rear-Admiral Woodward, transferred his flag to the carrier for the duration of the campaign. Also that day, despite the fact that the ship was sailing to war, the Crossing the Line ceremony was held on the flight deck, with Neptune and his entourage arriving on the flight deck via the forward aircraft lift. By the evening of 16 April *Hermes* was off Ascension Island which, despite the fact that it was 8,000 miles away, was to be the forward operating base for the Task Force; it was also the last land between the UK and the Falkland Islands. Next morning, at 8.15am, the C-in-C Fleet arrived on board via Wideawake Airfield for high-level planning meetings. On 18 April there was a submarine scare, and the whole Battle Group, including *Hermes, Alacrity, Broadsword, Glamorgan* and *Yarmouth,* together with the RFAs *Olmeda* and *Resource,* set sail for the Falkland Islands, with *Invincible* catching up later. The group had 12 days in which to arrive at the Total Exclusion Zone, and Admiral Woodward planned to enter it from the east, at night, and launch a dawn Harrier attack on Stanley airfield. He also intended to shell Argentine shore positions each day in order to

*Both HMS *Fearless* and her sister ship *Intrepid* had been victims of the 1981 Defence Review and were scheduled to be withdrawn and scrapped.

Hermes refuels the frigate *Broadsword* en route to the South Atlantic.　　　　　*(Fleet Air Arm Museum)*

destroy the morale of the offenders. There was no doubt that *Hermes* was vital to the whole operation to re-take the Falkland Islands for, in Admiral Woodward's words, 'Lose *Hermes* and the operation is over.' On 21 April, when the group was in mid-Atlantic, some 1,500 miles out from Ascension Island, there were problems with an Argentine Air Force reconnaissance plane which managed to evade interception and two days later, with the carrier butting her way into south-easterly gales, there came the first casualty when a Sea King of 846 Squadron crashed into the sea during the night of 23 April, a few miles away from the ship. Unfortunately the crew member, PO K. S. Casey, was lost and although a frigate and two RFAs searched the area until after daylight, there was no trace of him.

On 25 April, in atrocious weather conditions, the island of South Georgia was retaken by HM Ships *Antrim, Brilliant* and *Endurance* and, in addition, the Argentine submarine *Santa Fe* was severely damaged and forced to beach herself at Grytviken. This action resulted in the garrison commander, Captain Alfred Astiz, becoming an embarrassing prisoner of war as he was wanted by a number of countries in connection with the disappearance and, almost certainly, the murder of their citizens while they were in government custody in Argentina. Shortly afterwards the nearby Argentine garrison at Leith

surrendered. Next day, on board *Hermes* Admiral Woodward gave a press interview which, in retrospect, he had to amend somewhat after declaring, 'South Georgia was the appetizer. Now this is the heavy punch coming up behind. My battle group is properly formed and ready to strike. This is the run-up to the big match which, in my view should be a walkover.' By 29 April the Task Force was some 500 miles from the Exclusion Zone, and much of the day was spent in refuelling and replenishing. It was known that most of the Argentine fleet, including the cruiser *General Belgrano,* was at sea, and it would not be long before the submarine *Conqueror* detected her and the accompanying escorts. In the early hours of Saturday 1 May, a single RAF Vulcan bomber of 101 Squadron, which had made an epic flight from Ascension Island with the assistance of in-flight refuelling, dropped 21 1,000lb bombs on Stanley Airfield which, in effect, signalled the start of the British offensive on the Argentine forces in the Falkland Islands. That same morning Admiral Woodward's Task Force steamed into the Exclusion Zone and the first of the Fleet Air Arm's air strikes was about to be launched.

Almost simultaneously with the RAF's raid, while Admiral Woodward's Task Force was about 145 miles north-east of Port Stanley, the ship's company on board *Hermes* prepared to launch the first air strike on Stanley

168

RFA *Tidepool* refuels *Hermes* in the South Atlantic, whilst *Invincible* looks on.

(*Fleet Air Arm Museum*)

Airfield. In the event, at just before dawn, 12 Harriers took off from the carrier and led by Lt-Cdr A. Auld, they attacked defensive positions around the airfield, the runway itself and the Argentine airfield at Goose Green. The raid was a complete success with planes, buildings and the runways being damaged or destroyed. Although one of the Harriers was hit in the tail fin by anti-aircraft fire, all the aircraft returned safely to the carrier and it is best remembered today in the words of the BBC's reporter Brian Hanrahan who, being unable to quote numbers of planes involved, settled for, 'I counted them all out and I counted them all back.' It was not long, however, before the Argentine Air Force attempted to retaliate against the Task Force when aircraft from Port Stanley made for the frigates *Brilliant* and *Yarmouth* but, after being pursued by two Harriers, they jettisoned their bombs and returned to Stanley. There were other successes that day when the Harriers shot down a Mirage and a Canberra bomber, and a second Mirage which had been damaged was shot down by friendly anti-aircraft fire from Stanley. Following the initial air raids against Stanley and Goose Green airfields, units of the Task Force kept up the bombardment of the Argentine positions around Stanley from just over two miles offshore, with *Hermes* and *Invincible* providing combat air patrols.

On 2 May 1982, the submarine HMS *Conqueror* torpedoed *General Belgrano* which she had been following for two days and the cruiser sank with heavy loss of life. At the time, and for some years afterwards, there was controversy in some quarters about the sinking, mainly over the fact that she was some 36 miles out of the Total Exclusion Zone and on a course which would have taken her back to port in Argentina, but the simple fact that she was at sea and in the vicinity of the Falkland Islands meant that she was a very real threat to the Royal Navy. The course she was steaming at the time of the sinking was of very little significance and it would have been folly to allow her to continue her patrol. Had the submarines detected the Argentine aircraft carrier *Veinticinco de Mayo**** at sea, whatever her position, she too would have been torpedoed. Two days later, with the war escalating, the destroyer *Sheffield* was hit on the starboard side amidships by an air-launched Exocet missile. The massive explosion blew a hole in the side of the ship and a large fire was started which gave off huge quantities of thick smoke and fumes. Twenty men lost their lives and 24 were injured in the incident which crippled the destroyer. At just after 3pm local time, about an hour after *Sheffield* was hit, one of three Harriers of 800 Squadron from *Hermes* which had taken off to

attack Goose Green airfield, was shot down with the loss of its pilot, Lt Nicholas Taylor RN. Throughout the following days and often in atrocious weather conditions, *Hermes* and *Invincible* provided continual air cover for the Task Force and their Harriers detected and forced the surrender of an Argentine spy trawler, *Narwal,* which had been attempting to shadow and report the position of the Royal Navy's warships. During the night of 14 May, in rough weather with wind speeds of up to 75 knots, *Hermes* detached from the main Task Force off the north coast of the Falkland Islands to within 40 miles of Pebble Island which overlooked the North Falkland Sound and San Carlos Water. Once in position, four Sea Kings landed 45 commandos close to an Argentine airfield where they placed demolition charges on 11 Pucara aircraft which were parked there. Having destroyed the ground attack planes, the force successfully withdrew back to the helicopters which returned them to *Hermes*.

At 6.45am on Tuesday 18 May, in a position Lat 50° - 19'S/Long 52° - 55'W, some 200 miles east-north-east of Port Stanley, *Hermes* and the frigate *Brilliant* rendezvoused with the P&O liner turned troop transport, SS *Canberra*. A few hours later *Invincible, Broadsword, Arrow* and *Yarmouth* joined the group to provide protection as the assault force neared their destination which was to be San Carlos Water on the north-east coast of East Falkland Island. The landings themselves took place in the early hours of Friday 21 May and, as expected, the Argentine Air Force onslaught was directed at the ships anchored off Fanning Head. The first attacks began at 9.30am and it soon became clear that the Argentine Air Force was concentrating its fire on the gun line of anti-aircraft frigates which had been stationed in San Carlos Water, and although both *Ardent* and *Argonaut* were damaged (the former was hit by a number of 500lb bombs and was subsequently abandoned, and the latter was damaged by an unexploded bomb), by the end of the day a beachhead had been established. During the air attacks Harriers from *Hermes* and *Invincible* intercepted and destroyed four Skyhawks, three Daggers and a Pucara. On 25 May two Argentine Super Entendards took off with two of the remaining three air-launched Exocet missiles still held by their Air Force to search for both *Hermes* and *Invincible,* and after refuelling in mid-air from other aircraft, at 110 miles they located the carrier battle group on their radar. At a range of about 30 miles the missiles were launched, but with the carrier group alert to such attacks, defensive chaff radar decoy material was fired and one of the missiles hit the merchant ship *Atlantic Conveyor,* which did not possess any chaff. The resultant explosion and fire gutted the unfortunate vessel, but the second missile, obviously deflected by the defensive measures taken, missed the group completely. Fortunately the *Atlantic Conveyor's* cargo of Sea Harriers had been transferred to the carriers some days

***Veinticinco de Mayo* started her career in January 1945 as the Colossus-class aircraft carrier HMS *Venerable*. In 1948 she was sold to the Royal Netherlands Navy and renamed *Karel Doorman*, and in 1968, having been refitted with the boilers from the disused HMS *Leviathan*, she was sold to Argentina.

Bombs and missiles on the flight deck shortly before the aircraft are armed for an air strike. *(Fleet Air Arm Museum)*

earlier, although a number of vital helicopters were lost. Also that day the destroyer *Coventry* was lost to air attack.

With the main landings having been carried out successfully the eventual outcome of the campaign was never in any real doubt, but there were more tragedies to come, and with the ground troops ashore the Harriers from *Hermes* and *Invincible* had to provide air cover for the Task Force afloat and the air defences of the islands themselves. In addition to *Ardent* and *Argonaut*, HM Ships *Antrim*, *Broadsword* and *Brilliant* were damaged defending the amphibious forces in San Carlos Water and the frigate *Antelope* was sunk as she was overwhelmed by Argentine aircraft. On 8 June the LSLs *Sir Tristram* and *Sir Galahad* were attacked and hit by Argentine aircraft and both were abandoned, with heavy casualties. It was the biggest setback of the whole campaign, with 63 dead and 83 wounded. Meanwhile, *Hermes,* at sea east of the Falkland Islands, was troubled by machinery problems that forced the Engine Room department to carry out a full-scale boiler clean, which involved shutting down all four boilers in turn to descale and wash out the drums. In the furnaces the

washing of the water tubes built up a thick sooty sludge which had to be dug out and hauled up to be discharged over the ship's side. The whole job, which was normally undertaken by dockyard specialists, was carried out thousands of miles from home, more than 60 days since the carrier had last sighted land and while the ship was still within range of Argentine aircraft. The fact that it was completed in record time was a tribute to the dedication and teamwork of her ship's company. On 11 June the Battle for Port Stanley began with assaults on Argentine positions on the surrounding hills and three days later, to everyone's relief, the Argentine forces surrendered. During the final battle RAF Harriers operating from *Hermes* carried out air strikes on Argentine artillery batteries on Mount Tumbledown, overlooking Stanley, and they were to be the last air strikes of the campaign for soon afterwards, during the afternoon of 14 June, the Argentine Commander, General Menendez, requested a ceasefire.

Although the garrisons on the Falkland Islands had surrendered, Admiral Woodward in *Hermes* still faced the problem of the enemy Air Force, and the Harriers had to provide constant air patrols while the two carriers remained well offshore. By 17 June, however, with the overthrow of General Galtieri, it became clear that the war was indeed over and *Hermes* moved closer to the islands and anchored in Stanley's outer harbour of Port William. In order to help restore some sort of order out of the chaos which reigned ashore, a platoon of *Hermes'* ship's company, made up of volunteers from all branches, went ashore to support the land forces and were put to work guarding Argentine prisoners, thereby freeing front-line troops. On Sunday 4 July, Admiral Woodward sent his final signal to the Task Force, which read: 'As I haul my South Atlantic flag down, I reflect sadly on the brave lives lost, and the good ships gone, in the short time of our trial. I thank wholeheartedly each and every one of you for your gallant support, tough determination and fierce perseverance under bloody conditions. Let us all be grateful that Argentina doesn't breed bulldogs and, as we return severally to enjoy the blessings of our land, resolve that those left behind for ever shall not be forgotten.' Then, as he was about to leave *Hermes* there was a fly-past of the Task Force's Sea Kings and Harriers, some 80 aircraft in all, after which he departed to return home by air. Next day *Hermes* herself left the Falkland Islands for the long passage home.

After *Hermes* had left the hostile waters of the South Atlantic the atmosphere on board became more relaxed and two days after leaving Port William, Defence Watches were stood down. As she steamed north blue uniforms gave way to tropical rig which, in turn, gave way to blues once again as she steamed into the northern hemisphere. Finally, on 20 July, she reached the English Channel where she passed the new carrier *Illustrious* which was on her way to the South Atlantic. Later that day she anchored in Sandown

Sea Harriers ranged on the flight deck and about to be launched for a dawn air strike.　　　　*(Fleet Air Arm Museum)*

Bay to prepare for entry up harbour next morning. Before weighing anchor *Hermes* received a visit from the Prime Minister, Mrs Margaret Thatcher, who was accompanied by the Chief of the Defence Staff, Admiral of the Fleet Sir Terence Lewin, and in an 80-minute tour of the ship she thanked the ship's company and inspected the 'scoreboard', 46 silhouettes of enemy aircraft shot down by Harriers from *Hermes,* which had been painted on the side of the island superstructure. Finally, however, after 108 unbroken days at sea, the weather-stained old aircraft carrier steamed through the waters of Spithead where she was met by a flotilla of small boats, and along the Southsea seafront it was estimated that 100,000 people had turned out to cheer her in. As she steamed in triumph through the harbour entrance she was met by a deafening barrage of sirens, hooters, ships' bells and car horns, to which she replied with a 17-gun salute. Overhead there was a fly-past by Harriers, an RAF Victor tanker, Army Lynx helicopters and a veteran Swordfish of the Fleet Air Arm's Historic Flight based at Yeovilton. *Hermes* had been the leading lady in the greatest naval drama since the Second World War and she was given a homecoming that her ship's company would never forget. Ahead of her lay the refit which had been cut short at the end of March.

During her period in Portsmouth Dockyard whilst she

was receiving her much-needed maintenance, there was a change of command when, on Monday 20 September, Captain R. C. Dimmock RN relieved Captain Middleton. Captain Dimmock had entered the Navy in 1953 and qualified as a pilot in the following year. After a secondment to the US Navy he served in the aircraft carriers *Albion, Ark Royal, Eagle* and *Hermes.* He also served in the frigate *Murray* and in the early 1970s he commanded the frigates *Berwick* and *Naiad.* After a spell as the Chief Staff Officer to FOCAS he took command at RNAS Culdrose, and it was from there that he was appointed to *Hermes.* Many members of the ship's company also left the ship at this time for a lot of them had been due for drafting prior to the Falklands campaign, and they were relieved by men who had been due to join the ship in April and May. In the final weeks of the refit a 'Falklands Task Force Ball' was held on board in the hangar which was attended by representatives from all the ships, squadrons and units that had taken part in the campaign, as well as members of the Merchant Service, civil servants from the MoD and press representatives. However, in early December 1982, *Hermes* slipped out of Portsmouth Harbour at the end of her 12-week refit with a trials and work-up programme which promised a testing time for the ship's company. In mid-December, flying the flag of Rear-

Sea Harriers and Sea Kings are ranged on an icy flight deck during operations in the South Atlantic.

(Fleet Air Arm Museum)

Admiral Sir John Woodward, the former Task Force Commander, *Hermes* visited Brest in France, where the local and national news media showed considerable interest in the ship. Arriving back in Portsmouth after the visit, Christmas and New Year leave was taken before work began again in earnest.

After leaving Portsmouth on 18 January 1983, and before steaming north to Rosyth by way of the Irish Sea, *Hermes* had a very different operation to undertake at the request of the Independent Television Company, TV-AM. They had asked the ship to put the word 'Britain' into the company's breakfast show, 'Good Morning Britain'. For the occasion 550 members of the ship's company formed the word on the flight deck, while overhead in a Wessex helicopter the camera crew filmed the 'off caps' drill for the opening titles of the new programme. The split-second timing needed for the best effect was provided by the combined efforts of the carrier's two chief gunnery instructors giving the order in unison. In a painstaking two-day operation, the programme title was completed by people from a West Country village and by Trafalgar Square pigeons. The 5,000 villagers formed the word 'Good', and the pigeons were bribed with bird seed to spell out 'Morning'. With the public relations exercise over and

with the Harriers of 800 Squadron and the Sea Kings of 814 Squadron embarked, *Hermes* steamed north for 'Exercise Roebuck' which took place off the north of Scotland in some very severe weather. Also involved were units of the US, Netherlands, Norwegian and German Navies, and on its conclusion the carrier returned to Portsmouth for another short break before sailing again on 14 February, once again bound for northern Europe. Two days later there was a little light relief when the 30th anniversary of the ship's launch was celebrated, and on the following day she started a five-day visit to Hamburg. Despite the very cold weather a full sporting programme went ahead, and many younger members of the ship's company were introduced to the Reeperbahn. The end of February and early March saw the ship in Norway on 'Exercise Cold Winter 83', which lived up to its name, and during which 45 Commando and Dutch marines 'invaded' the Norwegian coast. Finally, on completion of the exercise, *Hermes* steamed south again and in mid-March she returned to Portsmouth for Easter leave and to prepare for her next deployment, a four-month WESTLANT stint which should have taken place the previous year.

When *Hermes* left Portsmouth again on 7 April she had on board 40 schoolboy sons of ship's company members

A weather-beaten *Hermes* anchored at Spithead on 21 July 1982, on her return from the South Atlantic. *(Michael Cassar)*

Crowds and small boats greet *Hermes* as she passes HMS *Herald* on her return to Portsmouth from the South Atlantic. *(Michael Lennon)*

Small craft of all shapes and sizes escort *Hermes* to her berth at Middle Slip Jetty on her return from the South Atlantic, whilst on the jetty crowds of relatives greet their loved ones.

(Fleet Air Arm Museum)

whose ages ranged from 12 to 17 years. After getting a grandstand view of the ship leaving harbour and the landing on of the Harriers of 800 Squadron, the young men had a full day of activities and a night at sea in a spare mess deck. Next morning, with the ship well down Channel, they were flown off in a Sea King to RNAS Culdrose. The transatlantic passage was extremely busy, with a full flying programme and a range of NBCD exercises. There was one day off, however, when a Sports Day was held on the flight deck, with the Royal Marines Detachment getting some funny looks when they were the only ones to turn out in fancy dress. On Thursday 19 April, in an unseasonal snowstorm, *Hermes* steamed up the Hudson River to berth alongside at Manhattan, right in the heart of New York, for a very popular six-day visit to the city as part of 'Britain Salutes New York Week'. As always the hospitality of the people of New York was overwhelming, with invitations to many private parties, and the visit was enjoyed by everyone, before the carrier left the port on 25 April to steam south for Mayport. During the passage a number of US Defence officials and press representatives were embarked by helicopter to witness 'Shop Window' displays by the Harriers and Sea Kings, and particular interest was shown in the Harriers and their launches from the ship's 'ski jump' ramp. At Mayport, where temperatures never dropped below 80 degrees, the ship was taken in hand for an assisted maintenance period. Meanwhile, the squadrons disembarked to Cecil Field, Jacksonville, where they were able to take part in the open day at the air station. During the visit the rare honour of the Freedom of an American City was bestowed on the aircraft carrier, when the keys of Jacksonville Beach were presented to Captain Dimmock by the Mayor. Music at the ceremony was provided by the Royal Marines Band of FOF3, and a Union Flag was presented to the city. The ship's company had plenty of time to enjoy the sights, with the most popular destination being Disneyworld. Once again generous hospitality was enjoyed here with many swimming pools in the sun, barbecues and ice-cold beer being offered by local residents. After leaving Florida, however, it was back to work with 'Exercise United Effort' with the US Navy and, for the Engine Room Department, a five-day boiler clean at sea, during which temperatures never dropped below the high 90s. The next call was the main US East Coast Naval Base at Norfolk, Virginia, and, being such a large base with every facility, many never ventured beyond its limits. One unusual sporting event which was laid on for the ship was the '*Hermes* Hurricanes' ice hockey match with the local Virginia Beach team, and a final late goal by the home side gave them a 12-11 victory.

When *Hermes* left Norfolk on 26 May it was the start of a three and a half-week spell at sea and the eastbound transatlantic crossing took the form of a major anti-submarine exercise code-named 'Ocean Safari', but once in home waters, instead of returning to Portsmouth, the carrier paused briefly in Mounts Bay off Porthleven to disembark 814 Squadron before steaming north for the Skagarrak where 800 Squadron took part in joint exercises with the Swedish Air Force based at Saterner. *Hermes* went on to visit the city of Gothenburg, which was voted a good run ashore by the ship's company. After leaving Sweden the GR3 Harriers of No 1 Squadron, RAF, were embarked for 'Exercise Mallet Blow' in the North Sea, following which, off Portland, 800 Squadron were exchanged for a flight of 845 Squadron's Wessex helicopters. Following this *Hermes* again missed Portsmouth and returned to the North Sea, and after a visit to Oslo she held further exercises in the Channel. Once again the carrier ignored Portsmouth and she steamed instead to Start Bay to embark Indian Navy Harriers for deck landing practice. Finally, however, on 20 July she flew off all embarked aircraft and headed home to Portsmouth where, on the following morning, she embarked 2,000 family members and friends for a 'Families Day'. The state of the tide meant that time alongside allowed little more than half an hour to complete the embarkation, which involved some fast moving over the brow. Once at sea the packed programme included displays by Sea Harriers, Sea King and Lynx helicopters, as well as Tornado, Buccaneer and Nimrod aircraft. There were performances by the Royal Marines Band and a replenishment at sea with RFA *Appleleaf*, and with a warm, sunny day everyone was able to enjoy the displays from the flight deck. That afternoon, having given the families a memorable day, *Hermes* steamed up harbour to begin a six-week maintenance and leave period.

On Tuesday 23 August 1983, while the ship was alongside, there was a final change of operational command when Captain K. A. Snow RN relieved Captain Dimmock. After having been educated in South Africa and attending the South African Nautical College, Captain Snow had entered the Royal Navy in 1952. By 1962 he was in command of the minesweeper *Kirkliston*, and after having qualified as a navigation specialist, in the 1970s he commanded the frigates *Llandaff* and *Arethusa*. Not only was there a change of command, but also a change of Flag Officers when Rear-Admiral R. G. A. Fitch, himself an ex-*Hermes* CO, relieved Vice-Admiral Sir Derek Reffell, who had served in *Hermes* in every rank from midshipman to flag officer. By now it was clear that *Hermes*' Royal Navy career was drawing to a close for the plan was that she would go into dockyard hands at Devonport for a refit in January 1984, and following that, in the spring of that year, she would sail to Portsmouth. She would then be employed on training tasks alongside and, 'kept in a state of readiness by operation', which in itself meant that the complement would be drastically reduced with many men increasing the 'pool' of available personnel who could man the new carrier *Ark Royal* in preparation for her trials and entry into service

On 25 November 1982, following her post-Falklands refit, *Hermes* leaves Portsmouth Harbour in pristine condition once more.
(Michael Lennon)

which was expected in 1985. Although no decision had been made on her long-term future, rumours of her intended fate, from a sale to the Australian Navy as a replacement for *Invincible,* to sales to either the Indian or Chilean Navies, abounded as 'buzzes' circulated round the ship. In the immediate future she remained very much part of the Royal Navy, and by the second week of September she was once again ready for sea.

It was on Tuesday 13 September 1983 that *Hermes* left Portsmouth, and two days later she was alongside at Devonport being loaded with a proportion of 40 Commando's war maintenance reserve of stores and equipment, with the rest being embarked in RFA *Resource.* On the flight deck were paraded the guns of 79 Battery RA, rigid raider boats and the Gazelle helicopters of A Flight, 3 Commando Brigade, as well as the Sea Kings and Wessex helicopters from 845 and 846 Squadrons and over 90 Landrovers and trailers from the Commando Group. Finally, over a two-day period, the 850 men of 40 Commando Group were embarked, bringing the number of personnel in *Hermes* to almost 2,000. With all the equipment and men safely on board the carrier sailed, although the original destination of Malaga, where 40

Commando was to have undertaken cross-training with Spanish marines, was cancelled and instead she headed for the north coast of Cornwall to disembark the Commando Group for a 36-hour exercise on Davidstowe Moor near Bodmin. The exercise was an excellent shakedown for both the ship's company and the commandos, for with the ship newly returned to large-scale LPH exercises the complicated series of assault procedures kept everyone on their toes. With the exercise over, however, and the commandos re-embarked, *Hermes* set course for a ten-week Mediterranean deployment during which she would be accompanied by the assault ship *Fearless,* the frigates *Leander* and *Ariadne,* and the RFAs *Resource* and *Brambleleaf.* With the call at Malaga having been cancelled the first stop was Naples where, having survived volcanic eruptions and earthquakes, the ruins of Pompeii were subjected to visits from the ship's company and the embarked force, and soon *Hermes* filled up with enough pumice stone to keep all hands clean for a long time to come. Whilst in Naples the Commodore Amphibious Warfare (COMAW), Commodore P. G. V. Dingemans DSO, embarked and hoisted his Broad Pendant, before *Hermes* sailed to play her part in 'Exercise Display

Determination'. Almost immediately there were problems when, at very short notice, the Greek Government withdrew completely from the exercise. The programme was quickly reorganized and a three-day schedule of training in the Brindisi training area of southern Italy was substituted for the marines, who might have imagined they were on the set of a spaghetti western film. Once the commandos were back on board, *Hermes* steamed south around Crete and then north for Saros Bay where the Turkish phase of 'Display Determination' was to take place. During the passage a machinery defect in *Illustrious* necessitated FOF3, Rear-Admiral Fitch, transferring his flag to *Hermes*. At Saros Bay there was a combined British/Turkish amphibious landing by helicopter, landing craft and rigid raiders in conjunction with Turkish Naval Infantry (the Turkish equivalent of the Royal Marines), which was watched by a large number of senior NATO and Turkish officers from a specially constructed observation point. To the Royal Marines taking part in the exercise it seemed that no expense had been spared in the construction of the VIP site, with three large marquees, porcelain toilets and the only piped water supply for miles around. However, the marines were amused to see a rainstorm turn the area into a quagmire of mud and, when a helicopter took off from the area, the down draught from the rotor blades blew down one of the marquees, enveloping the VIPs in soggy canvas. The five-day exercise saw a parallel inland advance of both 40 Commando Group and the 1st Battalion, Turkish Naval Infantry, with the Turkish Army in tanks and armoured personnel carriers acting as the enemy. With the exercise having been completed, both forces returned to the beach at Saros Bay to participate in an afternoon of joint sports and a barbecue.

With the conclusion of 'Exercise Display Determination', the Commando Group re-embarked and *Hermes* steamed through the Dardanelles and across the Sea of Marmara, to anchor off Istanbul. Once ashore the colourful bazaars and hard-to-refuse 'very special prices' offered by the traders took their toll on the pockets of sailors and marines alike, and those who escaped parting with their money in the bazaars were, after one or two drinks, often caught on their return to the quay which was festooned with traders selling 'unique' wares of all shapes and sizes. From Istanbul *Hermes* steamed south to Cyprus and the Akamas Peninsular where, in scorching temperatures, the rugged hills and scrub provided an ideal training environment for the commandos who enjoyed unlimited live field firing. For three days they carried out section and troop attacks, company group attacks and a full-scale Commando Group attack. Meanwhile, while *Hermes* and *Fearless* lay off the coast of the island, many members of the ships' companies donated blood for the American and French peacekeeping forces in Lebanon who had fallen victim to the factional fighting in that country,

and who had been evacuated to the British bases in Cyprus. The next stop on the agenda for *Hermes* was Egypt where the ship was 'attacked' by sections of the Egyptian Navy to test her ability to ward off swarm assaults by small, missile-firing craft. After anchoring in Alexandria Harbour on 28 October the Commando Group was landed for a period of cross-training with the Egyptian Army, while the ship's company enjoyed coach excursions to Cairo and the Pyramids at Giza. Meanwhile, back on board, the ship was visited by children from the British school and Captain Snow laid a wreath at a nearby war cemetery. After leaving Alexandria on 2 November and not being able to make a proposed visit to one of the Adriatic ports, either Venice or Trieste, *Hermes* steamed west to Gibraltar conducting exercises en route, arriving alongside the south mole on 11 November. During the visit the ship's final Rock Race was held, with the embarked force inevitably 'hogging' the prizes and a Royal Marines sergeant setting a new record for the race.

After a week in Gibraltar *Hermes* left for the last time to return to Portsmouth, and whilst off the coast of Cornwall there was a clue to the carrier's future when Indian Navy Sea Harriers were embarked for training exercises. As the ship steamed up Channel the C-in-C Fleet, Admiral Sir William Staveley, joined for the passage, as did a large press contingent. Finally, on Tuesday 22 November 1983, with her 750-ft paying-off pennant flying, *Hermes* steamed into Portsmouth Harbour to secure alongside the dockyard's North West Wall. Within a week of her arrival all aircraft and squadron personnel, as well as the Royal Marines, had left the ship, and all ammunition had been landed. Many members of the ship's company, both officers and ratings, had been drafted to other ships and establishments, and it was at this time that *Hermes* led the way for another innovation for the Royal Navy - that of women serving in HM Ships. Captain Snow's new Assistant Secretary was a member of the WRNS, Second Officer E. Nuttall, and she was the first woman to be appointed to a ship which was still on the Active List, with the C-in-C's permission to remain on board overnight whilst the vessel was at sea. On 29 November *Hermes* left Portsmouth to arrive alongside in Devonport the next day, to begin her four-month refit. A few days later, on 9 December, a farewell ball was held in the hangar which was attended by seven ex-commanding officers; Admiral Sir William O'Brien, Admiral Sir John Fieldhouse, Vice-Admiral Reffell, Rear-Admiral Fitch, Rear-Admiral Jenkin, Rear-Admiral Middleton and Captain Dimmock. By mid-December, however, with the carrier in dockyard hands, the ship's complement had been reduced drastically to 400. On 9 March 1984, in a farewell to their adopted Borough, the ship's company were given a stirring send-off by the people of Tiverton. Thousands lined the streets of the north Devon town as 200 men from the carrier, accompanied by the Royal Marines Band of

FOF3, marched through the streets with flags flying, drums beating and bayonets fixed. The salute was taken by the Mayor of Tiverton and Captain Snow whilst three Fleet Air Arm Sea Harriers flew past and later in the day the men were entertained to lunch by the town council. By this time the carrier's refit was coming to an end, and on 6 April 1984 *Hermes* left Devonport manned by her reduced ship's company to undergo six days of trials in the Channel. On 11 April, when *Hermes* was off Eddystone Light, there was a last historic meeting with her half-sister *Bulwark*, which was making her final voyage under tow from Portsmouth to Cairnryan for demolition. *Bulwark* had begun her slow passage the previous day and after saluting the 'Rusty B' as she was affectionately known, *Hermes* set course for Portsmouth, where she arrived the next day. It was the last time that the carrier would enter harbour under her own steam as a unit of the Royal Navy, and despite the small ship's company she looked extremely smart with her flight deck manned and with the White Ensign flying proudly.

Soon after her arrival, however, she was towed into No 3 basin and it was not long before her complement was again reduced in numbers to the 100 or so men required to keep the ship in a state of 'Preservation by Operation'. On 11 May 1984, her last operational commanding officer, Captain Snow, left the ship and *Hermes* began a period of semi-retirement.

With her reduced ship's company, on 12 April 1984 *Hermes* arrived in Portsmouth Harbour for the last time under her own steam. *(Michael Lennon)*

Chapter Thirteen

In Reserve And INS *Viraat*
May 1984 - August 2001

During her stay in Portsmouth Dockyard's No 3 basin *Hermes* remained in the care of a ship's company of 190 men, commanded initially by Cdr J. A. Bolger RN. Some of her compartments were dehumidified and sealed and steam was kept on the main boilers in A boiler room while the turbo alternators provided electrical power as the ship was kept at 30 days' notice for steam on the main engines. The term 'Preservation by Operation' meant that once a month basin trials were carried out and the main engines were tested, as was much of the machinery and equipment on board. In the autumn of 1984, BBC television crews descended on the ship to film an episode of 'Superteams', a series in which international sportsmen and women were filmed competing in different events. For that particular episode they had to compete in a number of naval-orientated

events on and around *Hermes*. In October 1984 there was a small celebration in the hangar when her commanding officer, Cdr Michael Morgan RN, and his men drank a toast to the ship and cut a specially baked cake to celebrate the 25th anniversary of the first commissioning. In early 1985 the ship was inspected by the Flag Officer Third Flotilla, Vice-Admiral Richard Fitch, who was, of course, himself a former commanding officer of the ship.

With such great care being taken of the ship it seemed unlikely that *Hermes* was bound for the scrapyard, at least in the short-term, and as was pointed out by the MoD to anyone who enquired about her future, '...she remains ready, if necessary, to support the carriers *Invincible* and *Illustrious*'. However, by the summer of 1985, with the new *Ark Royal* undertaking her trials and due to arrive in Portsmouth on 1 July, rumours regarding *Hermes'* long-

Hermes leaves Portsmouth under tow for Devonport on 17 March 1986. She was to have a long refit before being sold to the Indian Navy.

(Michael Lennon)

Looking extremely smart in her new darker grey livery, INS *Viraat* undergoes sea trials and work-up at Portland in July 1987.
(Michael Lennon)

term future began to circulate. These included immediate scrapping, preservation in Portsmouth's maritime heritage complex and, the most persistent of the rumours, that she was to be sold to the Indian Navy. Although the Indian Navy had bought the smaller Majestic-class aircraft carrier *Hercules* in early 1957, which had been commissioned as INS *Vikrant* in 1961, she had never been refitted to operate Sea Harriers and, having been launched in 1945, she was clearly reaching the end of her economic life. In fact secret negotiations with the Indian Government were under way but, as nothing of this was known to the public, there were attempts made to preserve *Hermes*. One of these came from the Portsmouth-based Maritime Preservation Society who would have liked to have seen her berthed on the Gosport side of Portsmouth Harbour, with her hangar providing space for all manner of attractions. Finally, however, in the spring of 1986, the speculation was all but ended when it was announced that *Hermes* would go to Devonport to undergo a long refit as it was likely she would be sold to a 'foreign' navy. The maintenance and essential repairs were expected to take a year and on Saturday 15 March 1986, under the command of Captain (E) John Price RN, who had joined her nine days previously, and with a skeleton crew of just 40 men, *Hermes* was towed out of Portsmouth

Dockyard bound for Devonport. It was appropriate that Captain Price should be in command for he had already spent five years of his naval career in the ship. He had joined the Navy as an artificer apprentice in 1966, and between 1974 and 1976 he had served in the carrier as the Senior Engineer. In 1979 he had returned to the ship as Commander (E), and he was on board to oversee the long refit and the handover to the 'foreign' navy. As he said when interviewed by the press: 'Any purchaser will want to know that she is in reasonable shape under the bonnet and we will overhaul the engines and boilers and check on the hull. In my experience *Hermes* has always been a good runner. You could always plan things and make them happen.'

On arrival at Devonport *Hermes* was berthed alongside No 7 Wharf, and soon afterwards the Indian Government agreed to buy her for £60 million. With initial agreements and contracts having been signed, the refit and refurbishment could begin. In May 1986 her first Indian commanding officer, Captain Vinod Pasricha NM, and 200 of her future Indian ship's company, who were mainly key executive and technical personnel, joined the ship, although at that stage they were accommodated in the naval barracks. In addition the Royal Navy's strength on board was

Leaving Portland after a successful work-up. It would not be long before *Viraat* set out for her new home in India.

(Michael Lennon)

increased to around 300 men who, in addition to helping bring the ship forward for service, had to advise and familiarize the Indian Navy personnel in both the ship and its technical systems. Initially, having been out of operational service for over two and a half years, there were difficulties in refitting the machinery and weapons systems and progress was slow, but with a combination of hard work and perseverance by both RN and IN personnel they were overcome. In November 1986 the new Indian complement were able to move on board their new ship, which was to be renamed *Viraat,* and soon their strength on board was increased to 450 as men continued to join the ship.

The workload involved in setting to work and restoring a ship the size of *Viraat* was enormous. As well as manning the ship for day-to-day work, which in itself would usually require a ship's company twice the size, the Indian sailors had the additional task of familiarizing themselves completely with all the machinery and weapons systems. During a prolonged docking period the underwater areas of the hull were shot-blasted, repaired and treated with preservative paint to ensure that, as far as possible, the ship would not require docking for another five years. Major

work was completed in all the machinery spaces, including retubing of boilers and the overhaul and replacement of many auxiliaries. The flight deck was stripped of its paint and recoated and, as visitors to Devonport noticed, the ship's hull and island superstructure steadily assumed a new dark grey shade. All radar, sonar, computers and radio equipment were set to work, and the Seamen Department grappled with cables, RAS rigs, davits, guard rails and nets, many of which were in a sorry state after standing idle for such a long period. Meanwhile, the Supply Department was busy acquiring all sorts of rare spare parts, as well as making and keeping the ship habitable for the ship's company. The Engineering Department celebrated a milestone at the end of January 1987 when, for the first time since the fires were put out on 26 February 1985, B boiler room was flashed up once again. This heralded the start of a run-up for full basin trials and the metamorphosis of the ship from being a dockyard-dependent hulk to an independent ship.

The 11-month refit finally came to an end in May 1987, and on Tuesday 12 May the formal handover, renaming and commissioning ceremony took place at Devonport.

A Sea Harrier of the Indian Navy's 300 (White Tigers) Squadron landing on board *Viraat*. *(Captain R. F. Contractor)*

Attending the ceremony, and representing the British Government, was the Under Secretary for Defence Procurement, Archie Hamilton, while the High Commissioner for India, Dr P. C. Alexander, represented the Indian Government and took possession of *Viraat*. Also in attendance was the Indian Navy's Vice-Chief of Staff, Vice-Admiral J. G. Nadkarni and, very appropriately, representing the Admiralty Board, Vice-Admiral Sir Derek Reffell, who had spent so much of his career in the ship. Hundreds of guests, including relatives, attended the ceremony, at which tribute was paid to personnel of both the Royal and Indian Navies for their work in ensuring the success of the transformation, and to all members of the dockyard at Devonport who were involved. There was a fly-past of Sea King helicopters and in her coat of new, dark grey paint, and dressed overall, with the Indian White Ensign flying, *Viraat* looked extremely smart for her big day.

With the ceremony over and her ship's company having been brought up to full strength, on 18 May 1987 *Viraat*

sailed from Devonport to carry out a programme of trials and shakedown exercises based on Portland. These were followed by another short period in Devonport Dockyard and as she left the base for the last time in late July, bound for India, her 800-strong ship's company manned the flight deck. As she steamed past Plymouth Hoe they came to attention, doffed their caps and gave three cheers as the ship displayed a huge sign saying, 'Thank You Plymouth'. *Viraat* arrived at Mumbai (Bombay) on 21 August 1987 and she soon became an integral part of the Indian fleet, which is the most powerful Navy in the Indian Ocean. Although her two quadruple Seacat anti-aircraft missile launchers had been removed during her Devonport refit, these were later replaced and despite the numerous additions and alterations which have been made over the years, *Viraat* remains distinctly recognizable as the former *Hermes*.

Today she operates from the Indian naval base at Mumbai and she carries the Sea Harriers of 300 Indian Navy Air Squadron - The White Tigers - armed with

30mm guns, air-to-air and surface missiles, bombs and rockets. She also carries the Sea King 42Bs of 330 Indian Navy Air Squadron - The Harpoons - which are primarily used in the anti-submarine role. Finally, she carries a flight of Chatek helicopters of 321 Indian Navy Air Squadron - The Angels - which have a dual SAR and communication role. In May 1999 *Viraat* began a two-year overhaul at Mazagon Docks Ltd, Mumbai, which included the installation of a new missile system, improvements to her main propulsion machinery and the fitting of long-range air and search surveillance radar systems. The modernization is intended to extend the ship's lifespan by ten years, and at (US) $71.4 million, it is the first major refit since 1987. In February 2001, commanded by Captain R. F. Contractor, who has also served on board *Viraat* as the Executive Officer, she took part in the International Fleet Review which marked the 50th anniversary of the Indian Republic and, anchored next to the new Delhi-class destroyer *Mumbai*, she looked as spick and span and as smart as ever. Once again rumour surrounds the vessel's long-term future and in this case it is that India intends to buy the redundant Russian Kiev-class aircraft carrier, *Admiral Gorshkov*, and if this is the case then it is almost certain that this newer ship will replace *Viraat*. Whatever her future, the fact that *Viraat* is still an efficient fighting unit, some 48 years after she was first launched, is a credit to her builders and to the Royal and Indian Navies who have taken care of the carrier in peace and, briefly, in war. It is perhaps fitting that the former *Hermes* should end her days not too far removed from the waters in which the ninth ship of the name so tragically ended her career nearly 60 years ago.

INS *Viraat* anchored off Mumbai (Bombay), India, in February 2001 for the country's International Fleet Review which was held to mark the 50th anniversary of the Indian Republic. *(Mike Critchley/Maritime Books)*

Appendix One

Principal Particulars - HMS *Hermes* 1923

Length Overall:	598ft
Beam Overall:	70ft - 3in
Standard Displacement:	10,850 tons
Deep Load Displacement:	13,000 tons
Draught:	18ft - 6in
Armament:	Three 5.5-inch guns, three single 4-inch HA AA guns. Two quadruple sets 0.5-inch AA guns
Aircraft: (as built)	15 Fairey IIID & Flycatcher seaplanes
1939	12 Fairey Swordfish
Main Propulsion Machinery:	Twin screw, two sets Parsons geared turbines. Steam at 235 psi supplied by six, oil-fired Yarrow water tube boilers
SHP:	40,000
Speed:	25 knots (2,930 miles at 18 knots)
Complement (with embarked squadrons):	700

Appendix Two

Principal Particulars - HMS *Hermes* 1959

Length Overall:	774ft - 4in
Beam Overall:	147ft -11in
Standard Displacement:	24,900
Deep Load Displacement:	27,800
Draught:	27ft - 10in
Armament: (as built) 1966	Ten 40mm AA guns Two quadruple Seacat SAM missile launchers
Aircraft:	28
Main Propulsion Machinery:	Twin screw, two sets Parsons geared turbines. Steam provided by four, oil-fired, Admiralty Three Drum boilers
SHP:	76,000
Speed:	28 knots (5,040 miles at 20 knots)
Complement:	2,100

Appendix Three

Commanding Officers HMS *Hermes* 1923

	Date Appointed
Captain The Hon A. Stopford CMG RN	20 February 1923
Captain C. P. Talbot DSO RN	15 July 1925
Captain R. Elliot CBE RN	25 July 1927
Captain G. Hopwood CBE RN	2 December 1927
Captain J. D. Campbell MVO CBE RN	17 January 1929
Captain E. J. G. Mackinnon RN	2 October 1930
Captain W. B. Mackenzie RN	8 January 1932
Captain The Hon G. Fraser DSO RN	15 August 1934
Captain F. E. P. Hutton RN	23 August 1939
Captain R. J. F. Onslow MVO DSC RN	7 May 1940

Commanding Officers HMS *Hermes* 1959

	Date Appointed
Captain D. S. Tibbits DSC RN	19 October 1959
Captain W. D. O'Brien DSC RN	24 November 1961
Captain T. T. Lewin MVO DSC RN	1 February 1966
Captain D. G. Parker DSO DSC AFC RN	23 October 1967
Captain J. D. Fieldhouse RN	9 December 1967
Captain D. G. Parker DSO DSC AFC RN	19 January 1968
Captain P. M Austin RN	2 July 1969
Captain C. R. P. C Branson RN	27 February 1973
Captain D. R. Reffell RN	9 November 1974
Captain R. G. A Fitch RN	21 September 1976
Captain D. C. Jenkin RN	22 April 1978
Captain D. J. Mackenzie RN	10 December 1979
Captain L. E. Middleton RN	4 November 1980
Captain R. C. Dimmock RN	20 September 1982
Captain K. A. Snow RN	23 August 1983

Commanding Officers INS *Viraat*

	Date Appointed
Captain Vinod Pasricha NM	12 May 1987
Captain Madhvendra Singh AVSM	16 December 1988
Captain Arun Parkash VrC VSM	31 August 1990
Captain Madanjeet Singh AVSM	27 December 1991
Captain Y. Prasad VSM	22 March 1993
Captain J. S. Dedi VSM	29 September 1994
Captain Vijay Shankar	14 October 1995
Captain N. K. Verma	9 November 1996
Captain S. K. Damie NM VSM	14 December 1997
Captain R. F. Contractor	16 June 2000

Appendix Four

Former Ships

The First *Hermes:*

The first of the Royal Navy's warships to bear the name *Hermes* was a 200-ton sloop, originally named *Mercurius,* which was armed with 14 guns. She was captured in 1796 from the Dutch by HMS *Sylph* when she was blockading the Dutch coast. She was renamed *Hermes,* which is another name for Mercury, the Roman god of eloquence, and quickly pressed into naval service. Her career did not last long, however, for in 1797 she foundered at sea with the loss of all hands.

The Second *Hermes:*

The second *Hermes* was a sixth-rate of 331 tons, armed with 22 guns and carrying a complement of 80. She entered service in 1798, serving in the North Sea before being sold in 1802.

The Third *Hermes:*

In 1803 the Royal Navy purchased the 339-ton, 16-gun sloop, *Majestic,* and after renaming her *Hermes* she was put into naval service. Her career, which lasted for seven years, was a quiet one and she ended her service as a stores ship in the Mediterranean. She was sold in 1910.

The Fourth *Hermes:*

This was one of the more spectacular ships to bear the famous name, and she was a 512-ton, sixth-rate, armed with 20 guns and with a complement of 121 men. Built in Portsmouth Dockyard and launched in 1811, *Hermes* spent her first year of service in the Channel and North Sea. During this period she was responsible for running down the French privateer *La Mouche.* Commanded by Captain Philip Brown, she assisted with the capture of an American ship which was laden with naval stores, together with two vessels carrying tobacco and ivory. These actions came at a time when, following the 1783 American victory in the War of Independence, ships from Britain and America were involved in tit-for-tat incidents on the high seas. Under Captain Brown's command she captured the American privateer *Swordfish* before, in 1814, Captain The Hon W. H. Percy took command. During the 1812-15 war with America, *Hermes* was sent to the Gulf of Mexico and in September 1814, in a combined operation with three other ships and 200 troops, she attacked Fort Bowyer at Mobile, Alabama. Having anchored off the fort she came under attack and, in order to avoid capture, her crew set fire to her. She lost 25 killed and 24 men wounded in the action.

The Fifth *Hermes:*

In 1830 the Royal Navy purchased the fifth *Hermes,* a 733-ton steamship named *George IV* which had been built at Blackwall on the Thames in 1824. Renamed *Hermes,* the ship spent four years in naval packet service before being renamed *Charger,* converted into a coal depot ship and being put into service at Woolwich. She was broken up at Deptford in 1854.

The Sixth *Hermes:*

The sixth *Hermes,* built at Portsmouth and launched in 1835, was an 830-ton, paddle wheel, steam sloop armed with six guns. Her first five years of service were spent on the Mediterranean Station, followed by four years on the North American Station and four active years on the Cape of Good Hope and East Indies Stations. During this period she rendered valuable service during the 1851 wars against the native peoples of South Africa. She then sailed for the East Indies where she joined a force led by Commodore Fox in the steam-driven frigate *Fox.* She took part in the blockade of Rangoon and the Army assault on the Burmese town of Martaban, and the capture of Rangoon. It was here that the first battle honour was earned. In 1854, with the Plenipotentiary, Sir George Bonham, on board she sailed up the Yangtse River as far as Nanking for the purpose of assuring the Chinese rebels in the area that Britain would remain neutral from their internal feuds. Once off Nanking she had to hastily weigh anchor to avoid a fire raft which had been sent out towards her. On passage back downriver she shelled Chinese rebel positions in front of Chin Kiang Foo and later, at Shanghai, she sent out boats to search for deserters from HMS *Salamander.* In 1854, having been in commission for four years and five months, during which time she steamed 75,000 miles and consumed 7,000 tons of coal, she was paid off at Woolwich. She saw another five years of naval service before, in 1859, she was sold for breaking up.

The Seventh *Hermes*:

Launched at Chatham in 1816, the seventh ship of the name was originally called *Minotaur* and she was a third-rate of 1,726 tons. She was renamed *Hermes* in 1866 when she was anchored downriver from Gravesend as a cholera hospital ship. Her career did not last much longer, however, and she was broken up at Sheerness in 1869.

The Eighth *Hermes*:

It was the eighth *Hermes* which, although launched as a cruiser, took a leading role in the early development of aircraft at sea. Launched in April 1898 as one of five light cruisers of the Highflyer class, she was a twin-screw ship of 5,600 tons and was armed with 4-inch guns. In 1906 she was the flagship of the East Indies Station, but in the following year she relieved HMS *Hyacinth* as flagship on the Cape of Good Hope Station. In October 1908 she recommissioned at Simonstown and again at Ascension Island, which was a coaling station, in 1910. In March 1913 she was relieved by *Hyacinth* and she returned home to pay off. She was converted at Chatham to a depot ship for the Naval Wing of the Royal Flying Corps, which subsequently became the Royal Naval Air Service. She was fitted with a launching platform forward and a storage platform aft for three seaplanes. She was actually recommissioned at Chatham in May 1913, and during seven months of trials she made a number of seaplane launches from her forward flying deck. In December that year, after seven months of trials, she was paid off and placed in reserve at Chatham. On the outbreak of war in August 1914 she was hurriedly recommissioned as a unit of the Nore Command, but on 31 October, whilst ferrying aircraft to Calais, she was torpedoed and sunk with the loss of 22 lives by *U27*, off the Ruyligen Bank.

The eighth *Hermes*, a light cruiser of the Highflyer class, was the first ship of the name to carry aircraft when, in 1913, she was fitted with a launching platform and carried three seaplanes. She is seen here in Simons Bay, South Africa, in 1899.

(Maritime Photo Library).

HMS *Hermes*
Altiora Peto
(I Seek Higher Things)

Badge shows the head of Hermes (or Mercury), the messenger of the gods

Battle Honours:

Burma 1852   Atlantic 1940

Falkland Islands 1982

Acknowledgements

My thanks to Rear-Admiral K. A. Snow CB, the *Hermes'* last operational commanding officer, for kindly writing the foreword to this book and to Captain Rusi F. Contractor, the current commanding officer of INS *Viraat* for his help.

I must also thank the following for their help and, in many cases, for the loan of their very valuable photographs: -
Bill Baptie, Chessington: Roger Beacham & staff of Cheltenham Reference Library: W. A. A. (Jock) Begg, Aughton: John Burrows, Barrow-in-Furness: Michael Cassar, Valletta, Malta: Derek Coombes, Cirencester: Mike Critchley, **Maritime Books**, Liskeard: Lt Norman F. Curnow RN (Retd), and Ian Curnow, Helston: Stan Curtis, Shrewsbury: C. L. 'Jan' Davey, Torpoint: Lynne Dunning, Arts & Museum Service, Barrow-in-Furness: Rear-Admiral D. M. Eckersley-Maslin CB, Hampshire: Charles Fisher, Honiton: Ossie Flowerdew, Enfield: Derek Fox, Southsea: Barry Guess **BAE SYSTEMS**: Peter Harris, Wath-upon-Dearne: Tony Kearns, Winsford: Lt-Cdr Maurice 'Jan' Larcombe RN (Retd), Sherborne: Michael Lennon, Waterlooville: R. W. 'Bob' Mason, Horsham: Terry McKee, Gloucester: Anthony G. Miers, Plymouth: George Mortimore, **Action Photos**, Ryde: Tony Perrett, **Royal Marines Historical Society**, Gosport: Trevor Piper, Winchester: John Proverbs, Gloucester: Jerome Rycroft, Hove: Mike Smith, **BAE SYSTEMS MARINE** (formerly Vickers Shipbuilders), Barrow-in-Furness: Don Smith, Hambleton: Ian Spashett, **FotoFlite**, Ashford: Adrian Vicary, **Maritime Photo Library**, Cromer: Bob Welch, Wellingborough: Keith Wood, Worksop: Special thanks also to my wife Freda and my two daughters Caroline & Louise for their invaluable help.

Special thanks also to Brian Conroy of Farnborough and John Morris of Dalgety Bay for their paintings and sketches of the two *Hermes*.

For details of other titles currently available Tel/Fax 01242 580290
Or write to:
FAN PUBLICATIONS
17 Wymans Lane
Cheltenham
Gloucestershire GL51 9QA
England